# BEYOND
# THE RÉSUMÉ

**OTHER BOOKS BY HERMAN HOLTZ:**

*Government Contracts: Proposalmanship and Winning Strategies*
*The $100 Billion Market*
*Profit from Your Money-Making Ideas*
*The Winning Proposal: How to Write It* (with Terry Schmidt)
*Directory of Federal Purchasing Offices*
*Profit-Line Management*
*The Secrets of Practical Marketing for Small Business*
*How to Succeed as an Independent Consultant*
*Mail Order Magic*
*Persuasive Writing*

# BEYOND THE RÉSUMÉ

## How to Land the Job You Want

HERMAN HOLTZ

## McGraw-Hill Book Company

NEW YORK · ST. LOUIS · SAN FRANCISCO · AUCKLAND · BOGOTÁ
GUATEMALA · HAMBURG · JOHANNESBURG · LISBON · LONDON
MADRID · MEXICO · MONTREAL · NEW DELHI · PANAMA · PARIS
SAN JUAN · SÃO PAULO · SINGAPORE · SYDNEY · TOKYO · TORONTO

2 3 4 5 6 7 8 9 D O C D O C 8 7 6 5 4

ISBN 0-07-029629-4{HC}
ISBN 0-07-029632-4{PBK}

LIBRARY OF CONGRESS CATALOGING IN PUBLICATION DATA

Holtz, Herman.
Beyond the résumé.
1. Résumés (Employment)       2. Applications for
positions.   I. Title.
HF5383.H64   1984        650.1'4        83-9878
ISBN 0-07-029629-4
ISBN 0-07-029632-4 (pbk.)

Book design by Nancy Dale Muldoon

**To Brandy Sherman**
for valuable suggestions and unwavering encouragement

# Contents

## 8 ENTER THE "SUPER-RÉSUMÉ" 133

A Functional and Logical Approach. A Few Tips for Coping. Special Cases. Why "Super-Résumé"?

## 9 HOW SUPER-RÉSUMÉS SOLVE RELATED PROBLEMS 142

Classic Résumé Problems. The Automatic Solution. Several Built-In Problems with Résumés. Closing. Using the Super-Résumé to Lead to the Custom Résumé. Associated Problems and Opportunities.

## 10 USING THE SUPER-RÉSUMÉ 151

How Much Information? Help-Wanted Advertisements. The Typical Requirements in the Help-Wanted Advertisement. The Bottom-Line Résumé. A Businesslike Approach. "Salary Desired." Tailoring the Super-Résumé in Responses. Difficult-to-Respond-to Solicitations. Tailoring a Super-Résumé to the Organization. How to Get the Information You Need.

## 11 THE FOLLOW-UP 171

Typical First-Reactions to Super-Résumés. Saying *Yes, But*. You Must Keep the Initiative. Making the Job-Hunt a Full Campaign. Laying It on the Line. How Frequently to Mail. How to Study Advertising: A Special Tip.

## 12 THE INTERVIEW 184

Some Facts about Interviews and Interviewers. Interviewing Styles. Preparing for the Interview. The Résumé Request. Taking Charge. Problems: Handling Them. A General Strategy. Handling Liabilities. Asking Questions about the Company. About Salary. After the Interview.

# Preface

ONCE, several months after I had accepted a new position to found and manage a Washington, DC branch of a company located some hundreds of miles away, I answered the telephone to find the company president on the other end of the line.

"Herm, I want to use your résumé in a proposal, and we seem to have lost our file copy. Can you send us another one right away?"

"Sure," I answered. "No problem. But you didn't lose your file copy of my résumé. You never had one."

Shocked silence. Then: "Of course, we had one. You couldn't have been hired without it. We insist on seeing a résumé before we even interview anyone."

I didn't press the point. There was no purpose to it. But what I had said to the president of that company was truth: I had been hired as a general manager of a new and independent branch (which I did, indeed, found for the company) at a substantial executive salary without ever having furnished anyone in the company a résumé.

I really had not intended to do this. Like everyone else who has ever had to seek new and better positions to advance my career, I had experienced the frustrations of mailing dozens and dozens of copies of my résumé to companies, sometimes in response to help-wanted advertisements, sometimes "cold," and sometimes on the basis of tips from friends that such-and-such an organization was hiring. And when few interviews resulted, I had agonized over what was wrong with my résumé—why did I not hear from people, as well experienced and well qualified as I thought myself to be?

Even when I approached executives I knew and inquired—for

example, when I ran into one at a convention or seminar—and was answered with something such as, "Sure thing. Why don't you drop me a résumé in the mail, and I'll see what I can do," it turned out invariably to be a don't-call-me-I'll-call-you kind of brushoff. The request for a résumé was simply a convenient and face-saving way of avoiding that distasteful rejection of a friend. Or perhaps that distasteful admission that he couldn't do anything for me, despite his affectation of being a highly placed muckety-muck in his company.

Among other things, I've had some intensive experience in value engineering. So it seemed appropriate to use some of that valuable and effective VE (value engineering) discipline to analyze my own situation. Among the things I subjected to that functional analysis which is the heart of VE was the résumé, first of all. I put some key functional-analysis type questions to it:

What *is* it?
What does it *do*?
What is it *supposed* to do?
How *well* does it do that?
What *else* would do it?
How well would *that* do it?

Put to the acid test of functional analysis, some answers popped out which were both surprising and enlightening. (Strange how much we take at face value, never questioning, never doubting—unless something happens that compels us to begin questioning.) Those answers are a major part of what this book will talk about, especially the answers to those last two questions. And to press on—in fact, to answer those last two questions—it was necessary to resort to still another area of past studies and experience: marketing and sales. For it did not require too much study to realize that the *job hunting* is a misnomer for what we do when we are unemployed. In fact, we don't "work for" someone else—that is, we should not work for someone else or, at least, we should not regard our employment as working for someone else; what we do is *sell our services to a buyer*, whom we call *the employer*. This whole idea of "working for" someone, of having "an employer," is at the root of our difficulties in finding the job we want, need, and should have. It's what compels us to accept a job that we do not want and that is entirely wrong for us.

I am going to tell you in these pages facts behind that telephone conversation with the company president to whom I had sold my services. I'm going to reveal exactly how I managed not only to sell my services to him for what was then top-dollar, but also how I did it in direct violation of what he regarded as an absolute requirement, a *sine qua non* for employment in his company, without his even realizing it. (And I did sell my services directly to him and his vice-president, in a lengthy series of discussions that continued over dinner and into the late evening.) But let's digress, for a moment, and approach this indirectly.

I once worked for a salesmanager who was fond of observing on every possible occasion that whenever two people meet and have an exchange of any kind, a sale is made. I found that he was right, too. My wife and I meet and have exchanges frequently about such things as doing the dishes and taking the garbage out, and she makes a sale every time—I do the dishes and take the garbage out. She happens to excel at this kind of selling.

Of course, that kind of persuasion is something like the persuasion I once used on an employee who had ignored or misunderstood my earlier orders, expressed on more than one occasion. I persuaded him, finally, to understand and obey those orders by getting red in the face, poking an angry forefinger at him, and bellowing loudly and belligerently, "One more time and you're fired." That did it. He was persuaded that I was an excellent salesman, on this occasion at least, and we had no more difficulty over the matter.

That kind of persuasion works well for absolute rulers of all kinds. It worked well for Caligula and Adolf Hitler, and still works pretty well in the Soviet Union and a few other slightly retarded societies in the world. But under other circumstances than marriage and absolute authority, it is necessary to resort to a somewhat gentler and more subtle brand of persuasion, usually called *salesmanship*. And getting a good job or the job you want and ought to have, as compared with getting just any job you can manage to fall into, is like the difference between selling a customer the package of cigarettes he came into your store to buy and persuading him to buy a $300 camera he had had no intention of buying.

In short, getting the job you really want and should have means selling your services, and that's SELLING in capital letters, not taking orders. No one ever won the really good job—the *career position*—without doing a first-class selling job (unless he happened to be the owner's son, and even then Dear Old Dad had to be convinced that Junior could handle the job without screwing the whole company up).

The message here is that of *marketing* yourself properly, of course, which is a subject that goes beyond even that of selling. Selling is the business of winning the specific job or kind of job you want, but marketing is the greater and prior business of deciding what kind of job you want and should have, where to seek it, and how to position yourself to win it. The message is that not only was my erstwhile salesmanager right about every exchange between people representing a sale, but he and others who were/are obviously graduates of the same school are right in asserting that we are all—each and every one of us—salesmen or saleswomen, and our success in careers and all other aspects of life on this planet depends largely on how good we are at that art of persuasion we call selling.

A great many people claim to detest the very idea of being a salesperson. Perhaps they have visions of the wearisome and thoroughly traumatic experience of having doors slammed in your face, of cruel and even arrogant rejections. Perhaps they envision selling as being the perpetual victim. To some degree, they are right. But those who work throughout the bulk of their adult years will generally face the job-hunting task a number of times in their lives—some statistics suggest eight to ten times, as an average—so you will probably play the marketing/selling roles at least that number of times. And when you consider what is at stake—your life and your career—it is not a role to be taken too lightly.

A few years ago a young firm prepared and published a job-hunter's manual, selling it via mail order and getting their orders through large newspaper advertisements in such publications as the *Wall Street Journal*. It was a far-better-than-average manual of its kind, drew praise, and became a good seller, eventually leading to the firm's establishing themselves as job-placement consultants. That is, they work in behalf of the job seeker, not the employers, so they are not the traditional "head hunters" or professional recruiters, but fall somewhere between the professional employment agency and the résumé-writing and consulting-services firm.

Currently, this firm is running large advertisements which describe what the copy claims are six myths about job hunting. They claim that these are commonly believed myths:

That if you can't find the kind of job you want it doesn't exist.

That most people know how to go about seeking a job.

That employment agencies can always place you.

That help-wanted advertisements are a good place to seek for openings.

That employers have all the control in the hiring situations.

That the best jobs go to those with the best qualifications.

The text makes that hoary claim made so often by such firms and writers on the subject of job finding, that by far the majority of job openings—this copy claims that it's between 85 and 88 percent of all the jobs—are not advertised nor available through any of the traditional sources that job hunters know of and utilize. And the copy goes on to claim that there are always some two million professional and executive jobs available, nevertheless. It quotes NFSB—the National Federation of Small Business—as maintaining that small business alone has one million jobs.

That alone is a strange statement, since Congressional committees and other sources have consistently taken the position that by far the greatest percentage of Americans are employed by small businesses—that some 60 to 70 percent of all the jobs are with small businesses. This copy suggests that only 50 percent of the openings are with small business.

In general, the claim that most openings are not advertised is a dubious one. That it serves the purposes of some—employment agencies, résumé writers, and such firms as the one referred to here—to propagate that belief alone makes it somewhat suspect. Personally, I have no trouble believing that *some* jobs are not advertised. Someone seeking a President or Chairman of the Board of a large corporation, for example, does not run help-wanted advertisements, and certainly a hospital seeking physicians would not seek them in the classified pages of daily newspapers or through employment agencies. But I find it highly unlikely that firms almost desperate to hire engineers, technicians, secretaries, accountants, and other specialists would keep their requirements secret.

As to whether most know how to seek jobs, the copy reports that standard résumés produce an average of one response for every eighty-five copies of a résumé sent out, and only one-half of these responses produce an interview. Theoretically, then, you must mail out 170 copies of your résumé to get one interview. And to get a job, you must therefore send out 1,700 copies of your résumé because (the copy insists) it takes ten interviews to produce a job offer.

This is hard to argue with, because the statistics may be right, but they are totally impossible to either verify or refute, and it makes no difference anyway because the statistics, even if valid, are meaningless. They are like actuary tables: they probably have absolutely no application to your own situation.

In any case, we will be addressing matters closely related to this throughout the pages of this book.

This advertiser claims that less than 7 percent of all managerial, professional, and executive jobs are listed with agencies because employers are unwilling to pay the agency fees. My personal observations certainly have not led me to observe any evidence that employers are reluctant to pay agency fees. Quite the contrary, many employers find it no more expensive than doing their own recruiting.

Of course, using the "want ads" in job hunting is always frowned upon and described as a poor way to find a job by all those who seek to persuade you that they can help you—for a fee. They cite statistics to "prove" that want-ads are not productive, particularly for professional, managerial, and executive jobs. For example, did you know that such advertisements can draw as many as 500 responses? Or that as many as 85 percent of employers, in some cities, reveal that they have never or rarely hired anyone via classified help-wanted advertising?

True enough. But what you do not learn is that as many as ninety-eight out of a hundred of those 500 applicants are totally unqualified and do not get even momentary consideration. Of those 500 applications, perhaps ten to twenty are truly worthy of consideration. That changes the odds considerably. And some of those employers do not use classified advertising because they hire through employment agencies or get enough applications and résumés "over the transom" to satisfy most of their needs.

The other two "myths"—that employers have all the control and the best qualified people get the jobs—will get no challenge from me. I agree that these are myths: employers do *not* have all the control—at least not when they need specialized people and applicants know what they are doing. And it is those who know how to market themselves properly who win the good jobs, whether they happen to be the best qualified for the jobs or not. That means, of course, that you can be very well qualified and still not get the job because you didn't sell yourself properly.

The real myth here is that you need someone else to do your job for you—to do your prospecting, write your résumé, coach you, find your leads, and otherwise do what no one can really do as well as you can do: sell you.

No one knows you as well as you do. No one knows what you can do as well as you do. No one knows what you really want as well as you do. Therefore, no one can write your résumé as well as you can. No one can prospect and find the proper leads as well as you can. No one can interview and sell yourself as well as you can.

What you need is not someone to do it for you, but someone to give you just a bit of guidance in how to do it for yourself. That is the purpose of this book—not to find a job for you, and not to offer you some magic formula for writing a can't-miss résumé, a surefire plan, or a gimmick of any kind, but to pass on to you a few things that will help you do the job for yourself:

> Some basics of sales and marketing in general—facts, not theories.
> Some hard facts—do's and don'ts—about finding a job.
> A few tips, based on practical, and successful, experience.
> Marketing strategies and tactics specific to job hunting.

This is what kept the author busy over many years of success in finding jobs, even through the Great Depression and beyond, and keeps him busy now, although self-employed, in finding consulting assignments which are themselves usually short-term, highly paid employment.

# 1

# What Is a Job?

*Even those of us who were most in demand a few years ago have not learned what we should have learned from the experience of being a seller in a seller's market.*

## THE BOOM YEARS FOR SKILLED PEOPLE

**T**HERE was a time for more than a few years when there was an acute shortage of skilled workers in a variety of industries, especially those involved with what has come to be called high technology. For the most part, the shortage was in scientific and engineering personnel, and it was a clear reflection of the needs for designers, technical writers, engineers of many kinds, and sundry related personnel to help produce all the modern technological wonders: rockets, missiles, and space ships; computers; radar sets; TV receivers; modern, high-speed jet aircraft; nuclear devices; and hosts of related systems and new devices.

Meanwhile, the government was swelling its ranks: Staffing new departments and hosts of new bureaus created to solve both technological and social problems, to wipe out poverty and illiteracy, to put an end to cancer and other killer diseases; and letting many support contracts, as well as hiring many new government employees. As a result, soon there was a shortage of secretaries and clerks as acute as there had been of high-technology workers.

For a time, then, most of us who had any skills at all, and especially those of us who had special, high-technology skills, were "in the driver's seat" as far as job hunting was concerned. Employers were pursuing workers more energetically than workers pursued jobs.

*1*

High-technology corporations would fly prospective employees across the country on expense-paid junkets for interviews, for example, and discovered later that many of the applicants weren't serious prospects—they were enjoying an expense-paid weekend in California or elsewhere!

Companies also set up "career weekends" in hotels in major cities where they interviewed prospects, hiring some on the spot and inviting others to visit company headquarters for interview at company expense. They also listed the openings with employment agencies and "head-hunters"—professional recruiters—and paid fees when hiring was done through these agencies.

Along with this, companies paid for relocating new employees and their families, usually allowing them thirty or sixty days' stay at a local hotel while moving their families and household goods. Some companies assumed the problems of selling the new employee's home in the city from which he or she was moving, keeping up the mortgage payments until the house was sold. And the larger companies who hired large numbers of new employees, also had special departments within their personnel functions to help the new employees find places to live and homes to buy.

There was also a frenzy of getting technical/professional specialists of many kinds on a contract basis, in which the company was not actually the employer technically, but paid an hourly rate to have the specialists work on the customer's premises as though they were employees. Under this arrangement, the customer paid a relatively high rate—perhaps $10 or $12 an hour when he paid his employees $5 or $6 an hour for the same work—and also paid a per diem living allowance, although no fringe benefits of any kind were included. Many specialists preferred to work under this arrangement—as "job shoppers"—because they earned far more money than they could as direct, permanent employees.

Not all of this was in defense and space projects. The boom years spanned primarily the fifties and sixties although they continued into the early seventies as well. Then in the middle sixties the government (under Lyndon Johnson) made an effort to wipe out poverty, ignorance, illiteracy, disease, and other social ills. The vanguard was the Office of Economic Opportunity with its Job Corps and other bureaus. Later came the Office of Education; the Environmental Protection Agency; the Department of Transportation; the all-but-exploding Public Health Service with its many institutions for a variety of disease and health-care projects; and burgeoning grants programs of many kinds, totaling some 1,200 programs for which the taxpayers were billed.

So, not only engineers and scientists were in the driver's seat, but also psychologists, sociologists, educators, administrators, secretaries, and clerks. There was now an acute shortage of secretaries, librarians, teachers, and many other specialists to match the perpetual shortfall in engineers and related scientific specialists. In fact, it was not too long before the Department of Health, Education, and Welfare (HEW) was so swollen that it had a bigger annual budget than the Department of Defense (DOD), NASA (with its $40 billion moon-landing program), and the EPA all put together.

Meanwhile, technological progress was being made at an ever increasing pace, with computers as an industry among the leaders in growth, but also as the instrument of growth for other industries. Myriad new jobs were being found for computers to do, helping expand the activities and the progress of NASA space programs and DOD weapons programs. And the term "weapon" no longer referred to a howitzer or a bomb: It was now "weapons system"—huge complexes of equipment, including radar, computers, communications, missiles, launchers, and a myriad of "GSE" (ground support equipment).

Of course, almost all this cost was being underwritten by the federal government under huge contracts, many of them on a cost-plus basis, so that the customers were reimbursed or had included these costs in their pricing when bidding for and negotiating the contracts.

It's not ended yet. There are still some of these activities afoot, despite the increasing rates of unemployment in recent years. Some of the activity survives; the message has not registered with most workers. Most workers do not yet today realize what all of this meant, or what it should mean to them in their job-hunting efforts now.

## WHAT MOST PEOPLE DO WRONG

Most people approach the whole problem of finding a job, or a better job, from a distorted viewpoint. They seem to believe that they must humble themselves to win an employer's approval. With that bias, job seekers turn out letters, résumés, and multi-page applications with the greatest of humility—trying earnestly to satisfy every request of the employer, no matter how trivial or irrelevant. Moreover, most applicants seem to believe that sincerity and willingness to work hard are the paramount requirements for impressing an employer. It's a mistaken notion. Most employers will not question your sincerity unless you give reason to question it—but assume that you will work for your salary.

Equally futile are those dreadfully trite claims to be an "idea man" and wanting a "challenge." In fact, the last thing an employer cares about is what *you* want. The employer wants you to help the employer's organization solve problems, win sales, operate profitably, and do all the other things an organization must do to survive. If an employer advertises for a technical writer, the employer wants evidence that the applicant can write reasonably well and has the necessary technical knowledge to work with whatever data is available, which may be raw indeed. Important but secondary to basic job skills, is whether the applicant will fit in with the team—can work with others. (Some very able people do not work well on a team, but only in more or less solitary functions.) Also, the employer wants to know what kind of employee the applicant will be—whether he or she is trustworthy, dependable, honest, and so forth.

Only when an applicant appears to pass these screenings does the employer agree to an interview. And a first objective of an interview is to verify the early impressions. The interview will continue to probe the full depth of the applicant's capabilities only after those impressions are verified, and then proceed to negotiation, if the employer is still duly impressed with the suitability of the applicant.

Unfortunately, most applicants fail to recognize this last phase of the interview as negotiation, but tend to permit the employer to dictate the terms of employment. Prospective employees could probably get better terms than they do, but they do not understand that they are negotiating with an employer who wants to hire them, and is simply trying to do so on the best possible terms.

Many applicants do not know how to handle the "salary requested" question—and it is most common for interviewers to ask applicants what they are seeking in the way of salary. Consequently, they underprice themselves for fear of demanding too much and "blowing" the whole interview. Getting hired at a lower salary than the employer was prepared to pay is not the worst of it—sometimes the applicant is not hired because the too-modest salary demand backfires and causes the interviewer to suspect that he or she has misjudged the applicant, after all. Rarely is an interviewer going to fill what is ordinarily a $15,000 job with someone at $10,000. On the other hand, it is rare for an interviewer to say, "Hey, you're under-pricing yourself. Ask me for $15,000 if you want this job." That may happen once in a great while—occasionally it does—but it would be naive and risky to depend on the chance.

What most applicants fail to recognize is that an interview is either terminated when the interviewer decides he or she is wasting time in an unproductive pursuit or, when it is a successful one, advanced to a negotiation which may very well result in a verbal [job] contract.

## WHAT IS A CONTRACT?

A contract is an agreement. It need not necessarily be in written form; verbal contracts are legitimate and binding. The reason for writing them is: (1) To document the agreements—often hammered out in protracted negotiation—so that no one needs to rely on memory; and (2) to prove later, if necessary, that the contract does exist and the terms are as alleged.

In fact, there are some occasions when a formal, written contract is drawn up between employer and employee. This usually occurs when an employer has induced a high-level executive or professional to leave lucrative employment, and the new employee insists on a written contract to protect his or her interests in the new position. However, these may be exceptional cases. Employment ordinarily entails a verbal contract: The employer specifies the terms—salary, fringe benefits, bonuses, insurance, paid time off, and/or anything he or she normally offers employees. A contract, however, is an agreement, and requires something from each of the parties. The employee may not stipulate his or her contribution to the *quid pro quo*—the exchange or trade between the two contracting parties—but it is nevertheless implicitly understood to be so many hours (forty, in most cases today) of his/her best efforts, performing some specific duties.

## EMPLOYMENT IS A CONTRACT

Although we use terms like *being hired, getting a job, being appointed, being employed, working for someone,* what we really mean is that we have entered into contract with someone to exchange our best efforts at performing some service in exchange for certain compensation—in cash and in other forms. A job is a contract, although it is a special kind of contract in some respects:

1. It is almost invariably verbal, although nonetheless binding.
2. It is usually for an indefinite term, unlike most contracts, and may easily run for a lifetime.
3. It is covered, controlled, regulated, and enforceable under and by more laws than are other, "normal" contracts.
4. It is a contract that is rarely violated by one party—the employer (who almost invariably delivers all the compensation promised)—and frequently violated by the other party—the employee (who quite often delivers less than forty hours of best effort).
5. Normally either party is free to terminate the contract and the relationship arbitrarily, usually on short or without notice.

The importance of this to you as a job-seeker is that it changes your point of view. You don't apply for contracts; you negotiate them. The process of job seeking and job finding has three major phases: marketing, selling, and closing. And these break down into sub-functions, as illustrated in the following simple flowchart (Figure 1) and table (Table 1).

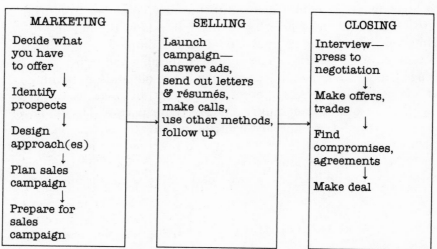

FIGURE 1. Basic functions in job hunting and finding.

## TABLE 1

### FINDING AND LANDING THE JOB YOU WANT

*The Marketing Functions*

DECIDE WHAT YOU HAVE TO SELL
:   Analyze your education (what you have learned formally and can show "paper" for), your experience (what you have learned informally and can account for and verify). Articulate these as specific work- or job-skills in terms that relate to specific jobs and job descriptions.

IDENTIFY PROSPECTS
:   Survey field, decide what kinds of employers (organizations) are most suitable or most promising prospects for employment at kind of job you want. (Short- and long-term objectives.)

DESIGN APPROACH
:   Determine how to best approach and reach the prospects you have chosen—mail, telephone, in person, via middle-agents or brokers, and others.

FORMULATE OFFER
:   Translate skills and past accomplishments into things you can *do* for employers (results you can promise). Rank-order these, select most important one(s).

PLAN CAMPAIGN
:   Draw up a specific plan of action to reach prospects with the most effective presentations you can devise. Consider résumés, letters, personal calls, speaking at meetings, writing articles, doing volunteer work, hiring out as temporary, and other methods. Consider also responding to advertisements, registering with middle-agents, mass mailouts of letters and résumés, and other methods. Make decisions and draft actual plan on paper.

PREPARE FOR CAMPAIGN
:   Draw up résumé, letters, cards, other materials, and have them duplicated in sufficient quantity for your campagin. Subscribe to services or periodicals you plan to use (e.g., *Wall Street Journal*, Sunday *New York Times*, other). Register with agencies. Gather mailing lists. Prepare to attend suitable conferences, conventions, trade shows. Plan situations-wanted advertising.

TABLE 1 (cont.)

## FINDING AND LANDING THE JOB YOU WANT

| *The Sales Campaign* |
| --- |

| | |
| --- | --- |
| THE ROUTINE SALES ACTIONS | Do mass mailouts, run situations-wanted advertising, touch base with agents, attend "career weekends," respond to advertisements, call on personnel offices, make out and leave applications and résumés. |
| THE NON-ROUTINE, OFTEN-OVERLOOKED SALES ACTIONS | Get your name listed as available and interested in a position in all the special places often available and as often overlooked: placement offices at your old college or trade school, the newsletter of your society or association, other special places. Post notices (abstract of your résumé?) in suitable places, such as bulletin boards at public library or town hall, and literature tables at seminars, meetings, and conferences or conventions/trade shows. Volunteer to speak at seminars and other kinds of meetings, and leave your literature on the literature table. |
| OTHER WAYS TO DEVELOP LEADS | "Get around" as much as possible to business meetings and wherever else you are likely to meet people who can be helpful. Let them know what you do, that you are looking for a position. Get names, addresses, business connections, telephone numbers, not only of those you meet, but also of those they recommend. (Be sure to ask for suggestions and recommendations, even of strangers. This is one of the richest sources of good leads.) Be sure to record all the names and numbers, with notations of where, when, how, and from whom you got them. Also, join "job clubs," if there are any in your area. These are informal associations of jobless people who help each other with ideas, leads, tips, and other assistance. |

TABLE 1 (cont.)

## FINDING AND LANDING THE JOB YOU WANT

---

### *The Sales Campaign*

---

MAKE
FOLLOW-UPS

Follow-up is extremely important. Do something about every lead you get: mail résumés, cards, letters. Make telephone calls, ask for meetings. (Interviews, that is, although you suggest meetings, perhaps lunches, if you don't mind buying lunch.) Important note: Never end a meeting, even a chance or casual one, without some resolution, which always is a plan for the next action. Always try to pin the other down to an agreement to do something, preferably meet for serious discussion. At the least, you announce your next action ("I'll call you on Tuesday"). The objective is always to keep momentum even if the initial momentum is slight. Most people can be pressed into action if you do it skillfully and tactfully.

---

### *The Closing Actions*

---

MEET AND
DISCUSS

The goal of marketing was to plan and prepare for the sales campaign. The goal of the sales campaign was to gain interviews. And the purpose of interviews is to negotiate. Therefore, all the actions until now have been to press for serious "discussions" and "meetings," your euphemisms for job interviews. (You'll find less resistance to "meeting" and "discussing" than to "interviewing.")

PRESS TO
REACH THE
NEGOTIATION
STAGE

Whether the other party agrees that the meeting and discussion is a job interview or not, press to reach the negotiation stage by selling aggressively during the meeting. Conduct the negotiations tactfully but aggressively, being proactive and not reactive. Stress the benefits you can deliver, with ample evidence that you recognize typical problems and can cope with them successfully because you have in the past. Try to reach agreement during the meeting.

TABLE 1 (cont.)

## FINDING AND LANDING THE JOB YOU WANT

---

*The Closing Actions*

---

| | |
|---|---|
| PLAN ADDITIONAL FOLLOW-UP ACTIONS, IF NEEDED | If you cannot reach firm agreement—close your sale—during the meeting, more follow-up is in order. End meeting with plan for follow-up—preferably *your* follow-up in some manner. Plan to call, and ask when would be the best time, what else you can supply to help, such as references, more information, details about past employment not already supplied, or other action (even if this is only a stratagem furnishing a reason or excuse for the follow-up action). |
| MAKE FOLLOW-UPS | Make follow-up—telephone calls to press on with your fight for the job, send detailed résumé (or *proposal*, preferably), copies of letters of reference, other follow-up. |

# 2

# Marketing and Selling Yourself

*No, marketing and selling are not the same thing. Not at all. Not even in job hunting.*

## WHAT IS MARKETING?

**E**VEN if it makes you feel like a side of beef, you must think of job hunting as a marketing and sales proposition, as the first chapter and Table 1 have already suggested quite strongly. You must sell yourself. If you entertain even slight doubts about that, think about all the individuals you have observed who are no more skilled, intelligent, or dedicated than you (and perhaps are even less so) yet get ahead faster and go farther. Why is this? Is it possible they manage to sell themselves more effectively than you? Call it "office politics" and "making points," if you will, but the results justify calling it good marketing.

If you have taken the time to study Table 1 and the little diagram preceding it you will have noticed that first came marketing, then selling. That's as it should be, for marketing includes a number of functions, including making decisions as to what, where, and how to sell it. That is, marketing itself is preparation for selling—deciding what you will sell, to whom, and how. And, not surprisingly, success in selling depends largely on how effectively the marketing is done. Planning makes the difference in selling, as it does in most things, and is an integral part of marketing.

## DECIDING WHAT YOU HAVE TO SELL

The greatest problem most people face in marketing themselves, lies in appraising themselves—in deciding what it is they have to sell. Admittedly, it is not easy to be objective in making this kind of analysis. But this can be accomplished, if you accept certain facts and adopt the methods to be described here. First, recognize and accept these facts:

* No one really .wants to pay you for what you are or what you know. An employer wishes to hire you for what you do.
* Note the wording in the first item: for what you do. Not for what you *can* do, but for what you *do* do. There is no benefit to an employer that you're a Phi Beta Kappa, or understand the finest implications of information theory, or even your being able to carry out highly complex mathematical operations, unless (a) these abilities are of use to the employer and (b) there is some assurance that you will act on this knowledge and skill.

Time and again we hear individuals complaining that they are not getting ahead as fast as others who have far less ability. But your abilities do not have an absolute value. They are only valuable when applied—put to work—in circumstances where they are of practical use. In today's economy, young people who have earned their Ph.Ds are often unable to find jobs suitable to their education and training, and some have even accepted jobs bagging groceries at supermarket checkout counters. Obviously, the supermarket can afford to pay the Doctor of Philosophy only for bagging groceries, at whatever rate of pay that job commands; the doctoral degree and scholarliness are of absolutely no value at the checkout counter.

That's an obvious case, but it also holds true in cases which are less obvious. If you accept a job that does not make use of your best skills and abilities you are not going to command what you should in salary and position. But the same is true of any failure on your part to negotiate properly—to make a realistic evaluation of what you have to offer, what it ought to be worth, and what you must insist on getting for it. Here is a case that illustrates this:

When several major defense contracts were cancelled in Philadelphia, some years ago, a busy Washington-area contractor, Vitro Laboratories, recruited many of the engineering people in Philadelphia who found themselves suddenly without jobs. A number were hired as technical writers on a Navy project, most of them at starting salaries of $7800 (a median salary for the job, in those days). But one man managed to get himself hired at $8700. When his fellow workers learned this, they became outraged at the patent unfairness in the difference, and demanded of the man how he rated so much higher a starting salary than they did.

He told them that he "rated" the salary simply because he had negotiated it. Whereas the others humbly accepted whatever the interviewer offered, he had asked and gotten more. He had made a more realistic appraisal of what his skills and services were worth and had little difficulty in persuading the employer. But it was that realistic appraisal of his own skills that gave him the courage and conviction to hold out in negotiations for what he believed was fair and proper, and which he was sure the employer would agree to.

## THE SKILLS ANALYSIS

Perhaps you are a professional of some sort—engineer, psychologist, lawyer, architect, accountant, or other—but do not think of what you are trained to do as a "skill"; for the sake of convenience in reference, however, bear with the idea that being able to write a will or design an atrium is a skill.

For the professional, the process of appraising his or her value is somewhat simpler than it is for others, because he or she has access to sources of advice and guidance in the field as to what typical salaries are for given degrees and experience. Although it may seem irrelevant, matters such as the name of the university play a part, too. (It's not truly irrelevant, for the graduate of a prestigious university may actually be able to command more profit for an employer simply by virtue of graduating from Yale or Harvard, rather than from Excelsior U night school.) For most, however, self-appraisal is not easy, but requires a great deal of work.

The task is best accomplished in stages, going from the general to the specific. Study the items in Table 2, for example, and check off whatever is appropriate in your own case as the first step in profiling what you have to offer. (The choices include what you want—your objectives—as well as what you believe describes your skills, abilities, and experience.) At least, this will help you gain some insight into what you project, or wish to project, to prospective employers. More important, it will compel you to do some thinking, make some preliminary analyses, and perhaps start pondering on short- and long-term objectives.

Many of these questions are things we don't think about until circumstances force us to. For example, you might believe that no one would wish to work in a stressful environment—a newspaper city room, for instance. But there are individuals who prefer such conditions, who are exhilarated and inspired by this atmosphere, and would be most unhappy in a calm, quiet room where work proceeded slowly and deliberately.

Think about past experiences, as you ponder over this chart and decide where to place your check marks. Perhaps you worked at a sedentary job and hated it, and would far rather work outdoors at a job that kept you moving around. Perhaps your chief "skill" asset is great physical strength, and you are not averse to work that requires the use of this ability.

Think carefully as you check off the appropriate boxes. But don't hesitate to add a category or two, if you wish to: Perhaps the categories you want are not included in this preprinted table.

The various items are not totally unrelated to one another. On the contrary, many are interrelated. For instance, if you prefer outdoor work, have great strength, and prefer work that utilizes your physical strength, you probably ought to be checking off "construction" as a kind of organization you envision as a prospective employer.

Where you have made multiple checks—for example, if you have skills which are highly specialized but also have skills which have quite wide applications, rank these in order; place a number in the box, instead of a check, with 1 representing the skill you prefer to use or which you believe most valuable, 2 being in the next-highest ranked skill, and so forth. Do the same for the other assets of yourself being profiled.

The result of this will be a thumbnail sketch of yourself as a job candidate, complete with your general, and perhaps even long-term, career objective. But you will have done some thinking about yourself and your career—or at least the job you want to capture next. And you will now have begun to attach a rudder to your job hunt, so that you are not shooting wildly at anything that pops up, like an unguided

TABLE 2

GENERAL CHARACTERISTICS FOR PROFILE

| *General Description:* | *General Types of Skills:* |
|---|---|
| [ ] Technical/professional | [ ] Intellectual, cerebral |
| [ ] Non-technical/professional | [ ] Motor, mechanical, tool-using |
| [ ] Specialist | |
| [ ] Generalist | [ ] Generalized, wide applications |
| [ ] White collar | |
| [ ] Blue collar | [ ] Specialized, narrow applications |
| [ ] No strong preference | |
| [ ] ———————— | [ ] Require great physical strength |
| | [ ] Not physically demanding |
| | [ ] No special skills |

| *General Preferences:* | *General Objectives/Desires:* |
|---|---|
| [ ] Routine duties | [ ] Manufacturing company |
| [ ] Diverse and unanticipated duties | [ ] Association |
| | [ ] Professional-services firm |
| [ ] Problems to be solved | [ ] Construction firm |
| [ ] Low-stress environment | [ ] Outdoors, active, mobile work |
| [ ] Stressful situations | |
| [ ] Work as part of team | [ ] Indoors, sedentary work |
| [ ] Work alone | [ ] Career opportunity |
| [ ] Meticulous attention to detail | [ ] Stepping-stone, experience-gaining work |
| [ ] Highly structured situations | [ ] Any kind of work |
| [ ] Unstructured situations | [ ] ———————— |
| [ ] ———————— | |

*Education:*

[ ] College (degree?)    [ ]
[ ] Trade/vocational school
[ ] Special courses (e.g., military schools)

missile or loose cannon on a pitching deck—now you have a general sense of direction and purpose.

The following step is to sharpen this purpose to a point where you begin to get fixes on the kind of job you want and can win. This will also help you determine whether the kind of job you want *is* the kind of job you can win—or what it is going to take to win that job and what you must do to reach that objective immediately or later. Let us suppose that you discover you do not have all the qualifications you are likely to need to become the production manager of a small manufacturing firm. You may opt for that "stepping-stone, experience-gaining work" listed in Table 2. You will then know that you are in pursuit of a job that is likely to either lead directly to the managerial job you want, or will provide the kind of experience that will later help you pursue that job.

Consider that the job you are after is not an end in itself, but is a means to a larger and more important end that you are not quite ready to achieve. It is certainly helpful to recognize this, especially in interviewing and negotiating.

## NEVER MIND "SKILLS"—WHAT CAN YOU *DO*?

Having come this far, it's time to look at this from the employer's view: Picture yourself sitting at the employer's desk. Here are your basic problems, the problems that every business faces regularly:

*Payroll:* It has to be met every week or whatever the pay period is. And it requires hard cash. You can't meet a payroll with receivables except by borrowing against them at high interest rates.

*Unions:* If you have one, you've got to manage to get along with them, and it's probably a rare month that you don't have to arbitrate a few grievances and general complaints.

*Overhead:* Rent, heat, light, taxes, insurance, printing, marketing, and all those other outrageously high costs of everything necessary to merely keep your doors open, whether you are doing enough business or not. Overhead—there's always too much of it.

*Profit:* Whether you're the owner, trying to make a living, the CEO (Chief Executive Officer), trying to satisfy the stockholders, or a manager trying to keep the owner happy, you need profit to survive. Profit—there's never enough of it!

*Production costs:* Like overhead, production costs are always too high, which is what makes profits too low. Keeping the cost of production down is always a major struggle.

*Sales:* Everything would be all right if we could get more sales, reasons almost every proprietor and CEO. Getting enough sales is a major endeavor of every company, even in the best of times, and these aren't the best of times.

It's a rare proprietor or manager who isn't afflicted by these concerns. What can *you*, an applicant for employment, do to help? Now that you're sitting behind the employer's desk, bowed beneath the weight of all these problems and wondering what ever possessed you to start a business in the first place, you look at those résumés and applications on your desk in a new light. What you're looking for are clues to who among all these eager beavers can *help* you overcome some of these problems? Who can help you increase sales, cut production costs, reduce overhead? If anyone is smart enough to promise to do any of these or other things that can help solve these problems, you are going to read that résumé and/or letter eagerly, looking for evidence that the writer can provide relief of these burdens.

Most of the time you look in vain. Almost everyone is *asking* for something. Rarely is anyone smart enough to *offer* something—to offer help. They simply don't understand what it is to be an employer, why an employer hires people, what an employer is looking for. They don't understand the difference between an application and an offer. They don't understand that you are not interested in what they want, but you are interested in getting help with your problems.

## AN OFFER OF HELP

The next step in your marketing analysis is to translate your various skills and desires into what they can and should represent to employers as offers of help. But even here it is possible to go astray and describe how you can help, but miss the mark. Take, for example, the hypothetical case of a typist who claims the lightning typing speed of 120 words a minute on a modern electric typewriter.

That's a pretty good speed, and the typist who reports this in her résumé with justifiable pride assumes that anyone reading that résumé says, "Wow! Wouldn't she be great to have in our office knocking out our letters or whatever we need typed." The sad fact is, however, that would rarely be the result for at least three reasons:

1. The reader of the résumé may not be aware that 120 words a minute is top-notch typing performance.
2. The reader may know what typing speeds mean, but the fact may simply not register because the reader must go through the reasoning process of translating that speed into estimates of daily production—and the busy executive is not likely to do that. Thus the point is lost.
3. At least some executives are aware that the speed achieved in a typing test has nothing to do with an average rate of production. Even the fastest typist does not work at such a speed all day, and the fast typist's average for a typical day may be 10 words a minute.

The last reason is the clue to what is wrong with how so many people report in their résumés and letters what they can do or have achieved: They express the ability or achievement in either somewhat abstract terms or by ways that have far more meaning to them than to the employer who reads the résumé. Suppose the typist who can turn out 120 words a minute in a test reports in her résumé that she customarily handles correspondence for half a dozen executives, and averages 25 letters a day. The employer can relate this information to his or her business workload directly, even though that probably represents an average over the day of about 50 words a minute. Typing 120 words a minute—or even averaging 50 words a minute throughout the day—is not an "achievement." Handling the correspondence load for a half-dozen executives and typing 25 letters a day is an achievement to be reported.

In short, the idea is to relate what you can, or offer to, do directly to the employer's needs. Anytime you require a reader to translate what you say into another set of terms so that he or she can see how it relates to his or her need, you defeat your own purpose: Readers simply will not do that very often.

Alan R. is a case in point. Al learned to write proposals fairly early in his career as a technical writer. A few years later, fate propelled him into a temporary assignment to write a proposal in Europe. It gave Al a taste for world travel, and the work paid rather well, too, far better than technical writing had. His familiarity with writing proposals to foreign governments and foreign companies, his freedom and willingness to travel, and his track record of winning proposals won him increasingly better jobs with companies who marketed to foreign governments and foreign companies. Al's ability to turn out winning proposals was a major asset, but his ability to handle foreign assignments successfully was the clincher: what he could do was win business for his employer. He doesn't bother relating, in his résumé, how many years he has been a proposal writer or how many countries he has visited on business. What he does list is simply how many foreign contracts he has won for his employers. That's all he needs to say to draw immediate interest. That's the language the employer understands.

Or take Henry G. as another example. Henry, an engineering writer, attended a meeting of his professional society one evening to hear a Dr. Jonathan P. Slupski speak about programmed instruction and how the organization of which he was a research director developed programmed-instruction products. Henry sought Slupski out later during the coffee-and-cake follow-up to the formal part of the meeting. Henry was interested to learn how Slupski's company managed to find qualified writers for so many different subjects in which the company wrote training programs. He was advised that the company contracted sometimes with freelance writers, and was invited to visit Slupski at the latter's office whenever he wished.

The upshot of all this was that Henry followed up this lead and was ultimately interviewed by the company's Editorial Director, who saw in Henry an ability that had been lacking and was needed in the company. Henry finally accepted what he found to be an attractive offer to join the company's writing staff in a responsible position.

In one sense, this is pure luck—many would so regard it—but it also is the result of maximizing the opportunities for Lady Luck to smile. Henry was busy and active, going to association meetings where he would be likely to meet people in his own profession. He also was interested in and followed up what may have seemed to be a rather slim lead, at first: The company Dr. Slupski worked for was not actively seeking to hire anyone. But employers will, surprisingly often, create openings when they have the opportunity to hire someone who shows promise of being able to help the organization succeed. Fortune, one sage has said, favors the prepared mind—the mind which is on the alert for opportunity, quick to follow it up and exploit it to the fullest extent.

Before you attempt to write a résumé, consider what you can do for an employer (not what the employer can do for you) to reduce costs, increase profits, expand sales, solve problems, and otherwise deliver much-to-be-desired benefits. See Table 3 and study it for guidance in expressing what you can do in the most direct terms possible— terms that the employer will relate directly and immediately to his or her own needs—preferably by explaining how you have performed in prior employment. Or, if you have not yet had the opportunity to do any of this in prior jobs or are seeking your first job, explain accomplishments in other applications, such as in pursuing a hobby, doing volunteer work, organizing something at home, helping a friend or relative. If absolutely impossible to claim some prior relevant achievement, project what you think you can do. Here especially you must provide some rationale and how-to-do-it detail if you are to be credible: claims without something that will pass muster as evidence, if not absolute proof, will simply not be accepted.

You will note in the table a great many suggestions of items that will usually be effective in persuading the reader of your résumé to accept what you claim. However, you must do these things, too:

1. Write up all the items that are suggested here and are applicable in your own case, creating a rough draft.
2. Sort through the items, decide which is/are most important and most impressive, rank-order them and use only a select few.
3. Use only some of the rationale/details—enough to lend your claim an authoritative air, an air of authenticity.

There are several reasons for giving only the most important and most impressive details. One is the obvious reason of keeping your résumé reasonably short: Your résumé should not appear so long that reading it would be a formidable task. But you also need "something for an encore"—for the follow-up interview. And you need to make it plain in your résumé that there is more—much more—to tell, so as to compel the employer to call on you to impart more details in an interview.

TABLE 3

## RÉSUMÉ ITEMS THAT MAKE THE DIFFERENCE

| *General Benefit* | *Rationale/Details to Explain & Validate Claim* |
| --- | --- |
| INCREASED SALES— GENERAL | Specific (quantified) reports on accomplishments: number of units/sales, dollar amounts, percentage increases, relative ranking on sales force, rate of improvement/increases in personal performance. Also 'as much how-you-did-it information as possible: ideas, methods, promotions, innovations. |
| REDUCED COSTS | What kinds of costs reduced (overhead, production, general, telephone, travel, printing, paper, purchasing, other specifics: the more specific, the more credible and the more impressive). Quantify as much as possible, dollars or percentages. |
| INCREASED EFFICIENCY | Quantify: where, how, by how much, with what results (dollars and/or percentages). Examples: reduced or eliminated overtime by improved scheduling (scheduling by computer?), redesigned assembly-line (give a few details; general claims will not be credible, without some idea of how you did it), simplified/improved product design, found better sources for raw materials or components, found it more efficient to subcontract some operations. |
| SOLVED PROBLEMS | Explain problem(s) so as to reveal the general nature and importance, show how you solved it and what it meant to the company in terms of savings of dollars and/or labor and time. Use percentages (your best estimates) where appropriate. Example: Searched for and found a substitute material when source of original material dried up or its cost became prohibitive, reorganized accounting department to meet difficult payroll schedules, decentralized purchasing to eliminate bottlenecks in getting materials to various assembly plants, found off-the-shelf computer programs to meet special needs. |

TABLE 3 (*cont.*)

## RÉSUMÉ ITEMS THAT MAKE THE DIFFERENCE

| General Benefit | Rationale/Details to Explain & Validate Claim |
| --- | --- |
| EXPANDED SALES BASE | Won contracts in related but new field, organized new department to handle, invented new product/ service, broadened marketing territories, found new markets, repositioned existing line(s), other. As in other areas, give some how-you-did-it detail and as much quantitative information as possible. |
| SETTLED LABOR DISPUTES | Name union and local, explain grievance/problems, give brief account of how you handled and settled it, what further trouble you avoided, such as possible strike, what your settlement cost and what it (probably—best estimate) saved company. Handle with care; labor problems are always delicate situations. |
| RECRUITED SCARCE SPECIALISTS | Many kinds of specialists are in short supply, even in these times, and employers often go to great expense in finding them and hiring them. (Sometimes the expense of not finding them is even greater). Helping in this area is an important achievement. Explain how you did it—wrote more effective advertisements, conducted successful career weekends and interviews, did innovative things (perhaps recruiting at national conventions, or other imaginative idea)—and with what results, quantified as much as possible (number of people recruited, cost per recruitment, and so forth). |
| ALTERNATIVE APPROACH TO PROBLEM | As alternative or addition to recruiting scarce specialists, you may have developed and successfully employed a training program in your company to retrain and upgrade suitable employees, thereby reducing and perhaps eliminating the need for additional hires of difficult-to-find specialists. If so, give a few details, especially costs of program and resulting average cost per newly retrained specialist. |

TABLE 3 (cont.)

## RÉSUMÉ ITEMS THAT MAKE THE DIFFERENCE

| General Benefit | Rationale/Details to Explain & Validate Claim |
| --- | --- |
| OTHER TRAINING | If you solved other problems, increased efficiency, reduced costs, or otherwise made contributions via training, explain, with details and quantified reports or estimates. (Many companies rely on training.) If your field is training itself, be sure to travel the breadth of experience in terms of subjects and target populations you've been able to handle successfully. |
| INCREASED PROFITS | Explain cost reduction, sales increase, other basis for increase in profits, such as more efficient operation, lower rejection rate on assembly line, better quality control, improved incoming-parts inspection, more effective work procedures, reduction in waste, other measures. Show linkage, provide quantified data (at least best estimates). |

If you can do this, the employer will not regard calling you in for interview as an onerous task he or she is obligated to carry out, but will call you in eagerly to question you and elicit valuable information. That is a prime purpose in doing your résumé in such a manner.

Note, too, that many items can be used as you see fit. Saving money by better purchasing, for example, can be cited as a cost reduction achievement, an efficiency-improvement, a better job performance (if you are a purchasing agent), and perhaps in other ways. You decide what will lend the greatest impact with regard to the kind of position you are after. Obviously, if you are a trainer, you'll want to show your various achievements in reference to your training activities—how you solved problems, reduced costs, raised efficiency, etc. via training. But you'll also want to show how efficient your training itself was—how you found the most effective and lowest-cost training programs, or perhaps created them. Similarly, if you are an accountant, you'll want to show achievements that are relevant to the accounting function, yet show how they produced beneficial results elsewhere in the organization. In short, the items ought to indicate to the employer these specifics:

1. General benefit in macroscopic terms—cost reductions, profit improvement, efficiency increase, sales expansion, etc.
2. More precisely what the achievement was—just what you did to achieve that general benefit.
3. How you did it—the logical rationale that makes the achievement believable.
4. The benefits that resulted, quantified—how much benefit.
5. Who benefited—all the elements of the company that benefited.


## DEVELOPING LEADS: THE SALES CAMPAIGN

Salespeople who do "cold selling"—approaching new prospects on every call, without any preliminary preparation—are doing the hardest kind of selling because they do not have the faintest idea whether the prospect they approach has the slightest use for or interest in whatever they are selling. They know, therefore, that they must depend on pure probability: some percentage of those cold calls will result in sales. The key to success lies primarily in making enough calls.

Somewhat easier is the lot of the salesperson who has leads— names of prospects who have indicated slight interest by responding to an advertisement, filling out a card at a demonstration booth, or otherwise giving the salesperson a reason to suspect that he or she is a true prospect—someone who is likely to buy. Therefore, for many kinds of sales campaigns, the marketing includes some method for getting a stream of sales lead. That's why so many advertisements include a "response card" or some other method for gathering names and addresses of people showing some interest.

Job hunting generally involves both types of selling. "Making the rounds" (visiting employment offices of companies) to fill out applications and leave copies of your résumé, mailing résumés and letters out to lists of prospective employers, and distributing résumés freely at suitable business gatherings is cold-calling, prospecting for sales leads—for someone to call you to discuss employment or to ask for

more information. Responding to help-wanted advertising is responding to leads: The advertisement tells you that there is a job available.
Being invited by individuals to send them your résumé should be (but
may not be, unfortunately) a sales lead: perhaps the individual doesn't know any other way to say, "Don't call me; I'll call
you."

Any time you respond to something employers or their agents do
as part of an effort to hire people, you are responding to sales leads.
A great many of the leads you can develop by more or less passive
means—by simply being alert and observing employers' and their
agents' overt efforts to recruit. Others you must develop by your own
active and aggressive measures, by taking the initiative, instead of
waiting for someone else to do something, by acting instead of reacting.
Table 4 lists the various kinds of passive and active ways to uncover
leads to which you can respond. The end-goal is to get job offers, of
course, but the immediate, direct goal of all this activity is to generate
good leads. Help-wanted advertisements, career weekends, and other
such things are general leads, but the kind of lead you are really
seeking is the one that shows real promise of producing the kind of
job you want—the invitation to come in for interview, the request
for more information (the sincere and obviously interested request, not the polite brushoff request to "drop a résumé off"), and
other such encouraging indications of impending success. Ideally,
you want to generate enough good leads so that your problem
is no longer winning a job, but rather deciding which is the best
offer.

## JOB CLUBS

A phenomenon that springs up in times of high unemployment
rates and job scarcity is the job club. This is an informal association
of unemployed individuals, who are having difficulty in finding suitable jobs and believe they can help each other. They generally gather
in a member's home, exchange tips, leads, and ideas, lend each other
comfort, advice, coaching for interviews, help with résumés, offer sol-
ace and aid. And, of course, those of such a group who connect—get
a job—are usually in a better position to help the others who also
win a job.

TABLE 4
## WHERE/HOW TO FIND LEADS TO RESPOND TO

| General Measure | What/Where/How |
|---|---|
| DISTRIBUTING RÉSUMÉS, LETTERS | Mailing: Rent mailing lists of suitable companies from mailing-list brokers, or compile lists from directories, newspaper advertising, association membership lists. Hand out at conferences and conventions; leave on literature tables; send to friends and acquaintances; leave at personnel offices of companies you visit personally. |
| ADVERTISING, SITUATIONS WANTED | Run your own advertisements in suitable publications—*Wall Street Journal, New York Times, Washington Post,* other major city newspapers carrying substantial help-wanted advertising; also some newsletters and magazines circulating amongst those in your field, including periodicals of associations. |
| TELEPHONE APPLICATIONS | Calling personnel offices—and managers, when possible—of companies, which is sometimes more effective, at least as opening gun, than sending résumés and letters. Tip: If you use telephone, try to learn names, titles of executives to whom you might send your résumé directly, bypassing personnel office, at least for the moment. |
| REGISTERING YOUR NAME WIDELY | Utilize every resource possible by registering your name with various placement services—commercial agencies and "head hunters," 40-Plus clubs, college placement offices, government employment services, local "job clubs," any others you can uncover. |
| CAREER WEEKENDS AND JOB FAIRS | Watch the advertisements for advertised career weekends and attend, armed with an ample supply of résumés, prepared to be interviewed on the spot. (Company managers and/or brokers often conduct preliminary interviews on the spot and select most promising candidates there and then.) Sometimes such an event is sponsored by a single employer who |

TABLE 4 (cont.)

| General Measure | What/Where/How |
| --- | --- |

is looking for a large number of people to staff a new project or an expansion of some sort. Sometimes the event is sponsored by a large agency or broker, who represents a number of employers and is looking for many people for many different jobs, different employers, different locales. Sometimes you can gather up literature of 20 or more different companies who are looking for help.

**CONVENTIONS, CONFERENCES, SYMPOSIA, SEMINARS**

These gatherings of people are excellent sources of good leads. Attendees are from all levels of many companies, including top executives and junior executives, sometimes secretaries and administrators, who are excellent sources of information. Attend as many of these as possible, circulate freely, meet as many people as possible, distribute cards and résumés, take notes, compile names and addresses, and be prepared to follow up. It may also pay to attend such events, even if not in your field—a gathering of personnel specialists, for example, may be a great help in finding good leads.

**DRAW ATTENTION TO YOUR SELF**

Speak at as many occasions as possible—guest at seminars, conventions, business meetings, association events—wherever and whenever you get the opportunity to make yourself known. Do the same in writing articles for newsletters, journals, other publications circulated among people who ought to know of your existence and availability. Somehow make your availability for employment known, perhaps by simply advising listeners and readers that you are freelancing or consulting temporarily, until a suitable permanent connection offers itself. (It's true enough that you are more likely to get offers if you appear not to be greatly in need of offers, but able to be independent and choosy.)

## SOME SPECIFIC RESOURCES

Most cities today have a Forty-Plus club listed in the local telephone directory. To get help, you are generally asked to give one day a week to the club, to answer the telephone and handle a few simple administrative chores. In turn, the club provides you a central source of information, takes calls for you and offers other kinds of help, including job listings.

Middle agents or brokers are listed under a variety of headings in telephone directories. Here are some of the headings:

| | |
|---|---|
| Employment agencies | Temporary help |
| Employment service | Executive search consultants |
| Employment contractors | Employment counselors |
| Industrial consultants | Labor relations consultants |

Some of these charge the applicant a fee, some charge the employers and list "fee paid jobs only." Legitimate agencies charge fees only after the successful placement is made. Beware any who want money "up front." Many of these have been the subject of exposés in newspapers, magazines, and on TV documentaries, which have revealed a poor record of success and rather flexible ethical standards among many such firms. (More than one has been subsequently forced out of business by the authorities or by the publicity.)

If you are interested in pursuing a job with the federal government, in addition to the civil service offices (now called Office of Personnel Management) of the federal government which exist in most cities and towns of size in the United States, there are several services that provide periodical publications and other aid and guidance in pursuing government jobs:

Federal Research Service, Inc., 370 Maple Avenue, Vienna, VA 22180, (703) 281-0200. Publishes *Federal Career Opportunities*, biweekly listings of federal job openings, 6 issues for $28. Also *How to Get a Federal Job and Advance*, by David Waelde, $10.

Federal Jobs, Inc., 10701 Lawyers Road, Vienna, VA 22180. (703) 471-1417.

*The Uncle Sam Connection: An Insider's Guide to Federal Employment*, by James E. Hawkins, Follett Publishing Co., 1010 West Washington Blvd., Chicago, IL 60607, (312) 666-5858, $4.95.

Army Times Publishing Co., 475 School Street, SW 20024, (202) 554-7100. Publishes *Army Times, Air Force Times, Navy Times,* and *Federal Times,* all listing at least some federal job openings each week. (*Federal Times* is for employees of all nonmilitary branches and civilian employees of military branches.)

*Managing Your Career Success,* by Terry D. Schmidt, Lifetime Learning Publications, 10 Davis Drive, Belmont, CA 94002, (415) 595-2350, $24.95.

*How to Sell Yourself to Others,* by Elmer Wheeler, Cornerstone Library, $2.95.

Directories which are useful for making up mailing lists and other prospecting activities are plentiful, and many of these are available in any good public library. (Ordering information provided for those not always found in libraries.)

*Career Guide to Professional Associations,* Garrett Park Press, Garrett Park, MD 20766, (301) 946-2553, $18.95.

Dun & Bradstreet's directories: *Million Dollar Directory, Middle Market Directory, Reference Book of Corporate Managements.*

*Encyclopedia of Associations,* Gale Research Co.

*Moody's Industrial Manual.* (Moody also publishes other directories.)

Thomas' Register of American Corporations (multi-volume)

*Standard & Poor's Register of Corporations*

# 3

## The Résumé Idea: Is It Any Good?

*One reason résumés don't work very well, as most job hunters learn sooner or later, is that most of us do not know what we are trying to accomplish with the résumé— what it can and should do (but also what it cannot do and should not be expected to do).*

### HOW DO YOU OR WOULD YOU WRITE YOUR RÉSUMÉ?

**T**RY this little quiz. If you don't know the answer, do a little thinking about the question and draw whatever appears to be the most logical conclusions. (That failing, make the best wild guesses you can.)
The best way to make up your résumé is as follows:

[ ]    As long and detailed as possible, putting in every fact that might influence anyone in your favor.

[ ]    Short and to the point, never more than one page. (Let the reader see how efficient and businesslike you are.)

[ ]    In an unusual format, such as a brochure, to get special attention and show how creative you are.

[ ]    On the most expensive paper possible, using color for both paper and ink, with copy typeset and your photograph featured prominently.

Now that you have decided how to have your résumé made up, let's think a bit about how to use it:

[ ]    Printed and mailed out in large quantity to every conceivable prospect, making probability work for you.

[ ]   Handed out discreetly, so you don't appear to be desperate for a job.

[ ]   Given only with a response to a help-wanted advertisement or handed personally to a personnel manager.

[ ]   Sent out as part of a large package of materials, in a full-scale direct-mail campaign, done as professionally as possible.

And, finally, let's take a shot at deciding just what a résumé ought to tell the reader about you or what its effect on the reader should be:

[ ]   Provide a complete profile of you, both as a set of job skills you claim and as a person, so that the reader has a total idea of what you represent.

[ ]   Concentrate entirely on your professional/technical or other job skills.

[ ]   Tell the reader what kind of *person* you are, which is sometimes even more important than your job skills are.

[ ]   Provide a complete biography, going back to your high-school days when you were a top scholar or athlete.

[ ]   Stick to only the experiences directly related to what you are looking for—be narrowly focused like a rifle shot.

[ ]   Be as broad as possible in describing your qualifications to maximize the kinds of jobs you might be considered for.

Periodically, as we work our way through the discussions in this chapter, check back on the answers you made here and see if you have changed your mind about any of them. I am not going to tell you that any one of them is wrong or right because none of the answers is entirely wrong or right. What is considered "wrong" or "right" depends on variable factors which are never absolute. The answer that is wrong on one occasion may be right on the next occasion. In fact, the philosophy is that whatever works is right, and whatever does not work—does not produce the desired result—is wrong. What you are going to read here is advice that is always based on certain logic and assumptions, but those can never be absolutes. Here is an example of how unpredictable results can be—how the merest chance can affect the outcome:

The contract on which Geoffrey Smith was working was about to expire (as space and defense contracts inevitably do). Geoff began to cast about for his next job, sending out up-dated résumés to anyone and everyone who appeared to be good prospects. For some reason, he happened to mention in this résumé having been a demolitions expert for a time during World War II military service, working with something called *shaped charges.* How that obscure reference crept into his résumé, Geoff still doesn't know—it had no logical relationship to his normal work. (He is a technical writer and writes about computers, radar, missiles, and other such gear.) It just so happened that one company who received the résumé had a division that was involved in the design and development of torpedoes and had an interest in the explosive phenomenon of the shaped charge, about which apparently few people knew. Voila! He was immediately invited for an interview and offered a job—which had nothing to do with torpedoes, demolitions, or shaped charges! But it was the shaped-charge reference that drew the attention of the reader of his résumé and was responsible for a job interview. (He did, in fact, accept an offer from this company to work on manuals for a naval missile system of advanced design.)

In theory, it would be irrelevant, by ordinary rules of logic and reason, to include that shaped-charge reference in the résumé. Yet, in a practical sense, it was as right as it could be because it was responsible for the résumé doing what a résumé ought to do: It aroused the reader's interest enough to provoke an invitation for an interview. At the same time—and this is important to note—this was a fluke and must not be interpreted to mean that a résumé ought to contain every possible fact about your life and working career. The fact that there are exceptions to the rule does not invalidate the rule or, as a fictional character on TV was fond of saying, "for instance" is not a proof. We must deal with both the rule and the *exception* to it.


## RULES AND EXCEPTIONS

The problem with most rules is that they are based on averages; and "average" is generally mediocrity. The average person gets discouraged easily; is not especially resourceful; is not especially ambitious; is not especially courageous; is not especially talented; and must, therefore, follow those rules established by and for average persons for average situations—to conform with what we call conventional wisdom—what "they say." That, however, does not mean that *you* must be an average person. You can be whatever you decide to be, and you can make your own rules, once you decide not to be average.

## WHAT HAPPENS TO YOUR RÉSUMÉ?

To go about the analysis of résumés and their usefulness, let's first consider what your résumé can do, not what you think it ought to do, for you. You'd like to believe that an employer is going to select your résumé and say, "Ahh, this is what I've been waiting for! Quick, let's make an offer and not let this one get away from us!" Of course, that's a fantasy. Even if you do happen to be the find of the year, you will not be able to prove that in a résumé and provoke that kind of reaction. (Even as an exception, that's a bit too much to hope for!) As a matter of fact, even in a seller's market, such as existed in defense and aerospace in the fifties and sixties, where technical/professional specialists were in demand and in relative short supply, résumés did not bring immediate job offers. They brought invitations for interview, if they brought a positive response at all.

That, in general, is all you can hope for when you submit a résumé—an invitation to come in for interview. Consider the typical situation, even in those situations where your résumé goes directly to the desk of the manager who does the hiring without preliminary screening by a personnel specialist.

First of all, even in days of great demand and short supply, an appeal for engineers, technical writers, editors, and others needed in the defense and aerospace industries brought a great many résumés flooding in—dozens, at least, and sometimes hundreds. Managers found themselves buried under the avalanche of résumés. As one manager who did a great deal of hiring explained to me, he spent a great deal of time just opening envelopes and stacking the résumés up on his desk, preparatory to reading them. Here is his own description:

"I began to read. I didn't attempt to read each résumé through. I'd never be able to spare that much time, and the bulk of that time would be wasted. I read a few lines and consigned the résumé to one of three stacks on my desk:

"*No way, Jose*: absolutely not right for my needs; no use wasting further time on those.

"*Possibles*: need to read these more thoroughly later on (perhaps).

"*Definite interest*: will read these carefully, probably interview at least some f these, may make all choices from this stack. (Will turn to *possibles* if I cannot fill all my needs from this stack.)"

One way or another, this is generally what happens, except that in larger companies, it is likely that the personnel department does the first screening and scraps all the *No way, Jose* résumés so the managers never even get to see them.

*Your* résumé is in that initial stack. Whether it goes to stack number 1, 2, or 3 determines whether you have the ghost of a chance to get called in for interview.

What résumé writing is all about is how to get in that third stack—*definite interest*. Once through reading and sorting all those résumés to screen out all the impossibles, the manager turns to that third stack and begins a search in earnest. What you are interested in now is what he or she is looking for in those third-stack résumés. But first you need to know what impels managers to consign so many— probably ninety percent—to the first stack, the impossibles. The answer is not a simple one. There are several factors that cause so many of the résumés to be scrapped with hardly more than a glance. And to bring you a complete understanding of it, let us look at some typical résumés and study typical errors.

## SOME BASIC CONSIDERATIONS ABOUT FORMATS AND HEAD DATA

Figure 2 is a portion of a typical résumé that would have landed rapidly in the first stack. It's not necessary to show all of it because what is shown here is all that most would read before consigning it to the oblivion of the first stack. What is of interest is *why*. What mistakes has Henry J. Tucker made in writing his résumé?

There are several mistakes apparent. Let's consider, first of all, why he sent his résumé: Henry Tucker should have been sending his résumé in the hope of getting an interview for a suitable job. What job is that? Tucker doesn't say. Eventually, he reveals that he has been an administrator and office manager, but he has not specified what he's looking for. Instead, he is leaving it to the employer to do that for him.

That won't work. It's Tucker's responsibility to decide what he is best fitted for and what he is seeking. Employers do not have the time or the inclination to do this job for him. Since he hasn't given a clue as to what job he's after, the employer loses interest. No, that's wrong; the employer fails to ever get interested, and that is curtains for Tucker's résumé.

He's committed some other errors, but we'll get back to those after a bit. Let us talk about *why* Tucker committed the basic error of failing to specify what he wants in the hope that you will see why *you* should never make that error:

---

**HENRY J. TUCKER**
17 Lincoln Lane
Feldspar, NY 10030
(917) 555-3232

OBJECTIVE:  Challenging opportunity

PERSONAL:  Protestant
Married to Mary Gillespie
3 children: Joseph, James, and Lucille
Hobbies chess and tennis
Member PTA, Hodgins County

EDUCATION:  BA Ancient Literature, Harkins College;
MA Philosophy, Notre Dame; MBA Jones
College.

EXPERIENCE:
Greenville Tool & Die Company, Greenville, KS: Office
Manager, August 1973–76. Supervised seven people.

Wheeler Brothers Construction Co., Inc., Harrison, NJ:
Administrator, September 1976–October 1980. Managed 18
people.

---

FIGURE 2. Portion of a typical résumé.

It is possible that Tucker doesn't know what he's looking for. He took undergraduate and graduate courses that would normally fit him for teaching only and, evidently, came to realize this later when he decided to pursue an MBA to fit himself for something in the business world. Even then he is either not sure what he wants to do or he doesn't care particularly so long as he gets a job. He probably reasons that if he doesn't limit himself to some specific job category, he'll stand a better chance—employers will then consider him for a variety of positions. Unfortunately, that rarely happens. Most often, employers simply move on and scan the next résumé in the pile.

There is some risk in being too narrow in defining the job you want, of course; it is possible that you may be passed over for some other job for which you might have been considered. The risk is rather small, however, for it is unlikely that anyone is going to take on the task of analyzing your résumé to see what you might be qualified for. The burden is on *you* to decide, and on you to prove your case. That stated objective, "challenging opportunity," is almost the ultimate cliché in résumés, found over and over. It doesn't really say anything; it appears to demand that the employer provide opportunity that challenges. But most significantly it fails to state an objective, because "challenging opportunity" is not an objective. "Technical writer" or "design engineer" are objectives. But they don't need the word "objective," they speak for themselves.

Some résumé writers believe that employers are interested in where they—the applicants—want to be ultimately headed. For them, a proper statement after the heading *objective* might be "Marketing management" or "executive management." But even then it is wise to use the term "career objective," to ensure that the reader understands that this is a career goal, not an immediate objective—unless you are, indeed, asking for consideration for such a slot.

The whole idea of including a statement of your career objective is the belief that employers are worried about the stability of those they hire, wanting to hire people who will remain with the company and make a lifetime career of whatever job they land. This is rather an old idea, not taken as seriously today as it once was because we have become so mobile in our society—relatively few people today remain with the same employer for their entire careers. There is some question as to the idea of including *objective* statements in résumés; it is probably as effective to simply identify whatever it is you wish to do—what kind of job you are after—by stating it somewhere in the head data of your résumé. The following straightforward and simple format, or some variant of it, works pretty well most of the time:

**NAME**

**ADDRESS**

**TELEPHONE NO.**

**JOB TITLE OR DESCRIPTION**

One thing you want to achieve with any résumé is an immediate impact or impression. But that does not mean that you want to dazzle the reader with fancy printing or other such irrelevant devices. The first impact you want to make is making your intent clear and giving the reader a hint of your qualifications. Remember that the reader is busy and doesn't relish the job of fighting through all those résumés, much less the job of deciding who to interview and who, in the end, to hire. Anything you do to ease that task will be gratefully utilized and deeply appreciated. Here, for example, is a format idea many have used with great success, and which enables a résumé reader to get a pretty good idea of the applicant in seconds, from the upper portion of the résumé alone:

Harvey Jones
22 Street Road
Terrycloth, OH 44553
216 555-7678

Design engineer, electronics, 17 years experience, 3 patents, communications and test equipment, weapons and aerospace systems.

Reading just these few lines enables a manager to determine whether he is interested at all and, if so, to drop this résumé in stack number

3 immediately. On the other hand, if this résumé is on the personnel manager's desk for screening, it will be sent to the appropriate line manager for consideration.


## YOU CAN'T TRUST TO LUCK

I mentioned earlier Geoffrey Smith's case, where luck took a hand and steered him to an acceptable job offer due to a fluke—to having mentioned something that had no logical reason for being in his résumé. There are other cases where pure chance plays a role, such as where your résumé just happens to be *exactly* what the manager is looking for. There is no denying that over a lifetime you are likely to "luck out" now and then. However it's foolish to base your actions on the possibility of luck dealing you a royal flush.

The other side of that coin is that if you wish to make something happen, you have to make it happen. Trust Murphy's Law; it's far more reliable than Chance. The basic message Murphy's Law and all its variants and derivative epigrams deliver is this: Left to chance, things always go wrong. The logical alternative, then, is to always take positive action to make things go right, if you are to have a chance of winning out in the end.

The message is this: Never trust to chance or luck that a kind manager will see your true worth, despite a poorly conceived résumé, and go to all the trouble of studying what you say and finding a good slot you can fill in the organization. You must tell the manager— point it out, as forcefully, as clearly, as *persuasively* as you can—what you can *do for the organization*. And that brings up another point: A basic and commonly made mistake of neglecting the only sales argument available to you.


## THE MOST COMMON RÉSUMÉ MISTAKE

You may recall that one of the basic mistakes Henry J. Tucker made in his résumé was to list as his objective "challenging opportunity." It was wrong for more than one reason, but the most basic reason is this: "Challenging opportunity" is virtually a demand made of the potential employer, delineating what the applicant wants. It ignores what the employer wants and, worst of all, it fails to specify what the applicant *offers*. Even in the days of the greatest shortages of workers, during and immediately after World War II, such a demand was unpalatable.

In short, conventional wisdom about how to write a résumé can be the wrong way to do it. There is no "right way" or "wrong way"; there are many different ways. Conforming to some standard format can be deadly. It's quite amazing how often someone reading résumés runs across several which are almost indistinguishable from one another, either because all the writers were guided by the same book on how to write a résumé or because all had their résumés prepared by the same résumé-writing company. (Many of those companies tend to make their job easy by having only a limited number of formats and virtually force-fitting all résumés into one of those formats.)

## THE GOVERNMENT RÉSUMÉ: SF 171

If you are in pursuit of a government job (federal, that is, although many state and local governments emulate the federal government in their forms and employment policies), you will have to fill out a "government résumé," the government's Standard Form 171.

Like many government forms, SF 171 is lengthy, tedious, and tiresome. Also like many government forms, despite its excessive overall length, it is far too brief in the most essential areas—where you describe experience and qualifications—and must be supplemented by your own additional pages. Yet its basic idea is not different from that of the résumé: it is intended to enable the reader to evaluate the applicant's qualifications.

The chief difference between the private-sector résumé and the federal government's SF 171 (as it is generally used) is that the government must furnish some specific criteria for evaluating the completed SF 171. The idea is to guarantee at least some degree of objectivity, whereas in the private sector there is no such requirement—except as an organization wishes to make one. By and large, however, in the private sector the manager will choose the résumés on personal preference.

Also, SF 171 is used in more than one way, depending on certain factors and conditions. For some kinds of lower-level jobs and for those that require specific manual skills, such as typing, tests are usually given and the resultant scores become part of the record. The applicant, on the basis of the tests and/or information furnished in the 171, is then graded and placed on a "register" of all those in that grade. When an opening occurs for a given grade and kind of job, the requestor (manager) is sent the top-graded 171s from the appropriate register. If the manager is not satisfied with any of these, the next three may be sent, until the manager finds one that is satisfactory.

A 171 may thus be filed for a specific opening that exists, or it may be filed for the general purpose of getting on a register and thus being generally qualified for a given job category and grade level. And because it takes a bit of time for the slow-moving bureaucracy to process a 171, it is wise to have filed a 171 as early as possible so that when and if you find an opening and a manager wants to hire you, there will be no delay in getting started. (That is, if you file a 171 only when you learn of a specific opening, it can take a long time to get to work even if the manager wants you.)

## RÉSUMÉ DO'S AND DON'TS

Do remember that even small companies and companies who are not advertising for help get a large number of résumés every week—every day, in fact—and whoever has the job of reading them is not going to spend a great deal of time on long résumés. *Keep it short.*

Keeping it short does not mean leaving out important information. But to make room for important information do omit all trivia. The yardstick? Is it important to the employer (not to you)?

Keeping it short also means having a focus. Even if you are a person of vast, diverse, and numerous major achievements, focus on only one or two—the most important ones and on those which are related to a specific area. Distracting the reader with too much leads to confusion but, even worse, it strains the reader's credulity and defeats you.

Get to the point immediately. Tell the reader what you want (in terms of the kind of work you are after), but couch it as much as possible in terms of what you have done, can do, will do for the employer. (See Tables 1, 2, 3.) Make your résumé an offer. Make your case and then stop.

Don't make claims. Report facts. The way to do this: Avoid hyperbole, adjectives, adverbs. Stick to the nouns and verbs. Quantify. Be specific. Provide details, especially how to or how you did it.

# 4

## What Do Employers Want To Know? What Are They Looking For?

*You must understand employers' problems if you want to understand their motivations and desires.*

### WHY EMPLOYEES ARE OFTEN CALLED "HELP"

**B**EING an employer is one of the world's more difficult ways of earning a living. The employer takes the risk of investing time and money, suffers the agonies of long hours, worries continually about a thousand and one things, and has the hope—often vain—of realizing a profit at the end of a difficult and frustrating year. The employer is the court of last resort in the company, the desk where the buck stops: It is the employer who must somehow meet the payroll every week or month. It is the employer who must comply with all those government regulations and reporting requirements. It is the employer who must satisfy the customers, pay off the bank loan, answer stockholders' questions and complaints, and somehow manage to keep it all together.

Some employers have the feeling that they are holding the entire enterprise together personally; that if they relax their grip for even a moment the whole thing will fly apart. It's not an uncommon sensation.

At the onset, in many cases, the employer does virtually everything alone—from purchasing to selling, manufacturing to packaging, accounting to driving the delivery truck. Ultimately, as the business

*42*

begins to grow, Mr. or Madam Proprietor begins to hire some people to help, literally to *help* with whatever the newly hired people can do—sell, deliver, post ledgers, or whatever.

When the hired hands are general workers, doing jobs intelligent people can learn to do on the job, they are regarded as "hired help." Only later, when the firm has begun to grow a bit and specialists are being hired—an accountant, a buyer, a sales manager—do they begin to become *employees*. But the employer never abandons the idea that everyone is hired to *help* in a variety of ways—cutting costs, increasing sales, boosting profits, raising efficiency, solving problems. It is for these reasons that employees are hired, and the employer is trying to hire the best salespeople, accountants, purchasing agents, and other doers and problem solvers, the best that can be found within whatever salary ranges the employer believes the firm can afford.

Early in the game the employer does all this hiring personally, and it's a most difficult thing to face. The employer has done so many of these jobs personally that it's hard to believe that any stranger can come aboard and get the jobs done as well. Most employers are convinced at this early stage in the typical founder company that every employee hired represents something of a compromise with what is really needed. But since it's not possible to get a hired person to do the job as well as he does it himself, the employer accepts what is available.

As the organization grows, the employer no longer does the hiring personally, but has subordinates take over the responsibility (except when the employer wants to hire a high-level executive). And when the organization is large enough, there is a personnel manager to help the line managers do the hiring. Or perhaps there is a general administrator who is also the purchasing agent and personnel manager. In any case, the *employer* is no longer the actual proprietor. He or she is now President, perhaps Chairman of the Board; whoever is doing the actual hiring at the moment may also be better known within the company as the engineering director, production supervisor, parts department manager, or by some other title.

Nothing has really changed, however, as far as the job hunter is concerned. The engineering director is looking for help, too, on behalf of the original employer. Both seek a competent engineer or laboratory technician with the right kind of experience, the ability to solve problems in the laboratory, the capacity perhaps for improving efficiency, or to provide whatever help the engineering director requires. Perhaps there are specific problems which must be solved; even if there are no specific problems at the moment, problem-solving is always of interest. Inevitably, the engineering director has problems—they come with the job—and he or she is just as eager to find problem-solvers as is the employer.

Problems are perpetual in the business world and employers are receptive to the prospective employee who can help solve or prevent problems. Don't make the mistake of assuming, however, that every manager is interested in only the technical problems of getting his or her own job done or managing his or her own department smoothly. Take the matter of costs and profits, for example: line managers are not usually directly accountable for profits, but indirectly they are accountable for costs connected with whatever department or function they handle. In many cases they are under constant pressure from higher authority to keep costs down and are constantly harassed. Even if they are not being harassed, cutting costs will always get one a pat on the head, consideration for promotion, and sometimes even a bonus. And although there may be no direct reward many managers are interested and dedicated enough to want to do their jobs as well as possible.

The point, then, is that everyone who hires employees is looking for help in doing whatever they do. Managers are the alter egos of the top-level executive(s) in the organization, doing what they believe their superiors want them to do: hiring the best people obtainable for what the organization has to offer. That word *employer*, then, refers to whomever makes hiring decisions in the organization no matter what their title in the organization happens to be. It may be a top executive who hires his or her own secretary, it may also be an office or personnel manager assigned to choose the secretary, making the hiring decision—selecting the best candidate for the job. It is that individual who is "the employer" as far as the applicant is concerned.

## EMPLOYERS' TYPICAL HIRING PROBLEMS

Hiring people is rarely a simple matter, unless you are hiring day laborers with strong backs on a temporary basis. (Even that is not as simple as it sounds; there are often unexpected complications in even apparently simple hiring situations.) Today there are exceedingly few jobs that do not require some skills or specialized knowledge, with the exception of retail sales in a store, or other jobs that require unskilled labor. For starters, the complications are at least these:

1. Verifying the claimed skills and knowledge. In today's litigious society, former employers are often reluctant to say very much, knowing that they may open themselves to lawsuits if they are critical. (It has happened.) They often resort to tests in their personnel offices as a result of having few other dependable ways to evaluate the potential of an applicant for particular positions.
2. Verifying educational background. An astonishing number of applicants falsify education and experience claims, and it is expensive and time consuming to track information down and confirm it. Consequently, many employers do little or no checking of such data, unless the applicant does something to arouse suspicion about the reality of his or her claimed education, past employment, or other qualifications.
3. Verifying the applicant's ability to work harmoniously with others. In some cases, the personnel office administers special psychological tests or sends the applicant to a clinic for testing, to get a psychological profile and satisfy themselves that the applicant is psychologically acceptable.
4. Checking on the applicant's honesty and general attitudes, which poses the same problem as item (3) and is often handled in the same manner.

These special tests and clinical evaluations are not entirely satisfactory. (In one case reported, the head of a large company applied, incognito, to the personnel office of his own company and underwent psychological aptitude tests that demonstrated clearly his unsuitability for any job in the entire establishment.) Some companies have implemented tests only to discontinue them later. The simple truth is that hiring an employee is always a risk. At least it may represent a waste of money when the employee proves unsuitable, for it is a great expense to hire someone only to terminate the employee and seek a replacement. In some cases, it's more than a waste: It may be a disaster of some proportion since some employees manage to do great damage as a result of their incompetence before being let go. (In one case, an employer wryly offered to pay a large bonus to someone he was letting go if the former employee agreed to get a job with his main competitor.) In other cases, a discharged employee costs the employer additional sums of money by instituting legal actions even if the complaint does not make it to trial in court; or a discharged employee simply makes trouble within the company, causing managers to waste a great deal of time in handling the matter.

## THE COST OF HIRING

There are "capital intensive" enterprises—those which require relatively large investments for capital equipment and operating funds, with correspondingly few employees (such as manufacturing plants). There are also "labor intensive" enterprises, which are the opposite in that they depend on human labor—individual efforts—more than on capital investment (such as advertising agencies). And there are enterprises that require both substantial capital and large labor forces. But, in general, the terms are used to suggest whether an enterprise does or does not use a great many employees. Even for those enterprises designated as *labor-intensive*, substantial capital is often required because the two terms are relative, not absolute. For the enterprise that requires a large number of employees, hiring to replace employees leaving—"turnover" of labor—is usually a continuous problem. There is a constant overhead cost for terminating and initiating employees, whereas for the enterprise with relatively few employees the cost of hiring and firing is often an occasional, rather than a constant, one.

There are firms that are outstanding examples of what *labor-intensive* means; the enterprise depends entirely on a large force of people with an assortment of specialized skills: engineers, chemists, technical writers, and support technicians. Some of these firms maintain help-wanted advertisements 365 days a year in various media— the *Wall Street Journal*, the *New York Times*, the *Washington Post*, and other newspapers and various journals (magazines) circulated among those in the relevant technical and professional fields. Despite high levels of unemployment in recent years, people with the desired skills and experience to handle the "heavier" jobs in these companies are in a less-than-abundant supply, and they tend to be rather mobile. Most of them change jobs on the average of once every three years. This is partly due to desire for a change of scenery; sometimes it is an opportunity to move into management or to a higher-paying position, other times it is sheer boredom or disenchantment with the firm. And, of course, there is still another factor at work; in some cases, a firm completes a contract and does not get another immediately, and is therefore compelled to let some of its workforce go. On the other hand, the firm who wins new contracts must expand its force of technical and professional experts and "raids" its competitors with advertising placed judiciously to attract applications from competitors' employees. There are also firms in certain industries, which are never fully staffed, subject to the conditions outlined here. They advertise continuously for help because they always have openings. Terminations and new-hires tend to balance each other, and the firm never catches up.

All of this is a great cost to the firm, of course; usually several thousand dollars (minimum) for each specialist hired, even when the firm manages to accomplish the hiring through its own resources—advertising, recruiting campaigns, and other activities of its personnel department. For this reason—because it costs several thousand dollars to hire each specialist—it makes good economic sense to many firms to accomplish their hiring by paying fees to employment agencies and "head hunters."

## THE INEVITABLE RESULT OF SUCH HIGH HIRING COSTS

In the face of such costs—easily $5–10,000 to hire a fairly high-level technical/professional person—you may expect even the most eager employer to exercise some caution in making hiring decisions; mistakes cost far too much money in both hiring and firing. Few employers today, especially in such high-mobility fields as aerospace, computers, and electronics, truly expect to get many lifetime employees or are especially dismayed by a résumé that shows a record of changing jobs every few years—particularly not when that record reflects a structured movement upward (professional growth) or movement with the vagaries of contract awards and completions. For that matter, in fields that are almost entirely dependent on government contracts, no employer can promise long-term or "steady" employment. So employers in these fields simply do what they can to control the high hiring costs, while they recognize that the more mobile employees are the ones that they should be most interested in: These are the very people they need, the ones with the right kind of experience. The chief concern is that the hiring manager distinguish between the mobile specialist who proceeds from one contract to another, but makes his or her contribution to each, and the "grasshopper" employee who moves *too* frequently. That, of course, raises the suspicion that the individual is unstable or not competent. In either case, a consistent pattern of changing jobs more frequently than every two to three years is likely to cause automatic rejection unless something is done to overcome the implications of such an employment pattern.

## THE YARDSTICKS BY WHICH AN APPLICANT IS MEASURED

There are no universal standards for measuring employee performance, but here are some typical ones used both for hiring and evaluating at each annual review period. They provide a useful insight into how to present yourself to a prospective employer because in one manner or another, every employer finds it necessary to take these basic factors into account in hiring and evaluating. First consider why an employee is hired—as a clue to what an employer must be seeking. Here are the typical situations leading directly to recruiting—hiring—efforts:

* A new contract award or other expansion, which requires additional staff.
* Special problems or special requirements, as the result of a new contract, calling for help.
* A special, troublesome problem which no one in-house appears to be able to cope with.
* A new system, calling for a new class of employee.

For example, the manager of an art department resigned to open his own business and was replaced by the former assistant manager. Almost immediately that department, which had never given trouble in the past, became the focus of many problems. Investigation proved that the new manager was a good illustrator and staff worker, but was simply unsuited to lead or manage others. Replacing him with a new hire solved the problem.

Growth compelled manager Gallen to hire an accountant for the firm where she had previously managed with clerks and a bookkeeper. After a while, the new accountant proved to be the source of greater problems than they had experienced without an accountant—the solution was to hire and train a bookkeeper in their systems.

Adding a small in-house printing capability compelled the owner of an editorial services firm to recruit print shop personnel, a class of employee never hired before in that firm.

With this as background, let's consider the yardsticks and how we manage to guess so poorly so often:

In most cases, the first factor considered in evaluating an applicant for a job (and keep in mind that "evaluating an applicant" usually means evaluating the applicant's résumé) is job skill and what we might call *technical qualifications* in general. Promoting the assistant manager to art department manager was based on his known technical skills and ability as an artist. He had had suitable training as a commercial artist and could perform all the functions normally associated with the job in a technical publications organization: lettering, operating the headliner and other machines used in the department, preparing roughs and dummies, proceeding to comprehensives, and finally preparing the mechanicals for printing. These were the technical skills required, and he could do them personally and—presumably—supervise others in this work. Were he an applicant from the outside, he would have faced sterner reviews of his qualifications and supervisory experience; but because he was already on-staff, he was accepted with far less consideration—in fact, his qualifications as a manager did not get serious study. The fact that this man did not have management experience, despite being an assistant manager, was never considered: He was not a leader—not only could not inspire others to follow and work with him, but aroused their resentment and so made a shambles of discipline and production in that department. (Oddly enough, he recognized and admitted that his department was not performing well, but he had no idea what the problem was.)

One factor other than specific job skills that must be considered is the ability to work with others; if the job is such that the applicant will have to work with others as part of a team of employees. There are those who are excellent workers and highly proficient in job skills, but totally unable to work with others through certain personality defects. In the case of that new art department manager, he could work harmoniously with others as their peer, but not as their superior. The ability to lead is itself a job skill when the position calls for leadership.

That deficient accountant, it turned out later, had never been the *chief* accountant. In former positions he had always been supervised, and he was not yet ready to assume the major responsibility for the function. This was a matter of job skill *at the level* of the job— he was still an *assistant* accountant, not yet capable of being *the* accountant in a one-accountant office in terms of his abilities.

The point here is that specific technical skills are not the sole criterion by which to evaluate a prospective employee or the résumé an applicant submits, and sometimes they are not even the most important consideration. Some of my own worst mistakes in hiring were because I had not given enough thought to other factors, and some of my most successful hirings were of people who did not have the qualifications "on paper" but turned out to be excellent employees because other factors more than compensated for some apparent shortcomings in job skills. I say "apparent" because in many cases, an individual with a quick grasp and a strong will to succeed can "pick up" job skills rapidly. For example, on more than one occasion I hired writers who could not demonstrate much in the way of training or experience—much less accomplishment—in the field, but who turned out to be quite satisfactory on the job.

Note how factors other than specific job skills manifest themselves: in the examples cited here, there were individuals who could not give orders effectively, but there are some who cannot *take* orders properly, and there are others who for one reason or another cannot learn by example or specific guidance. There are individuals who try to bluff their way into jobs for which they are not qualified. And that invokes the third factor an employer considers when evaluating a prospective employee: general honesty and attitude.

*Honesty* is something more than telling the truth and not stealing. It manifests itself—or fails to—in a great many ways:

- Giving a full day's efforts and giving best efforts.
- Submitting honest expense accounts.
- Spending the company's money conscientiously.
- Submitting a truthful résumé.
- Protecting the employer's interests.

Disillusioning experience has brought more than one employer to the preference for the best efforts of an employee of modest talents over the "get by" effort of a brilliant or highly talented employee. Experience proves again and again that a highly capable individual who doesn't give his or her best efforts every day—who decides how much result the employer is entitled to every day—is no bargain. It makes sense to determine what the employee's general attitude is; whether there is *enthusiasm* for the job and the work, for example, and what the applicant thinks the employer is entitled to. When an applicant is foolish enough to say that his or her main interest in the job is that it is close to home, it is a clear signal to end the interview as swiftly as possible. And there are many individuals who manage to "get by" on only a couple of hours of real work, and therefore never exert themselves for more than half of each day. The important factor here is not what the prospective employee is *capable of,* but what the employer will get. The employer is less concerned with what you *can* do than with what you *will* do.

Some people feel that an employee who spends a company's money should spend it as though it were his or her own. The message here is to exercise caution and conservatism. But that is based on the supposition that employees spend their own money carefully and conservatively, and that is assuming facts not in evidence. The fact is the opposite is good advice: As an individual, you have the right to spend your own money any way you wish; but as an employee, you do not have that right. You must not be foolish, extravagant, or careless with your employer's money. *Don't* spend your employer's money as though it were your own; spend it conservatively, responsibly.

Spending the employer's money is not confined to expense accounts or making disbursements. Many employees who do not have expense accounts, do any buying, or make any actual disbursements still spend the employer's money in a variety of ways, direct and indirect. Making unnecessary copies on the office copier, a common enough fault, is spending the employer's money carelessly. So are requesting unneeded supplies and equipment, discarding still-useful tools, and other wasteful practices. In fact, most employees spend the employer's money in one way or another.

Being caught telling deliberate untruths in a résumé or application is almost universally considered cause for immediate rejection and, when discovered after being hired, often leads to instant dismissal. It's true enough that relatively few employers go to the trouble of verifying everything you represent to be fact in your application or résumé, but some do. Also, sometimes the "facts" just don't hang together: They appear illogical and provoke the employer to check them out.

Misrepresenting yourself in a résumé or application is a dangerous game; often the frank admission that you do not have some qualification ordinarily deemed necessary will do more for you than having that qualification, if you are forced to respond directly to the question. (Never volunteer such information, however.) Employers will reject your résumé when it is discovered to be not truthful, not because of lack of qualifications so much as because such an offense stamps the applicant dishonest and therefore unreliable. It may be the only time in his or her life that the applicant has ever told a lie or falsified anything, or it may have been done in desperation, but those factors are not likely to be considered.

Honesty has still another facet, perhaps not as widely recognized, yet important to the employer. It is protecting the employer's interests in other ways than those we have already discussed here—loyalty. Consider, for example, the interests of an employer in a highly competitive industry where certain proprietary information may be involved. That information may concern a secret design, confidential research, customer accounts, a planned new product or new package, an impending advertising or sales promotion, or any other matter. Even the humblest employee is often unavoidably aware that the company is about to launch a new product or is about to close an important new account. Competitors would dearly love to get such information, and many companies spend a great deal of money in efforts to learn what their competitors are doing or are about to do.

An employer has the right to expect employees to be loyal, and not to blab to everyone about what goes on at the office or in the plant. The applicant who suggests to a prospective employer that he will reveal secret and proprietary information about his present employer, if he is hired, arouses the suspicion that he will be equally disloyal to any new employer. It is therefore dangerous to even suggest that hiring you is tantamount to engaging a valuable spy. And that is not inconsistent with remarks made earlier about what special assets you can bring to the job; it is a matter of what is fair to reveal to a new employer and what is foolish to promise. A salesman, for example, often develops a personal following and brings many of those customers along with him. On the other hand, the company accountant should regard what he knows about his employer's finances as confidential and not to be discussed even with a prospective new employer.

This is because an accountant is usually in a *sensitive* position, whereas a salesperson is usually not. A great deal of judgment is required here; there are no hard and fast rules to guide you. You have to have a sense of what is *ethical*, particularly if the position you are in quest of is normally somewhat sensitive—makes you privy to highly confidential information about your employer. Employers are bound to be more cautious in hiring someone who will be in such a position.

## REFERENCES AND CHECKS

The three factors that employers tend to consider are: job skills, which include experience, training, and education; compatibility or ability to be part of a team; and honesty, which covers general attitudes, dependability, willingness to work, and other such considerations. (Compatibility is often considered as part of honesty and general attitude or personality, but is a definite factor in most job situations.)

It may occur to you by now that most résumés do not offer many clues to these factors. How, then, does an employer manage to evaluate them? The fact is that it is rarely possible to evaluate all of these in a résumé—which is one reason for the interview and checking references. (Employers are far more likely to check references when the job under discussion is of relatively high level and therefore represents a high risk for the employer.) At the same time, the employer will try to read between the lines of the résumé to spot any clues there, a factor we'll take into account later in discussing pros and cons of résumé practices.

Aside from the fact that there is a risk of being sued when supplying adverse information to an inquirer checking on a former employee, there is a great reluctance to supply adverse information about anyone, particularly if the former employee was terminated "without prejudice"—left on good terms and with no "hard feelings."

In general, checking references is not the most reliable way to learn the facts about a prospective employee, and most employers are well aware of this. Still, employers will check, at least perfunctorily. It is surprising, however, how often employers either do not check or make a hasty and ·casual check that has little impact on the final decisions. For that reason references are not of great value in your résumé. (Moreover, many employers will not bother to check references until after an interview has gone favorably for the applicant, on the theory that it's a waste of time and money to check on an applicant who is not yet a solid prospect for employment.)

There are exceptions, however. If you happen to be fresh out of college, or for any other reason have little or no work experience, references assume a greater importance simply because there is so little else to check to evaluate you. Of, if you are pursuing an especially sensitive position, one that involves placing great trust in you, an employer may check and investigate your references with more than usual intensity. Or if the position is a high-level one (part of top management, for example) your references are likely to get more than passing attention.

In checking references, especially in those cases where there is special interest, an employer is going to be checking on all the factors: job skills and abilities, honesty and trustworthiness, general attitudes, cooperativeness, dependability, and anything the employer believes to be of special importance in the job. And in such cases, the employer is going to verify not only the employment experience, but also the job titles and responsibilities you claim. If you have given yourself a few "promotions" in reporting past employment, it may come to light and be regarded as an act of dishonesty. An indication that you are not to be trusted.

There are documented cases of employees being tripped up, years after they were hired, by lies in their applications or résumés. And in more than one instance, the information led to swift dismissal.

Recently I had a telephone call requesting information on someone whose name I could not recall immediately because he had worked for me some 15 or 16 years ago, and then for a relatively short time. Fortunately for him my memory has not deteriorated too badly over the years—I was able to recall him and that he was a satisfactory employee. Had I "drawn a blank" in trying to remember him, his claim might have been taken as a false one. There is a hazard in using as references individuals you haven't seen or heard from in years or whom you didn't know too well.

## WHAT DOES "EXPERIENCE" MEAN?

Far too many people operate on the somewhat naive belief that a number of years' "experience" is automatically qualifying for whatever position is the subject of the pursuit. For example, the man who can claim fifteen years as a salesman with a given company believes this history proves he is a capable salesman (would the employer keep him for fifteen years if he were not capable?), and often even believes that it proves his capability for a targeted job as sales manager.

In fact, some personnel people and employers share this assumption—*assumption*, not *belief*, because an assumption is often an acceptance of an idea without serious study, whereas *belief* implies that the individual has seriously considered the matter. Fortunately, this is not a universal aberration, and there are employers who recognize the difference between fifteen years' experience and one year's experience repeated fifteen times.

But that is not the only flaw in the premise that fifteen years' *employment* means fifteen years of qualifying experience. It is possible to *survive* in a job for fifteen years, and yet never do that job really well. That is especially true in large corporations and government agencies, but is often true even in smaller organizations. It's true because there are some individuals who do enough to "get by," but never turn in really good performances; and there are even some who do rather poorly, but are fairly clever at covering up and so "getting by." Sometimes this is due to the nature of the individual's ability— he or she is doing his or her best, but the best is not very satisfactory; and sometimes it is a case of an individual who simply doesn't try very hard—just enough to draw a pay check and avoid being fired.

Of course, the former is a case of marginal or inadequate job skills, and the latter a case of unsatisfactory attitude. How and why many such individuals manage to survive indefinitely in a job in which they are not doing very well is not germane here: It is sufficient that we recognize that such is the case and that we know that there are employers wise enough to want to know just what that fifteen years of claimed *experience* really means.

It's fairly easy to check up on experience, in the case of a salesperson. The employer can demand to know in quantitative terms how effective the individual was, e.g., how many sales or how many dollars' worth of business resulted every year, or even how the individual ranked on the force, since many sales organizations rank-order the salespeople in terms of the volume of business each produces. It's not so easy in the case of many other occupations, such as that of chief accountant or shipping clerk. And, as you will see in later discussions, solving that problem can make all the difference in how effective your pursuit of a given job is.

## INTERVIEWS

Presumably the interview is supposed to enable the employer to do several things not usually possible without conducting a personal interview:

- Gather details not provided in the résumé or application, which will answer some of the questions raised here.
- Get acquainted with and gather a personal impression of the individual—perhaps judge whether the application or résumé was prepared by a specialist and is or is not an accurate reflection of the individual.
- Ask some searching questions and gauge the individual's answers.
- Put some pressure on the applicant, and see how he or she holds up.
- Put the individual through some scientific testing (in the personnel department).
- Judge the applicant's general attitudes and motivation, to estimate his or her suitability as an employee.

In some cases, an applicant has made such an impression through the résumé or by other means that the employer wants to meet the applicant and try to decide where and how the company can best employ the individual. Even when the company does not have a specific opening, an employer may try to create one if an applicant appears to be desirable enough as an employee, particularly if he or she appears to be well-suited to some job that is usually not easy to fill, such as a key managerial slot or a marketing position. And if an applicant appears to be able to deliver business or something equally valuable, the employer can hardly help but invite the applicant in for discussion.

There are many styles and techniques used in interviewing, and we'll explore some of those in depth in another chapter. However, understand this: Only rarely will you find yourself being interviewed by someone who is truly skilled in interview techniques or has any specific plan for conducting the interview. Usually the interview is spontaneous, unstructured, and conducted by a manager who has little enthusiasm for the job, doesn't know precisely what he or she ought to be doing (other than in most general terms), and may also be quite nervous and uncertain about the whole thing. It's not always clear which party, interviewer or interviewee, is more nervous.

If job hunters are blundering blindly—without clear objectives, not knowing exactly what they are looking for—they are not alone. Employers, too, are often blundering without clear objectives, not knowing exactly what they are looking for. Employers do know in general terms what final results they hope to realize by making good hiring decisions, but they are far from certain that they know how to go about finding and selecting the individuals to produce those final results. The successful job hunter—the job hunter who winds up with the right job, not just any job—is quite often the one who learns how to help employers make those analyses, conduct the interviews, and make those important final selections. That is largely what this book is all about: how to help employers do the right thing and hire you for the job you want.


## HELPFUL REFERENCES FOR INTERVIEWING

*Winning the Salary Game: Salary Negotiation for Women*, Sherry Chastain, John Wiley & Sons, Inc.

*You Can Negotiate Anything*, Herb Cohen, Lyle Stuart, Inc.

*Sweaty Palms: The Neglected Art of Being Interviewed*, H. Anthony Medley, Lifetime Learning Publications, 10 Davis Drive, Belmont, CA 94002.

*Negotiate Your Way to Success*, David D. Seltz & Alfred J. Modica, Mentor Executive Library.

# 5

# Résumés Are For Marketing

*The résumé idea is not a bad one; the way most people execute the idea is bad, and it has given the very word résumé a distasteful reputation. The way most résumés are written defies common sense.*

## RÉSUMÉS NEED CHARACTER

**W**INSTON CHURCHILL is reported to have once sent back a serving of pudding in a London restaurant with the condemnation, "It has no theme!" Unfortunately, a great many résumés are guilty of the same thing; they have no theme or character. They have a disconcerting sameness about them. There are at least a half-dozen characteristics that can be found in well over 90 percent of the résumés that cross anyone's desk. To view some of the most common—and most inexcusable—faults in the résumés that land in the "No way, Jose" stack see Table 5.

If any single fault were to be selected from this table as generally true of most résumés, it would be the first one listed: a lack of focus or theme. Surprisingly, the résumé often reflects a complete lack of direction; the writer appears to be wandering aimlessly, looking for opportunity rather than having a specific objective and pursuing it. And that is itself a strategic mistake.

TABLE 5

## COMMON RÉSUMÉ FAULTS AND THEIR CURES

| *Common Faults* | *Recommended Cures* |
|---|---|
| Lacks focus; makes too many claims, tries to reflect too many achievements; rambles. | Decide on your main objective (type of job you want) and which is your strongest qualification for that job. Focus sharply on that; save anything else for the interview and discussion. |
| Takes too long to make main point, perhaps never really makes it at all. | Use format that makes main point as close to top of page as possible. Specify what kind of work you do or your chief skill and go immediately into demonstrating your credentials. |
| Includes wealth of trivia, such as personal family data and other nonessentials. | Such data is occasionally important, but even then should not be presented until specifically requested. Stick to what you can do for employer and where/how to reach you for interview request. |
| Apologizes for weaknesses, such as lack of college degree, limited experience, other shortcomings (real or perceived). | Never apologize; never sound defensive in a résumé or in any other communication or exchange regarding employment. Stick to what you have and can offer; never mind anything you don't have. Why draw attention to things you are unable to offer? |
| Pompous, inflated prose, presumably an effort to demonstrate erudition and otherwise "snow" reader. | Follow these basic rules in writing: Avoid adjectives, adverbs, all hyperbole and superlatives; don't use words not found in smallest pocket dictionaries; *report* facts, instead of making claims, by supplying details and specifics; quantify. |
| Too long—4, 5, 6 (and even more pages). | Screen, edit, eliminate all personal trivia, anything that does not bear directly on main point(s), anything not connected directly with main strategy. (Telegraphic style acceptable in résumés.) Also, do not include attachments, such as transcripts and certificates. (Mention their existence and be prepared to supply them at interview, not before.) |

Table 5 (cont.)

## COMMON RÉSUMÉ FAULTS AND THEIR CURES

| *Common Faults* | *Recommended Cures* |
| --- | --- |
| All "gussied up" with ribbons and bows, fancy covers, other ostentatious trimmings. | Résumé should be businesslike—may be typeset and printed on good quality paper, even carry your photo (although not recommended, unless you are applying for job as model or actor), but not pompous and inflated in physical appearance. May be distinctive, however, such as different size than 8 ½ x 11 inches or may be folded down to 4-page 5 ½ x 8½ inch brochure. |
| Focuses on what applicant wants—e.g., "challenge" or "opportunity," instead of showing understanding of what employer wants and needs. | Be sure to consider employer's problems and needs, and make your résumé an offer to help the employer. Everything in the résumé should be conceived and expressed with due consideration to what the item offers to do for the employer, not for the applicant. |
| "Achievements" are applicant-oriented—brags and self-congratulations (such as being an outstanding chess player or captain of the college football team). | Include only those achievements which have helped a prior employer or reflect capability for benefiting the reader, such as having helped a prior employer get more business, improve a product, outdo competition, expand. |
| Tiresome, excessive, unnecessary details, some not entirely relevant. | Even when dealing with main point(s) and focusing on prime strategy it is necessary to be brief and businesslike—come straight to the point. Time enough in the interview to supply all the details. |
| So much information; not only is tedium a possible hazard, but the reader may gain the impression that the résumé tells all; hence, there is no need for an interview. | Show that only highlights are in résumé. Make clear implications that there is far more to learn. Purpose of résumé is to arouse interest, not to tell your entire story. Use expressions that make this clear—*such as, for instance, for example.* |

## THE IMPORTANCE OF DIRECTION

In sales and marketing, as in other things, focus and direction are essential to success. Success requires concentration on a single objective and a single effort. Singlemindedness of purpose enabled Thomas Edison to perfect the incandescent light. He is reported to have tested some 10,000 different materials in his quest for something that would work. That dogged pursuit of a clearly perceived single objective brought about the invention of the self-starter for the automobile, the real breakthrough that was responsible for the commercial success of the "horseless buggy." It was the reason the Wright brothers succeeded in creating a craft that actually flew through the air under its own power. It was the way Jimmy Carter confounded the political experts and came "out of the woodwork" to become President of the United States.

That failure to establish a sharp focus is the most common fault found in résumés. It is difficult to correct this problem, admittedly. First of all, it is not easy to be objective about yourself, your talents and abilities. You may not be able to judge what your greatest ability or talent is, much less your most *valuable* talent or skill. They are not, of course, the same thing. Perhaps you are an excellent computer programmer, perhaps excelling by a considerable margin in some specialized field in that profession. However, if you are only one of many who can do the same thing quite well, or if there is not a great deal of demand or application for that ability, it may be of far less *value* to a potential employer than your skill in "documenting" (writing instruction manuals about) your programs.

Value is an elusive idea, and many of us tend to confuse it with level of skill when evaluating what we do and can do. In this hypothetical case, for instance, the ability to program solutions to difficult scientific problems, using FORTRAN, is probably much more difficult and possibly more of an achievement than the ability to document such programs. Yet the ability to write clearly is far from abundantly available in the scientific and professional communities. Even if somewhat less of an achievement in terms of difficulty and talent, it may well be considered valuable because it is harder to find. In fact, what you offer that has the greatest value may not even be central to the functions of the job you are after, but that has nothing to do with the marketing/sales problem you are trying to solve; your objective ought

Herman P. Wilson
34 Gravelley Road          Sales
Silver Spring, MD 20910     Market Research
301 555-1212

SUMMARY       Sales/marketing experience since 1959, including marketing research, supervision and training of sales personnel, purchasing, and merchandising. Recently completed real estate courses and passed Maryland Real Estate Salesman and Brokers Licensing examinations.

OBJECTIVE      Sales position in real estate.

Experience:
1965–Present:      College, full and part-time, with variety of spare-time jobs to support college attendance—taxi driving, post office clerk, etc.

1961–1965:      <u>Associate Buyer</u>, Modiste Department Store, Washington, D.C. Performed marketing/sales research for planning of sales, advertising, purchasing, merchandising. Worked with Head Buyer, as part of team, to select and make purchasing decisions for linen, domestics, bedware. Supervised, trained salespeople; prepared and made presentations to top management.

                <u>Assistant Buyer</u>. Handled customer correspondence, inventory, sales reference books to schools, libraries, individuals. Planned, coordinate sales activities, coordination, marketing research, recommending sales promotions (e.g., special sales), attended trade shows. Promoted to Associate Buyer.

FIGURE 3. A typical résumé with some common faults.

| 1959–1961: | Salesman, Instructors Publishing Corp., Chicago, Ill. National sales of magazines and reference books to schools, libraries, individuals. Planned, coordinate sales activities, strategies. |
| 1958–1959: | Teaching Assistant, at small, rural agricultural college, N.L., Mexico. Assigned to Department of English. Tutored students in English language, graded examinations, translated textbooks, abstracted newspaper articles, magazine articles, texts. |
| EDUCATION: | B.A. Political Science, American University, 1970. Real Estate courses Montgomery College, University of Maryland. |

REFERENCES AND DETAILS AVAILABLE ON REQUEST

FIGURE 3. (cont.) A typical résumé with some common faults.

to be to focus the employer's attention on something that has great appeal, whether it is the main skill you offer or not. Never forget that you are engaged in preparing a sales presentation, not a thesis or dissertation.

Consider Figure 3 as an example. It's a fairly typical résumé of a young person, with some work experience and some educational background. (An actual résumé, disguised so that even the subject of it would not recognize it as his own, this example was based on the original of a real résumé.) Note that Mr. "Wilson" was not quite sure whether he wanted to identify himself as a salesman or a market-research specialist. His summary statement covers sales, research, and supervisory experience, although his objective is stated as a sales position in real estate. The result is that he has managed to dim the focus of his résumé, possibly creating confusion for the reader. If a sales position *per se* is his true objective, as stated, everything ought to be focused sharply on his qualifications for that job, and all other experience and abilities relegated to second priority and certainly subordinate in importance. He has even gone so far afield in his summary statement as to bring in purchasing and merchandising background, experience almost irrelevant to his stated objective. His résumé does have the saving grace of being brief, although that is more or less dictated by his youth and lack of working experience. What could this recent grad, with only a little relevant experience (who also majored in a totally unrelated field) have done to his résumé to add impact? Let's consider this by making some logical analyses.

If you wish to be hired as a salesperson, and that is the only job that really interests you—if a sales job is your true goal—why waste time and energy (both yours and the reader's) on anything that does not pertain to your abilities and potential value as a salesperson? Admittedly, the accepted and expected format of the typical résumé more or less *dictates* that you must incorporate some information of limited relevance. Perhaps some is totally irrelevant but must be present for fear that otherwise your résumé will show gaps, which leads to the suspicion that you've something to hide.

That is one of the problems with most résumés and with the résumé idea itself, *as it is commonly interpreted.* Making your résumé read as though it were a somewhat detailed biography is not dictated by anything except custom, conventional wisdom, common practice, or whatever you wish to call what has come to be expected as the "standard" résumé format. There is no special logic in this notion. As some wry wits have remarked about the U.S. Army, many large corporations, and other bureaucracies: It doesn't have to make sense; it's policy.

We are saying here that instead of analyzing the whole résumé idea and deciding what is in our own best interests in résumés and their use, we blindly pursue what we think an employer expects or demands from us, whether it helps or hinders our efforts to find and win the job we want. Obviously that does not make good sense, yet individuals pursue this course of action every day.

## DOING THE UNEXPECTED

Some years ago in Chicago, a youngster answered an advertisement for an office boy—these were days in which most busy offices hired an office boy as a "gopher" and general helper for miscellaneous small tasks—and found nineteen boys already waiting in line to see the boss, Hiram W. Johnson. The boy took up his position in line and thought intensely about the situation. Then he took a scrap of paper out of his pocket and scrawled something on it. He implored Mr. Johnson's secretary to place this on Mr. Johnson's desk immediately, and managed to persuade her to do so.

The young man wound up with the job. His note had read, "Mr. Johnson, please don't hire anyone until you've had a chance to talk to me. I'm number 20 in line." Mr. Johnson was obviously convinced that not only should such resourcefulness and imagination be rewarded, but would probably be of great value to him as the employer of such a clever lad.

There are several morals here. One of them is to *turn your liabilities into assets*. The long line appeared to be liability, but this bright youngster made an asset of it. Without it, he would not have had an excuse for displaying his flair for originality and salesmanship.

Another moral is to *be different*. Do the unexpected. Draw attention to yourself—in a favorable way, of course.

Still another is *be positive*. Some boys might have become discouraged at the long line, and decided that their chances were too slim to waste time here. You can't win when you program yourself to lose.

The most important thing to learn from this example is that you have to think for yourself about what best serves your interest, without regard to whether that's what others do. It isn't others that concerns you, and what "they say" is meaningless claptrap if it does not serve your needs. Think *functionally*—what you wish to accomplish and what measures or actions are most likely to help you accomplish that. Focus your attention on the end, not the means. It's only to the true bureaucratic intellect that the means is more important than the end. In bureaucracy, the focus is on avoiding even the remote possibility of being criticized, and one way to minimize that possibility is to be as conservative as possible.

Being conservative means several things. It means minimizing risk, for one thing. But what does that mean? That means, to the bureaucratic mind, doing things according to well-established patterns. The presumption is that there is little chance of going wrong if you pursue well-defined paths. Of course, that's a rationalization;

the true reason for conservatism is that it is easy to defend yourself against criticism for failure if you pursued the most classical or time-honored ways of doing things. It is *that* risk, the risk of criticism being leveled against you, that is the true concern—"worry item"—of the bureaucrat.

Being conservative also means "don't make waves" to the hunkered-down bureaucrat. Making waves means drawing attention to oneself, and drawing attention to oneself is risky. So doing things as they have always been done or as "they say" they ought to be done minimizes the risk. Why take chances?

Of course, the opposite of conservatism is innovation, invention, initiative, pioneering. If you ever have the opportunity to hear Donald M. Dible, author of *Up Your OWN Organization!* (The Entrepreneur Press, 1971, 1974), you may hear some of his observations about pioneers and missionaries. Pioneers, he'll tell you, are the ones who get arrows in their backs. And missionaries usually wind up in the stew pot. Still, despite those cynical comments—and I cannot deny there is an element of truth to them—it was not conservatives and don't-make-waves advocates who put man on the moon; developed TV, computers, and jet airplanes; conquered dozens of hitherto "incurable" diseases; conquered the wilderness; and built the railroads, to name just a few advances that required running the risk of arrows in the back.

It requires courage to be different, to pioneer, to do things according to the logic of achieving a goal, rather than the logic of playing it safe. Obviously, if the goal itself is to play it safe, by all means shun everything that is creative, inventive, pioneering, innovative, or in any way entails *thinking*. Those kinds of things always entail risk—you might get and be tempted to try an original idea, which would only draw attention to you and might even be successful. (Success sometimes draws even more attention and criticism than does failure, especially if you have the audacity to succeed with something others have assured you could not be done.)

On the other hand, there are some things in which the only way to be successful is to be different. But not different merely for the sake of difference itself. Be different in a positive, constructive way, in a way that does more than merely draw attention . . . or show a degree of initiative in a way that contributes directly to achieving your goal.

One young man owned a special "interview suit." He had paid

$250 for that suit (before modern inflation when that represented a price only the very prosperous man would ordinarily spend for a suit; it was an extravagant price for anyone). Certainly there were exceedingly few young men, at the start of their careers, who thought that they could afford a luxury on that scale.

For this young man, however, his $250 suit was not a luxury, but an *investment* in his own career. That suit hung carefully preserved in his closet between jobs, for that was his interview suit, to be worn only for job interviews. It was a magic suit, this young man explained. When he wore it, he felt ten feet tall, for he knew that it was almost impossible to buy a better suit of clothes anywhere, and wearing it did something to him psychologically. Wearing that suit gave him a sense of success and security, and he found that he radiated a sensation of power and confidence when he wore it, which helped him enormously in making the right impression in an interview.

## UNDERSTANDING THE CUSTOMER

Perhaps the best way to understand the difference between what you sell and what a customer buys is to consider how successful advertising is designed. Take that most familiar of all advertising, the TV commercial. Toothpaste commercials are an excellent example. The advertisers are selling their products, toothpaste in a rainbow assortment of colors, scents, and flavors, with probably not two cents' worth of functional difference among all, yet with each advertiser working at proving the superiority of that advertiser's product.

Logic might suggest that the way to do this is to present a wealth of scientific evidence—and that would mean, of course, largely technical evidence, but also any other evidence to prove that given brand was more effective than the others. You can imagine an array of white-coated specialists presenting the evidence, the rows of figures resulting from laboratory tests, the testimonials from satisfied users. But is that how it's done? Yes and no. *Some* of this kind of evidence is offered, but far less than you might expect. Note something else that might strike you as being curious: that kind of evidence is not only presented far less than you might have expected, but it is clear that this is secondary to the main advertising appeals. These are *backup* offerings, supporting the main presentations, which are of an entirely different nature. The main presentations promise certain *results*, such as:

* Shining bright, attractive teeth.
* Greatly enhanced sex appeal.
* Better "checkups"—healthier teeth.
* Fresh breath.

The advertisers are not selling toothpaste at all; they are selling romance, personal image, security against the embarrassment of bad breath, and other such benefits. They also sell healthier teeth, although by far the majority of toothpaste advertisers ignore dental health. They don't think it has nearly as much appeal, motivational influence, as romance.

Note, too, that the dental-health appeal—"better checkups"— is made to parents as parents, while the other appeals are made to those who buy and use the toothpaste themselves. This is "segmenting" or "positioning" advertising: Selecting a group of prospects and deciding what the appeal should be in terms of what the motivation of the prospect is to be.

The two are not unrelated. If you wish to use the dental-health appeal, it is futile to address your appeal to the user directly; finding romance and avoiding embarrassment are far more powerful motivators than are commonsense appeals of any kind. The dental-health appeal is most effective when made to parents who have to pay for children's dental care and who can be made to feel responsible for compelling their children to use the right toothpaste—or guilty if they fail.

In any case, note the really significant fact: The advertiser wishes to sell toothpaste, but the prospect does not wish to buy toothpaste. The prospect wants love, freedom from fear, freedom from the guilt of children's dental problems, freedom from backbreaking dental costs, to be attractive, and other such emotional goals. *Those* are what the advertiser must *promise* to motivate the prospect enough to close sales. Which would *you* rather have—a toothpaste that is compounded of superior ingredients in a superior formula, or a toothpaste that gives you a dazzling smile, a fresh breath, a fatal attraction for the opposite sex, a movie-star appeal? No contest, is there?

To sell whatever it is you wish to sell, you must promise the prospect a result that has powerful emotional appeal. The prospect does not want to buy the product; the prospect wants to buy some result or set of results. That's a universal truth, and it's true in all advertising, TV commercials, print, billboards, radio, direct mail, and other media. It's true despite the fact that advertisers also offer some "logical" evidence. (We'll discuss that, too.) Why this is so is that we are all creatures of emotion, and we "think" with our emotions far more than we do with our gray matter. But even in terms of pure logic, it makes sense that we all want to buy results, not products. We want to buy what the products do, not what they are. Consider the purchase of an automobile. How many of us really want to spend thousands of dollars on something we can all recall as selling for far less (hence, is "way overpriced," we all agree), and tie ourselves down for three to five years of monthly payments which tend to last longer than the automobile does, at exorbitant interest rates? Few of us really want to do this, but we do want the convenience of personal transportation in a comfortable, even luxurious, vehicle of our own. We want this badly enough to suspend reason and surrender to emotion. If ever the public were to begin using *reason* as the chief criterion in making buying decisions, a great many important industrial and commercial structures would come crashing down, not the least of which would be the advertising industry. But there is no danger. Customers will continue to buy what they want, which may or may not coincide with what they need.

## THE IMPORTANCE OF PERCEPTIONS

A former President of the United States, Jimmy Carter, was unable to understand why he did not win reelection; why he was so universally unappreciated by the citizens of this nation. He thought himself bright, sensitive, firm in his resolve, rational in his decisions, unflinching in facing unpleasant truths. The public saw him as hesitant, wavering, indecisive, fearful, and confused. Whether Jimmy Carter was truly what he thought he was or what the public thought he was did not matter on Election Day 1980. What did matter was what the American public *thought* Jimmy Carter was. The public voted according to their perception of Jimmy Carter. And Jimmy Carter's bewilderment reveals as clearly as anything can that his perception of the American public and of his own image was cloudy and far short of reality.

Success in marketing depends heavily upon the prospect's perception. What you *are* is not the deciding factor. The deciding factor is what the employer *thinks* you are, how the employer *perceives* you as a potential employee. There are individuals who are wizards at selling themselves; people who advance rapidly in their companies even though they are really not very good at what they do. But they are very good at manipulating and shaping their superiors' perceptions of them— at selling themselves, to be blunt. And it is that skill that every job-seeker needs to master to some degree.

Of course, it is necessary first to make a realistic assessment of what the employer *wants* to see, and then to pursue some method that will bring this perception about. Bear in mind that an employer is not really different from any other customer-prospect; the employer may be hiring a human being, a person, but what the employer really wants is some set of results, something a person can do for the organization. For example, the employer is not interested in personal trivia unless it bears directly on the job you will be expected to do. Suppose you are applying for a job as office manager of an appliance manufacturer, and you mention an interest in golf and other sports. You're wasting your time and the employer's and unnecessarily risking incurring displeasure. However, if you are applying for a position in a sporting goods company of some sort, your interest in golf and other sports is entirely germane and certainly should be mentioned.


## RÉSUMÉS AND PERCEPTIONS

In the past few years there has been some reversal of popular thinking about résumés. Since the Second World War, as our commercial and industrial base became more and more technological and specialized in various ways, the need for rightness of résumés—of the basic résumé idea—achieved a sanctity rivaling that of God, Country, and Motherhood. It became almost automatic, a reflex action to say, "Drop off a résumé," to anyone who approached you with an inquiry about job leads.

There have been growing doubts and many questions about this over the past few years. Books have been appearing which exhort readers to forget about résumés, to throw their résumés away because résumés don't work and only defeat the user's purpose. Arguments are raised against the basic résumé idea, against résumés *per se*. The arguments are not without merit, but they do suffer from the myopia of authors who assume that because most résumés do not work very well the résumé concept is a bad one. They evidently do not consider that perhaps part of the problem is due to the fact that few résumés are intelligently conceived and designed, let alone well written. Further, they appear not to consider perhaps another part of the problem: the common prejudice about what a résumé ought to include.

Examine any of the books of advice on how to write résumés, examine any of the samples published as examples of well-written, well-planned, and presumably effective résumés, and study them with regard to what has been said here about marketing and customer perceptions. What you will perceive, if you think about it, is that without exception those résumés are written with the applicant's needs and desires in mind, rather than with the prospective employer's needs and desires in mind.

In the face of these facts, do you think that any prospective employer is interested in your biography, your dreams and ambitions, or anything else you want? The employer is not trying to sell you; you are trying to sell the employer. Therefore, whatever you call that piece of paper you send to prospective employers in your quest for interviews, it is in fact a *sales presentation*. Study all those published examples of what are believed to be good résumés and see how many qualify as effective sales presentations. How many accomplish the following:

1. Offer specific benefits, clearly defined?
2. Focus sharply on one or two major benefits?
3. Provide some evidence that the applicant can and will deliver, as promised?

The problem is not inherent in the résumé idea but in how the whole idea has become distorted by those who are so full of themselves that they believe a résumé must be a personal monument. The typical résumé writer never even thinks of the reader's perceptions, but only of his or her own ego needs. Perhaps being Homecoming Queen or President of the Chess Club was important to you, an achievement, but what is it to an employer who wants someone to take over the troublesome chore of managing the inventory? Let's take a look at a typical chronological résumé and see how it stacks up as a sales presentation. (See Figure 4.)

This résumé offers only one blessing: it's brief. If the employer does take the time to read it—and it's possible that this will happen primarily because the résumé is brief—the positive assets *suggested* may surface in the employer's consciousness: Three patent developments, successful telemetry designs and customer commendations, and outstanding computer-programming accomplishments. The success of this résumé as a sales presentation depends on the possibility that the employer will read it through, will note the accomplishments reported, and will interpret the latter as an indication of what Hugh Rogers, engineer, can and is likely to do for the employer's organization.

That's pretty chancey. Good sales presentations do not depend on the probability that the prospect will see the benefits implied or suggested in the presentation; they do things to ensure the prospect will be made completely conscious of those promised benefits.

Another fault of this résumé is the chronological presentation of the writer's earliest experience first, which presents the least impressive experience first. Assuming most readers will read only the first few lines of a résumé before deciding whether to spend time reading the rest of it, why not present the latest—and presumably most responsible and highest-level job to date—first? Is it not likely that the latest (and probably current) work experience is going to be more significant than your early experience? It usually is, and it's generally a better practice to use a reverse chronology, if you use a chronological résumé, starting with current or latest position and working backwards. (Quite often you will not want to go all the way back to your earliest experience, but will find the experience of current and perhaps one or two earlier positions more than adequate for your purposes.)

There is another type of résumé some think preferable: a functional résumé. Let's consider the pros and cons of this approach. (See Figure 5.)

This résumé is far from being everything it ought to be as a sales presentation, but it does have some advantages over the one shown in the previous figure. For one thing, it does deal primarily in accomplishments of the writer, in terms of the benefits other employers have realized from Hugh Rogers' efforts. It also uses an approach that is

Hugh Rogers          9722 Hopeful Lane—Madison, OH 45544
                     513-555-0677

EDUCATION:
    Madison High School, graduated 1964
    Powerful University, BSEE, 1968

EXPERIENCE:          Engineer, Blackford Electronic Indus-
1968–73:             tries, Philadelphia, PA. Developed several
                     models of CB radios; designed circuits
                     for telemetry in support of satellite pro-
                     grams. Developed three circuits patented
                     by company.

1974–79:             Development Engineer, Sigma Chi Elec-
                     tronics, Houston, TX. Developed teleme-
                     try systems for NASA, leading team of
                     three other engineers and four techni-
                     cians. Conducted successful field tests,
                     including preflight checkout on launch
                     pad. All firings successful. Wrote all final
                     reports. Commended by customer.

1979–Present:        Engineering Manager, Communications
                     & Weapons Department, Blue Star Avia-
                     tion Corporation. In charge of static
                     missile firings in instrumented cham-
                     bers, programming data for analysis, in-
                     terpreting results and preparing all final
                     reports. Programs I have written have
                     reduced total computer time required by
                     nearly one-half, have produced final re-
                     ports within six weeks after firings.

FIGURE 4. Typical brief chronological résumé.

Hugh Rogers        9722 Hopeful Lane—Madison, OH 45544
                   513-555-0677

EDUCATION:
    Madison High School, graduated 1964
    Powerful University, BSEE, 1968

EXPERIENCE AND CAPABILITIES:
Electronics engineer, design of missile test instrumentation
and telemetry, computer programming, conducting field
tests, report writing.

Designed and conducted instrumented static firing of missile in test chamber; developed new computer programs to
process test data, reducing computer time required by one-
half; wrote all final reports.

Designed telemetry for missile; personally conducted successful field tests, including preflight tests on launch pad;
wrote all final reports; received customer commendations.

Holder of three telemetry patents developed for employer.

FIGURE 5. A functional résumé.

not bound to the sequence in which Rogers gained his experience or achieved his sterling professional deeds, giving him the freedom to structure his résumé more effectively.

Still, the benefits to the prospective employer are only suggested, and the result therefore depends on the reader's inferring benefits from employing Smith. Moreover, engineer Rogers is made to appear a specialist in telemetry, with a bit of computer-programming capability thrown in as a bonus. This is okay if Rogers wishes to consider only telemetry-connected positions; otherwise, it's a bit confining and restrictive, limiting Rogers to only those positions connected with telemetry.

Finally, this résumé lacks a sharp focus. It has some of the shotgun elements of those polypharmacal medical prescriptions mentioned earlier, offering several achievements and skills and suggesting that engineer Rogers is good in more than one "department" of his profession. That subject merits some discussion, for it is an important consideration in marketing.

## SPECIALIST VERSUS GENERALIST

For quite a number of years now we have been trending away from the notion that people can or should be generalists, able to do many things well. Read the help-wanted advertisements in the newspapers today and take notice of the specialized skills called for. Look at the job titles used in organizations today, for further evidence of this idea that everyone must be a specialist.

Even in the medical profession, where specialization has existed for a long time, it has been carried to such an extreme that the general practitioner, that friendly neighborhood doctor you called when Sonny Boy had a bad cold or was developing spots on his face, has almost disappeared. The closest thing to a GP (general practitioner) today is the *internist*, who is a specialist too. But the ultimate irony is that the medical profession now recognizes that there is a need for GPs, and few physicians are willing to become them, probably because they have been conditioned to the notion that one has to be a specialist to be a true professional. An effort had to be made to make being a GP more prestigious and respectable, and it was made into its own specialty. The modern GP takes a residency in "family medicine," so the GP is now a specialist too!

It's important to understand this trend and how it has affected business and industry, as far as hiring and employment practices—and perceptions—are concerned. Again, we must segregate reality from perceptions, and sell to the perceptions while planning for the realities.

The reality is this: To be seriously considered by most employers—proprietors, managers, and personnel specialists, many of whom tend to be the least understanding of this anomaly—you must go along with the perception that you must be a specialist. It is an absurdity because it is carried to extremes. Obviously, the basic concept is rooted in fact: Being an electronics engineer is being a professional specialist. However, the field of electronics has become so broad that it is almost impossible to be equally proficient in all areas. So the electronics engineer tends to specialize either in the types of equipment he or she uses (e.g., radar, communications, computers, television broadcasting, controls, automation, etc.) or in terms of the types of engineering functions (e.g., design development, technical writing, field engineering, maintenance, etc.). But it can get carried to extremes. A technical writer, for example, tends to work with equipment classes most familiar to him, but some employers will insist that an applicant engineer-writer be directly experienced with and knowledgeable about some military manual specification. The able writer knows that this is absurd: Any able technical writer can work with any military writing specification, given a copy of the specification and an hour or two to study it. (The differences between the various writing specifications for the military are usually not great.) Still, if an employer thinks that such experience is necessary, rarely will that perception be changed by an applicant.

## PERCEPTIONS MAY BE PREJUDICES

The perception mentioned here, that of an employer that an applicant technical writer must "know" some particular specification, is in fact a prejudice. The employer has already decided that no applicant who fails to demonstrate that specific knowledge will be considered, despite the fact that the perception is false. If the employer has stated in an advertisement that such knowledge is a required qualification, a frontal assault on the notion can only bring about even more polarization of the employer's view. Certainly, it would be a rare employer who agreed with you when you said "You don't know what you're talking about."

Does that mean you should not make an effort to win the job when you are sure you can do the job well, you find the job attractive, and the only problem is an employer's false perception? No, it does not mean that at all. People who do not meet all the idealized qualifications specified for jobs are hired every day. There are various ways to address this, all of them based on the technique of avoiding the subject as much as possible, and certainly not challenging it. If you manage to get to an interview, you have already met with preliminary approval; and if you make a good enough case for yourself, you stand an excellent chance of getting around the problem. (Of course, you should have some advance ideas about how to field that question if and when it comes up, as it is likely to. But we'll discuss that further in the chapter on interviewing.) Bear in mind that the employer may not have really meant that knowledge of that specification was an absolutely rigid requirement; it may have been a wish for someone who had prior experience with that specification, without the full-blown hope of finding such an individual. In short, ignoring it may result in the matter never being raised at all.

Successful sales presentations never fly in the face of known prejudice. Prejudice can be overcome, but not by logic or other direct attack. Prejudice is overcome by indirect means, such as by making the desire to gain some promised benefit far stronger than the prejudice against doing whatever that prejudice prohibits. Even bankers have been induced to invest in risky undertakings by the lure of extraordinary profits, when they would never have considered the investment for a moment had the profit margin been an ordinary one.

## THE MOST IMPORTANT ITEMS IN A RÉSUMÉ

Sales and advertising people often use the acronym AIDA to explain sales and advertising rationale:

A — for get Attention
I — for arouse Interest
D — for generate Desire
A — for ask for Action

A simpler and perhaps more direct explanation of sales/advertising presentation and argument is Promise and Proof. These are the two major factors you will find in every successful sales and advertising presentation. And these two "Ps" explain everything that AIDA does. That is, if the promise you make is sufficiently attractive, it will get attention and arouse interest swiftly enough. And if you furnish convincing evidence—proof—you'll have no problem generating buying desire and getting the order.

Even this discussion of the difference between AIDA and PP illustrates an important point about the subject. *Get attention, arouse interest, generate desire,* and *ask for action* are aims—what you want to make happen—but *making promises* and *offering proofs* are the ways in which you will make those things happen. They are more specific, more concrete explanations. AIDA attempts to explain what your sales presentation or advertisement ought to bring about, but it does not tell you *how* to bring it about.

This applies to résumés too. Consider the items of Figure 4, even those positive achievements and the potential benefits they imply (not specifically promise): they are stated as *claims*, with no proof offered. Thus they are almost as unconvincing as such commonly used (and *mis*used) terms as "idea man" and claims to being extraordinarily "creative" and "imaginative."

Like any other sales presentation, therefore, the résumé must present an alluring promise and some good evidence of the validity of the promise. And it must manage to focus on a sharply defined promise while avoiding being too narrow and restrictive. And there are still other considerations in addition to these. One of them is: No sales presentation can be effective if it is too clever and sophisticated. Clever and sophisticated advertisements and sales messages tend to be subtle ones; they rarely succeed in accomplishing their purpose because far too many people miss the message.

## GETTING THE MESSAGE ACROSS

The résumé, you must remember, is intended to persuade, as are all sales presentations. Promises and proofs are the principal persuasive techniques and tactics here, but for promises and proofs to do their work they must be both sharply focused and highly communicative; they cannot do the job if the reader *does not get the message*. And advertising history is chock full of tales about artistic, clever, sophisticated copy that won art awards but failed to sell the product because the prospect didn't get the message.

A local bank has been running a TV commercial with great frequency to advertise its money fund investment offer. The commercial shows a man working at a desk, apparently at home, for his wife and small child show up with cans and buckets as water begins to pour into the room. The voice-over says something about the money funds and emergencies, but the impact is badly blurred by the visual in two ways: One, it distracts attention from the audio, and two, the connection between money-fund investments and the scene is vague— it's not at all clear what the scene is supposed to convey. I've seen the commercial at least a dozen times now, and I've still no idea of the main point of the thing. It's amusing, and well-staged, but it does not deliver the message. It neither makes a promise of any kind nor gives any kind of focused argument for buying the advertiser's product.

Résumés make the same mistakes. The promises are implied in some cases, perhaps, but rarely are they clear. The employer is expected to infer the promise, in most cases. In fact, most résumés are stronger on evidence by virtue of their weakness on promises.

There are those who go to the opposite extreme and make promises they do not and cannot support with evidence, such as being people who can solve problems, who have wonderful imaginations which constantly spew out great ideas, and who want nothing more than an inspiring challenge.

The latter are not promises, really, nor even evidence, but are unsupported claims. They are self-appraisals, judgments that the résumé writer is trying to force down the throat of the reader. It won't happen. The readers of the résumé won't swallow it because they see the same thing over and over, and they recognize it for what it is; so they will only sigh and go on to the next résumé in the stack.

Don't make claims or vague promises. Make specific promises and only ones you can back up.

## DON'T TELL THEM, SHOW THEM

Somewhere in his education the fiction writer is advised, "Don't tell them; show them." By this is meant bring the characters and situations to life. For example, instead of explaining to the reader that a certain character grew very angry, describe what could be observed—his face reddened, his knuckles went white as he clenched his fists, sparks virtually darted from balefully glaring eyes, etc.

Similar advice applies to achieving credibility in any writing, but especially in making a sales presentation and the general area of presenting claims. If, for example, you are tempted to claim a great creative imagination and many great ideas, *prove it* by furnishing specific examples in adequate detail. Details lend credibility. Name names, dates, and places. In that Figure 4 example, Hugh Rogers could have added a great deal of impact to his résumé by furnishing a little detail about those designs he patented, or about the nature of his other work.

Now here you may perceive an anomaly: Overly long résumés are anathema to most employers (who has time to read such lengthy résumés when there are so many to be read?). So how can you present all the necessary detail to prove your case, and yet offer a brief résumé?

In fact, the two notions are not only entirely compatible, but actually work in your interest in other ways, as you will see. It is far more effective to make a single promise and present an abundance of proof for it than to make a dozen promises and present only scant evidence to back them up. And this is entirely aside from the consideration of achieving a· necessary sharpness of focus, although that is a consideration too.

"Showing them" means presenting the details—anyone can make a general claim to be the producer of great ideas, but actually describing specific cases in documentary detail is another matter. It entails, however, thinking graphically, as though you were describing an actual scene. Think of it as *reporting*, if you wish to be truly objective; minimize your use of adjectives and adverbs. Stick to nouns and verbs and short sentences. That alone will tend to keep you more objective and reportorial. Report things that have happened without trying to interpret what they mean. That will not interfere with achieving the result you want, if you are careful to report the event or achievement *and the result*.

For example, if you are reporting on a device you designed which your employer was able to patent, explain the device and what it does, but explain also *how your employer benefited* from it. It is that latter item that will be of greatest interest to a prospective employer. These are the main areas of interest to any and all employers:

Increasing sales
Stimulating growth
Increasing profits
Reducing costs
Solving problems (especially those related to any of the above)

When you think of achievements you can lay claim to and how they have benefited your employers, or when you wish to make promises of benefits you can produce, think in terms of these items, for all employers recognize these and agree that they would like to achieve these as general goals.

Different employers, by virtue of both their individual characteristics and the characteristics of their organizations, tend to focus more sharply on one of these goals than on the others. Some individuals and organizations, for example, are entirely sales oriented because they are essentially sales organizations. Therefore, they are more likely to respond to prospects for increasing sales (and for growing generally) than to other inducements. The manufacturing organization which produces a large volume of products and depends on large-volume sales, is usually quite sensitive to costs, and responds to any prospect for reducing them. The organization that works on a narrow margin is naturally sensitive to possibilities for increasing profit margins. The firm that by its very nature must solve problems frequently is always conscious of the need to solve problems. It is therefore wise to consider such factors when designing your résumé and try to appeal to the areas of greatest concern.

There is hardly a job in any area of any organization that cannot be linked to the history or promise of benefits in one or more of these areas. The linkages are obvious in some cases such as sales and purchasing positions; but every employee can contribute to one of these goals or the position would not exist at all. So, in structuring a résumé, then, study these typical employer goals and decide to which ones you can make the greatest contributions. Once you have decided this, *get right to the point.* If you've been through college, there is no need to document your high school diploma; it's obvious you must have one, and it's of no interest in any case. In fact, unless your education is of some critical importance for one reason or another, don't take up valuable headline space at the top of your résumé with it. Tack it on at or near the end, and allot that valuable headline space for the most important item: the promise that constitutes the main reason for hiring you.

## "ME TOO" WON'T DO

The federal government spends some 85 percent of its annual procurement budget—upwards of $150 billion a year currently—on what is referred to as *negotiated procurement*. This means that price is a secondary consideration to other factors, and it may or may not be the low bidder who wins the contracts. In fact, is is relatively rare that the low bidder does win, for the government requires each competitor for the contract to prepare and submit a proposal. Each proposal is evaluated by the government for various qualitative factors, such as estimated probabilities of success, experience of the proposer, quality of the staff, and sundry other considerations. The effort is to select the *best* contractor, not the cheapest one.

In such a competition there is only one winner. There are no awards for second- or third-place runners-up. And among the most common mistakes proposers make in pursuing such a contract is to write a proposal that says, in effect, "Me too," meaning "We can do a good job too, as good as anyone else." But *me-too* doesn't win contracts. The government wants someone who demonstrates a quality or ability far better than anyone else's, not simply as good as anyone else's.

Too many résumés also appear to be written with the me-too philosophy, and the employer seeking someone for any but the most routine sort of job will certainly prefer to hire the *best* candidate for the job, not just a me-too candidate.

You must write your résumé with that philosophy, finding and expressing some *specific reason for selecting you*. The employer is a customer prospect, to whom you wish to sell your services. Like any customer prospect, he or she needs to be given a *reason* for buying what you are selling.

# 6

# Make Your Own Rules

*Your résumé is your sales presentation, designed to do something for you. Never mind what anyone else thinks— what "they say"; design and develop your résumé to do what you want your résumé to do for you.*

## THE BASIC STRATEGY THAT SHOULD UNDERLIE ALL RÉSUMÉS

**I**N show business, the professionals have two sayings that are useful to remember when you're planning and carrying out your job quest:

1. Save something for an encore.
2. Always leave them wanting more.

If the only legitimate reason for making up and sending out résumés is to gain interviews so that you can sell yourself into the job—so that you can negotiate a trade of your services for salary and other considerations—the résumé must logically be designed to bring the interview about. Let's consider, then, the best way to cause the employer to request your presence for interview.

You've already seen ample arguments directed to the point that everyone, including employers, acts out of self-interest. With that as a premise, you should design your résumé to aid the employer in seeing it in his or her self-interest to have a face-to-face talk with you.

That invitation to come in for a chat is not provoked by any burning desire to hire you. Not yet. No résumé is likely to be that motivating or to provide enough information to create that desire. In fact, that invitation to come in and talk is not necessarily aimed at verifying your suitability for employment. If you are depending on your résumé to do that, you are going to be compelled to send out a great many résumés before you get an interview, and you may never get an invitation to talk. A far sounder general strategy for your résumé is to provoke a desire—even a need—for more information. Here is why:

Employment is the reward you are seeking. It's what *you* want. True enough, the employer wants to hire someone, to give someone a job, but hiring someone is not the employer's true desire—not the end. It's the means. What the employer wants is the help the right new-hire can provide. And the résumé cannot, normally, satisfy the reader that you are that help. So if you want to *motivate* an employer to want to talk to you, you must offer some reward for doing so—some powerful motivational influence.

In short, persuading an employer to interview you is a selling job, and you need to *offer* something to make the "sale." The question, then, is what can you offer? And probably the only thing you can offer immediately is information—the promise of useful information. If, somehow, your résumé delivers a credible promise of useful information, the reader will want to talk to you.

That is the primary reason for keeping your résumé brief. You do not want to give away what you have to "sell"—valuable information. But you also want to make it clear that your résumé merely skims the surface of a store of valuable information; that there is far more valuable information to be mined. Obviously, the only way to mine it is to invite the writer of that résumé in for a chat. The writer then has the opportunity of doing the selling and pressing for negotiation. The logical progression is shown in Figure 6.

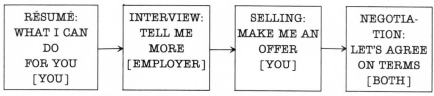

FIGURE 6. The fundamental résumé strategy.

## THE "RULES" OF THE GAME

Obviously, you cannot state in your résumé that only if the reader
will invite you in for interview will you impart important and valuable
information. The commonly accepted "rules" of job hunting and hiring won't permit that. Most employers would be totally affronted by
that approach, although they are not offended when other things are
sold to them on that basis, when they are told plainly that they can
derive certain benefits only by shelling out their money. The difference
here is that the employer is "in the driver's seat" when it comes to
hiring people. Despite modern attitudes and legislation concerning
the rights of those who work for others, many employers still react,
perhaps unconsciously, like the feudal barons of long ago. The image
of an employer as the boss lingers on, and is an unconscious, or at
most semiconscious, prejudice. So it is necessary to be somewhat
subtle in implementing the strategy of you've-got-to-interview-me-to-
find-out-what-I-know-that-you'd-like-to-know. But that is not especially difficult to do. It requires a little imagination, a little writing
skill, and the courage to think independently.

The biggest obstacle most résumé writers face is their own chained
thinking. Most people who go out to seek jobs are still chained to
whatever passes for conventional wisdom, to what "they say," whoever
"they" may be.

The very concept of the "standard" résumé format illustrates
that. Select any of the many résumé books to be found on the book-
shelves of any well-stocked bookstore—there must be at least twenty-
five such books in print at this moment, and new ones are still appearing. Study the literally dozens of résumés that appear in these
tomes. You will discover that although many purport to be examples
of how one may tailor a résumé for special purposes or to one's own
special needs, there is a startling sameness among all. Few, indeed,
are truly distinctive, except in such fine details that no employer is
likely to see a difference.

That points up one of the basic weaknesses in the whole résumé
idea: As the "standard" or accepted résumé format is conceived by
most people, it demands that the writer provide a complete education
and work-experience biography, and that it be in some chronological
sequence, with all periods accounted for. Any gap in the sequence

becomes grounds for great suspicion that the writer has something to hide and is trying to cover up.

This is not truly a weakness in the résumé concept as much as it is a weakness in how we have permitted what "they" think, do, and say to dictate to us what we shall think, do, and say, whether it makes good sense or not. The previous chapter made several brief references to being different, being independent, doing the unexpected. The point was not that being different is valuable for its own sake, but that one should think in terms of function—what will do the job most effectively? You must analyze the problem *objectively—unemotionally*—if you are to find the most effective way to get the job done. There are two principal steps in the process:

1. *Where Do I Wish to go OR What Do I Wish to Have Happen?*

Get a clear picture in your mind of what you want. In this case, presumably, you wish to get a letter or call inviting you to come in and be interviewed. Be sure that you understand that as your goal, then think and plan in terms of that goal.

2. *What Are the Things I Can Do to Make That Happen?*

Now you must totally disregard anything you believe "they" say, think, or do. It is not "they" who need and want a job, but *you*. No one is keeping records of how you do whatever you do to achieve your goal, and certainly no one is going to reward you for playing by some imaginary set of rules. There are no rules. There are only notions about how to do things and what things to do. There are notions referred to as "conventional wisdom," which means what is commonly accepted as being the best way to do things or the truth about things. Sheer nonsense. There is absolutely nothing sacred about those notions, nor are they either wise or always correct.

Decide for yourself all the possible ways to achieve your goal, evaluate them and select whatever you believe to be the way most likely to produce the result you want, and then do it.

For example, one man was faced with the necessity of sending out résumés to companies with hardly any knowledge of the companies except that they were in lines of endeavor suitable to make them prospects. He was well aware, as are most experienced job seekers, that only a fraction of the résumés which reach the desk of a personnel manager find their way to the desk of a decision-making manager who might hire him. He was also aware that when he sent a résumé to a company addressed to no one especially, the mail room would open it and, recognizing it as a résumé, would send it on to the personnel office.

He found an effective way to deal with the problem. He made up a brief form letter to go with his résumé, advising the personnel manager that he had something to offer the company, that he needed help in finding the right managers to whom to offer his services, and that he knew that the personnel manager, wise and dedicated to personnel work, would be glad to help him and the employer by sending the résumé on to the right managers. His ploy worked well— either because he flattered the personnel managers and made them feel important or because he appealed to their consciences and made them feel a bit guilty. He was rewarded with several interviews and accepted an offer made to him. A paraphrase of his letter is offered in Figure 7.

He was not afraid to be different, and he was not reluctant to think objectively about his problem. He finessed his problem in the way others have tried to achieve what many thought impossible: He freely recognized the obstacle, acknowledged to himself that there was no practical way to avoid it, neutralize it, or plow through it, so he found a way to make it work for him. He turned a liability into an asset; something which is quite often possible for those not afraid to think independently and creatively—to be different. Where a great many personnel managers appear to believe that their main function is to screen all résumés and prevent most of them from getting to line managers' desks, he showed personnel managers a new way to accomplish something, to carry out the true mission, which is to *help their employers find good employees.* Getting what you want usually requires helping the other party get what he or she wants.

## SOLVING PROBLEMS: METHODOLOGIES

The entire process of finding and landing a suitable job is usually one of solving a series of problems. There are the problems of finding or identifying the opportunities—companies with specific openings suitable for your needs. There are the problems of making your applications in the most effective ways—in the ways most likely to bring

Rita McCullough
Personnel Manager
Accurate Tool Mfg Co., Inc.
Factorytown, PA 18766

Dear Ms. McCullough:

I can offer your company a number of important new manufacturing techniques I have developed over the past few years as a methods engineer in tool manufacturing. These techniques have reduced costs by as much as 22 percent in some areas, and have raised efficiency everywhere they have been used.

Of course, I do not know anyone in your organization, although I know the fine reputation your company enjoys. I need your professional help in directing my résumé (enclosed) to the most suitable manager(s), since you will know best how my services can best be used to benefit your employer.

Thank you for your help.

Cordially,

Hiram Walters

Enclosure: Résumé

FIGURE 7. Appeal to personnel manager for help.

you interviews and serious consideration, of course. There are the problems of getting through the interviews successfully and inducing actual job offers. And there are the problems of successful negotiation—getting offers which include terms acceptable to you. Of course, each of these is a major problem, but there are many smaller problems within the framework of finding answers to the major problem.

Job hunting is as much a problem-solving task as it is anything else. Getting past the personnel manager is only one problem—and there appears to be almost unanimous agreement that personnel managers are an obstacle to getting your résumé presented to a hiring manager. And, as you have just seen, the solution is not always to detour or bypass the problem: sometimes it is possible to nullify the problem, even to turn that liability into an asset. There are generally four ways to cope with a problem:

1. Go around it. (Detour.)
2. Blast through it. (Push it out of your way or demolish it.)
3. Neutralize it. (Counter it in some manner.)
4. Convert it. (Turn it around and make an asset of it.)

## LIABILITIES TURNED INSIDE OUT BECOME ASSETS

You're all familiar with that old cliché about the pessimist being someone who sees the cup as half empty, while the optimist sees the cup as half full. Old though this platitude is, it embodies a message that seems to escape most people: The way you look at some things determines what they are, liabilities or assets. A young person worries that prospective employers will find him or her too inexperienced for the job, and so works overtime at being defensive in the résumé, where the "experience" areas are concerned. But that young person is also a new broom that sweeps clean, an open mind, a fresh perspective, and many other assets—*if these are cleverly pointed out and highlighted in the résumé.*

In general, defensiveness in a résumé (as elsewhere) is negative, and the negative tone is self-defeating. Make it a rule to always be positive; sell what you have, and never mind what you don't have. There is absolutely no benefit in dwelling on what you cannot offer, why you cannot offer it, what you propose to do about it, and so forth. It is totally ineffective to explain what a quick learner you are, and how swiftly you will catch on to things, for example. In fact, aside from being ineffective, it is positively harmful, for it merely highlights and stresses your apparent weaknesses. Far better to leave the subject entirely alone, if you cannot say something positive about it. At least, your job hunt won't die in the dishonor of self-inflicted wounds.

Fortunately, you can be positive, with a little imagination and a proper mental set. Let's consider some typical problems job hunters have to cope with.

# TYPICAL PROBLEMS AND HOW TO COPE WITH THEM SUCCESSFULLY

Here are some problems which will be discussed here:

Changing fields, hence experience not totally relevant.
Age—too old or too young.
Experience—not enough or the wrong kind.

Observe, as you read these discussions and suggestions, the methods by which these problems can be approached—sometimes avoiding or detouring around the problem, sometimes finessing it and turning it into an aid, sometimes simply ignoring it because some problems exist only in your mind. And that is something to consider carefully: Is the problem you perceive truly a problem, or is it a chimera—something which will be a problem only if you permit it to be a problem? Be absolutely sure that the problem exists before you conceive and attempt a solution, or you may create a problem where none really existed.

## Changing Fields

Many people find themselves pursuing jobs in a new field. Whether by choice or by force of circumstances, the change engenders feelings of insecurity in most people. And they begin to write defensively, trying to compensate for their lack of experience in the new field to which they aspire and for which they fear they cannot show adequate qualifications. One way to address the problem is to search out the common denominators between the two fields—the one you are pursuing and the one in which you have been working—and focus on them. For example, if you have been a purchasing agent for an aerospace company and are pursuing a job as a purchasing agent for a chemical company, stress your prior business dealings with chemical companies in which you purchased rocket fuels, plastics, paints, solvents, and other chemical products. If you are an engineer with background in mechanical design but want to get into aerospace engineering areas, address those areas in aerospace that can make the best use of your experience. But even this is only one way to attack the problem. There are other ways, some of them even more positive, offering special benefits to prospective employers:

One way is by invoking the modern concept—and goal—of

"technology transfer." This is a relatively new idea which recognizes that we have become so specialized that our various technologies exist in some degree of isolation from each other. While we are not quite ready to go back to the idea of hiring generalists (with some exceptions), we have begun to see the need for better communication and transfer of technical know-how among the various fields. If you are changing fields, therefore, from one technology to another, you can offer to bring some specialized knowledge along, as an asset in your employment.

There is another consideration in making special appeals to employers when you are changing fields. Depending on the nature of the job you are leaving and of the one to which you aspire, you may be in a position to guide a new employer to new or additional business prospects. You may be able to suggest specific customer prospects or specific kinds of customers, as well as methods for approaching these new fields of business.

You may even have some specific ideas for a new employer as a result of observing the new employer's company or industry objectively from an outsider's viewpoint. This can be a powerful asset in your bid for a position with the new employer.

## AGE AND EXPERIENCE

Age is a worry item for many résumé writers. I have already suggested some approaches for those who fear that they are too young and too inexperienced to be considered seriously. But what about those who are over forty and who believe the myth that they will be considered "over the hill" and virtually unemployable?

There is no denying that to some degree the fear is well founded. For some fields, over-forty status is no problem; for others it is a real problem. Still, the problem is not solved by defensiveness and an apologetic tone. Once again, concentrate on what you have to offer, never on what you do not have to offer. You must study yourself in terms of what you can offer, even if it is readily available from younger people.

In general, you can offer experience, but what does that word mean? The trouble with experience as an asset or qualification is that too many of us assume experience means number of years employed in some type of job in some type of industry. Ergo, twenty years' experience is better than fifteen years' experience as a cost accountant in the machine-tool industry. Most who write résumés tend to lay stress on the number of years they have been successfully employed at some kind of work. Perhaps most employers go along with the evaluation of measuring one candidate's years against another candidate's simply because they've nothing else to measure.

The mistake you make as a job seeker is to assume a few things about employers which are false, such as:

You assume that all employers follow the same principles and methods in assessing candidates for jobs. Not so. Employers are individuals; some are bright, perceptive, hard-working, and imaginative, but others may be quite dull, obtuse, lazy, and unimaginative.

You assume that all employers have large staffs or some ways to check applicants out carefully and find out what loyal, devoted, hard working, energetic employees they were for previous employers. Not so. There is far less staff work done on applicants than this fable suggests—often little or none. In most cases the employer knows what your résumé says and no more, and his image of you is whatever leaps off that printed page at him or her.

You assume that employers will take the time and have the capacity for reading the résumé carefully and weighing everything on it. Not so. Employers tend to skim résumés quickly, or grab quick impressions from the first few lines, sometimes even from the general appearance of the résumé, and discard most of them before reaching the middle of the first page.

Also you tend to forget how many other résumés are competing with your own and how ordinary it will appear when it is one in a stack of dozens, perhaps even hundreds, of others. If you expect an employer to pay more attention to your résumé than he or she pays to any of the others, it's a vain hope—unless you do something to make the attention positive. Here's a basic rule which I like to think of as Holtz's First Law:

> Nothing but disasters happen all by themselves. You have to *make* the good things happen.

The best thing to do about your age, as far as your résumé and other aspects of the job hunt are concerned, is to *forget it*. Ignore it. Never mind when you were born; it's totally irrelevant. I myself sought and won more than a half dozen jobs after age forty, in addition to many consulting assignments and job offers I chose not to accept. And on some of those occasions, I was "between jobs" too, one of the unemployed.

As far as your résumé and other "paper" is concerned, don't do anything to focus attention on your age. Focus on what you can offer, stressing experience not on the basis of years, but on the basis of specific things you have done—situations you have faced, problems you have solved, contracts you have won, and whatever other things you have managed to accomplish *for your employers*. And that is a point that needs some explanation, for again we are going to indulge in a bit of iconoclasm and demonstrate that what passes for conventional wisdom is wrong.

## ACCOMPLISHMENTS, SUBTLETY, AND MODESTY

Most books on résumé writing exhort you to write an "accomplishment-oriented" résumé. This has been noted here already as good advice; the logic is inescapable. And the point has already been made that the "accomplishment" or "achievement" must be in such terms that the employer who reads the résumé instantly sees something the writer can and is likely to do for him or her. There is one more thing to be said about this: To make it absolutely clear that any subtlety or false modesty is not misplaced, but totally self-defeating. A résumé, like a proposal or any other sales or marketing presentation, is about the last place in the world you should be modest or subtle. Nor do you have any need to be. It is not at all difficult to give yourself full and complete credit for your accomplishments and to make that credit and those accomplishments crystal clear without giving offense or being in bad taste. It's a matter of exercising good judgment and being a bit careful in your phraseology.

It has already been pointed out that your writing style should be one that minimizes adjectives, superlatives, and hyperbole, and strives to present unemotional *reports* rather than *claims*. It is never immodest or in bad taste to report facts, if they are simply stated, not embellished, especially when they are stated quantitatively. It is not necessary to state that you are the greatest salesperson in shoe leather to make your point. Consider the following "before and after" or "right and wrong" examples. (Figure 8.)

### RÉSUMÉ SUMMARY

I was the leading salesman at Excelsior Tapered Bearing Co., Inc. for nearly 15 years. I produced more sales volume than the other three salesmen and the Sales Manager combined. I managed to get this volume of sales out of the smallest of the four sales territories.

"BEFORE"—CLAIMS WITHOUT EVIDENCE

### RÉSUMÉ SUMMARY

As one of four salesmen at Excelsior Tapered Bearing Co., Inc., I generated $14.65 million in sales last year out of a total company volume of $27.75 million, despite a territory that included less than 35 percent of the company's accounts.

"AFTER"—A REPORTORIAL FORMAT

FIGURE 8. Right and wrong ways to present accomplishments.

## FINDING A JOB IS A TRADE OF BENEFITS

Never underestimate or misunderstand the prime motivator: selfishness. And that is not said in a derogatory sense, either, for we all must be selfish if we are to survive, let alone prosper in this society. But successful people report frequently that one great lesson they have learned, which was contributory to, if not responsible for their success, is this: The best bargains are those in which both parties are satisfied that they have benefited. But no one is going to agree to any bargain unless he or she believes he or she will benefit. To induce anyone to enter into a bargain with you means inducing the other party to believe that he or she stands to benefit directly from it.

In the end, then, your résumé, letter, application, personal presentation, or whatever action you are pursuing in your job quest, is an *offer*. You are offering a trade: Your services to perform certain functions, especially to deliver certain benefits and bring about certain results, in exchange for the typical and traditional benefits of a job—salary, fringe benefits, and whatever else is important to you. Consider that your résumé or other action as a sales presentation, which is an offer—a sales presentation is always an offer of some promised benefits in exchange for [usually] money.

Once you begin to think about your résumé in that manner, your entire approach tends to change. You begin to consider what it is that you can offer and how to make your offer—not your appeal or solicitation—most attractive. You must then think positively, not negatively, and begin to perceive the futility of worrying about your age, or whether your education is a match for what others think qualifying education for the job ought to be, and other matters which are truly irrelevant. Think, instead, how closely your personal work experience resembles the business your prospective employer is engaged in.

Study yourself, not as an individual, but as a set of capabilities. In pursuit of government contracts, many companies find it necessary to develop a "capability brochure." Quite often, when a government agency is planning many months ahead to conduct a competitive contest for a contract, it will publish a request for "capability statements." This is to help the government agency determine which contractors have suitable qualifications to bid for the job, and only those who submit acceptable capability statements will be invited later to submit their proposals and bids. In these statements, the government is not interested in what or who the contractor is, but in what the contractor is capable of doing.

This is how to study yourself before preparing a résumé. Decide what your capabilities are, rank order them (in descending order of your "strength" in each capability). Decide also which capabilities are in greatest demand and of greatest value in the marketplace judged by their relative demand and values. Then correlate your lists and decide not only what kind of job(s) you wish to pursue, but what kind of job(s) you have the best chance of winning. Finally, develop your résumé *strategy*, for that is critical.

## POSITIONING AND OTHER STRATEGIES

All successful sales, marketing, and advertising campaigns are based on successful strategies. Those professions have a lexicon of their own jargon, terms such as *positioning*, but basically strategies entail such factors as identifying the best prospects, finding the most compelling reasons for them to buy, and determining the ways to make the greatest impact with your presentations.

For example, the typical job hunter goes in search of those employers who appear to have an opening or two most of the time. That translates into responding to advertisements, making the rounds of employment agencies and other such recruiters (those recruiting executives and professionals find the term "employment agency" beneath their dignity and use other terms, such as "professional recruiter"), and visiting all the company personnel offices they can find.

There is nothing wrong with doing this. But it is wrong to confine your activities to this alone, even if you also try advertising yourself with "situation wanted" advertisements. What is wrong with it is the notion that the only jobs available for your efforts are job-openings which already exist. That is, it is wrong to assume that only requirements already recognized, identified, and/or listed by employers represent possible employment for you. Quite the contrary, there are many situations in which a job-seeker can actually create a job opening—many cases in which an employer can be persuaded to create a job for the right individual. Or even a number of jobs, to staff an entire new division or new branch office, as in the case of U.S. Industries' divestment of a division several years ago:

Certain circumstances led U.S. Industries to sell their Education Science Division to a Chicago firm which had been one of the division's leading customers. Hardly any of the division's employees went with that division to the new owners. Most chose to remain in the Washington, DC area where the division had originally been, and two groups of the division's former employees went on to two other companies to start new departments for those two companies. In both cases, the concept was sold to the heads of those companies.

It is not unusual for an employer to have an expansion idea or a need in the back of his or her mind, but to keep the idea shelved until such time as a suitable candidate to implement the idea can be

found. That's why you can be invited in to interview for a position
as a marketing manager or purchasing agent, but suddenly discover
that you're being considered for a position to be newly created:
head of advertising, or manager of a new branch office, or a new
division. Employers will often create new jobs when it appears to be
viable.

Bear that possibility in mind when you are seeking to present
yourself. Make it a consideration in your basic strategy—in your
*presentation* strategy, that is. It is one of the more compelling reasons
for avoiding too narrow a focus in the presentation of your capabilities.
While you must not make that presentation so broad that it becomes
a generalization saying very little, neither do you wish to make it so
specific that it qualifies you for only a very narrow range of jobs. If
you are a sales or marketing manager, for example, be sure that you
don't link your sales or marketing abilities to a narrow range of products or services. Be sure, too, that you show a capability for initiative—
for being a self-starter, for creating ideas, for being a take-charge type.
But don't merely claim to have these abilities; demonstrate that you
do by citing the evidence for it.

Consider the things cited in earlier chapters as perpetual and
universal goals of all employers: growth, increased sales, increased
profits, reduced costs, and solved problems. Incidentally, do understand that growth and increased sales are not synonymous, although
to most employers increased sales are integral to growth. But in these
times everything becomes obsolescent rapidly, and growth means
keeping up, as well as swelling in size. Lack of growth, in this sense,
has been responsible for many failures of small and large companies,
even for such large and once-successful companies as Korvette's, W.T.
Grant, and Robert Hall. And neither Chrysler Corporation nor other
American automobile manufacturers are in the healthiest state at
present.

Bear in mind then, particularly if you are a specialist in some
rapidly changing field, that one thing you can offer to do for a prospective employer that is of great value is helping him keep up with
the state of the art and thus help him grow in the truest sense of the
word. The way to do this, to say again that which cannot be said too
often, is not by simply claiming the ability, but by showing how you
have done this for previous employers and what it has meant to their
growth.

## THE IMAGE YOU WANT TO PROJECT

An integral part of your presentation strategy is the image you want to present. You must decide whether it is in your best interests to project yourself as imaginative and innovative, conservative and dependable, bright and energetic, or whatever you think enhances your appeal.

To some degree this must be governed by your profession, although individual circumstances are a large part of it too. For example, if you are an accountant seeking a senior position, perhaps that of comptroller, you probably should try to come across as conservative and steady. Still, special circumstances may change that idea. Suppose your role is that of financial manager and you are in some kind of go-go field that requires a great deal of highly imaginative financing tactics and techniques. In that case, the daring and innovative image might be better suited to your needs.

This could apply to any field. An electronics engineer in a fast-moving field, such as micro-miniaturization and especially small computers, will probably want to show that he or she has a great deal of imagination, is inventive, not reluctant to try new approaches. But that might not be right for a civil engineer whose work tends more to require the solid and dependable image, especially if the specific field is public works, such as bridges, tunnels, and dams, where public safety is such an important consideration.

For some, the résumé is itself a sample of ability. The writer and editor, for example, must be especially careful. Employers will usually scan résumés of writers and editors as examples of their writing and editing abilities. Analogously, if you pursue a position in sales, marketing, advertising, or something related, your résumé ought to reflect your abilities. Perhaps not every employer will so regard your résumé, but it's risky to assume that such will be the case. It seems logical to assume that any vague, rambling, or otherwise poorly written résumé reflects a lack of writing and editing abilities. And if the résumé has obviously been prepared by a résumé-writing firm (which is often obvious because most such firms have certain standard practices, easily identifiable), that is evidence, too, that the individual is not a writer or editor. Also, if applicants cannot explain their own background and capabilities clearly, it suggests that they are not the clearest of thinkers. A poorly written résumé may therefore project an unfavorable general image of you, no matter what kind of job you are trying to qualify for and win. At the least, then, your résumé ought to be crisp, clear, and businesslike. In the next chapter, we'll discuss some techniques for achieving this tone and get into writing considerations generally. And we will delve into the strategies of the physical presentation, the actual résumé itself, for there are some important matters to consider there.

# 7

# The Written Word: Rhetoric, Semantics, and Formats

*Semanticists are fond of pointing out that "the word is not the thing." But it might as well be, because to most people the word is the thing. Most of us have at least some unconscious bias.*

## JUST ONE WRONG WORD . . .

**A** "WRONG WORD" can kill a sale, demolish a friendship, destroy your chance for a job. There are "right" and "wrong" words, but the idea does not apply to words alone; whole phrases, and even sentences and longer passages can be ill-conceived, can fail to anticipate the prejudices of respondents.

In northern states of the United States, for example, history records the American conflict of the middle nineteenth century as the Civil War. But in the southern regions of the United States, the citizens insist that the conflict was the War between the States. Why is the nomenclature important? Because the two titles of that war each suggest a different legal situation. The title Civil War suggests a conflict among the citizens of the same nation, which is how the federal government views that war. The southern states, however, believe that they had a legal right to secede from the union as they did, and that therefore the war was not a civil war, but a war between sovereign states. To those holding that view, accepting the term Civil War is admitting that the southern states did not have the right to secede. It is therefore a *faux pas* to refer to that war as the Civil War when talking or writing to citizens of those states.

On the other hand, finding the right words and phrases can have a salutary effect, making otherwise unpalatable information acceptable, making palatable information attractive, and making attractive information overpoweringly desirable. That, in fact, is the heart of advertising effort: achieving the latter ideal.

Prejudice applies to formats, too. We tend to assume, without examining it, that whatever we see is what it appears to be. Or, conversely, that it is not what we think it ought to be because it does not appear to be that thing. We tend to have prejudices, for example, about what a résumé is, in terms of how it is structured and what information appears in it. Anything that departs sharply from that prejudice—from that *image* of a résumé—is immediately suspect. Even if it is labeled RÉSUMÉ, the reader circles it cautiously and suspiciously: It doesn't look like a résumé; therefore it probably is not a résumé, goes the reasoning.

Here are the basic "rules"—prejudices—that dictate what most people believe ought to be in your résumé, and what they therefore expect you to do when preparing your résumé for their inspection:

1. Specify details of your education.
2. Present your entire working history, if you are young enough to tell it all in a page or two or, alternatively, if it does not cover more than fifteen or twenty years.
3. If your working history is long and checkered, go back at least fifteen years and/or describe and explain all *relevant* working experience. (You may omit those odd jobs you had while going to college or while you were between jobs and picking up a few dollars to keep going.)
4. For as far back as you do go, leave no gaps in the record. Account for all time, including periods of nonemployment, sabbaticals, or anything else that created a gap in your work-experience.
5. Specify your employers, your job titles, at least a general idea of your responsibilities and duties in each job.
6. Present the record in chronological order, preferably starting with the present or most recent job.

Failing to follow these rules, especially leaving gaps in the chain of your career history, arouses suspicion. That would be all right if it also aroused curiosity and led to calling you in for an interview to explain the gaps. Unfortunately, that rarely happens. Instead, it is assumed that you have something you'd rather not present, and if your résumé otherwise arouses nothing but polite yawns, it is dispatched to limbo.

Consequently, the traditional résumé poses many difficulties, such as:

There is a period you'd rather forget, for one reason or another. Perhaps you worked for an unreasonable so-and-so who is almost certain to put you down if anyone calls for a reference check. Or perhaps because of circumstances you accepted a job beneath your normal level and it's no asset on your résumé.

Your choice: Risk lying by covering up that period in one way or another, explain frankly that this is not a suitable past employer for a reference check, or say nothing and cross your fingers. All bad choices.

The best job you ever had, and the one that is most qualifying experience for the job you now want, was one you had a few years ago. It's not at either end of your résumé, and you'd like it to be the first experience cited, and the one with the most detail. But you can't get it up top and stick with the chronological-sequence format. What to do?

None of your past jobs sounds really qualifying when you explain your past job titles and duties. Your whole résumé is somehow rather lackluster.

Your formal education is less than exemplary, although you've had lots of useful practical experience, and you have held respectable job titles and job responsibilities. Skimming over educational background may stand out like a sore thumb, and lying about it is both distasteful and risky.

All in all, it seems as if the résumé idea was designed specifically to make it as difficult as possible for you to present yourself properly— to take suitable credit for your accomplishments and abilities, and to make a reader perceive what you have to offer. Whoever came up with the original résumé idea must have either been stupid or fortunate enough to shine in all departments—formal education in the best "name" universities, job titles that couldn't have been better if he'd written them himself, jobs with prestigious and well-known corporations, and no bad periods or jobs to cover up.

It's because of this that the previous chapter stressed the need to make your own rules. It's not how you play the game or whether you follow someone else's rules; it's whether you win or not. And your rules are just as good as anyone else's—or better. So let's make a few rules of our own. And never fear that you are cheating in any way. The résumé is supposed to help you and the employer find each other for your mutual benefit. If it fails to do that, it's a bad résumé; if it succeeds in doing that, it's a good résumé. No matter whose rules prevail.

## RÉSUMÉS ARE NOT USELESS

A recent entrant in the job-hunting/résumé-writing book field (and I have personally counted more than two dozen titles already on the shelves, with new ones coming along as the unemployment figures continue to climb) exhorts the reader to "throw away your résumé." The author is presented as a former group vice-president in some corporation, who explains in his preface that most authors of résumé guides are those who did the hiring, not those who had to learn how to find jobs. (Obviously, the view from that side of the desk is quite different and so often fails to reflect a real understanding of the problems of job hunting.) His own experience, after he lost his job as group vice-president, led him to the conclusion that résumés do not work at all, and compelled him to find another way to get a job, which brought him results quickly, he reports.

I won't quarrel with that author; in fact, I tend to agree with him. Résumés *don't* work in a great many cases, with the possible exception of those situations where the job-seeker is in a seller's market, as in the salad days of defense contracting and enormous shortages of skilled technical people. But there is also the problem of the difficulty in reaching agreement on the definition of *what a résumé is*. He was undoubtedly referring to that common conception of what a résumé ought to be—that tedious biography so structured that in a stack of 200 résumés, 150 of them are almost indistinguishable from each other and the other 50 are gauche and hopeless.

It parallels a myth about proposals for government contracts. The myth has it that when a government agency requests bidders to write and submit proposals in a competitive contest for a contract, it's all a silly game because the winner has already been selected, and the competition is a fraud. Successful contractors have excellent reasons for knowing that that is a myth because they have won many contracts solely on the basis of submitting the best proposal and winning the competition. Yet the myth continues. The myth was originated and is propagated and sustained by those who cannot write a good proposal or won't make sufficient effort to write a winning proposal. They are unable to face their own deficiency in this regard, so they rationalize their failures by propagating that myth.

We have something of the same situation here. Most of those who believe that résumés do not work at all are the ones who have never managed to create an effective résumé. It is, after all, something which must be created, and imitation—especially imitation of unsuccessful and undistinguished models—is not the way to create an effective résumé. To say that résumés do not work at all is equivalent to Korvette's or Robert Hall maintaining that newspaper advertising doesn't work as they sink into oblivion, while Sears and others are using newspaper advertising with great success. There are a great many individuals whose résumés do produce job offers for them, so the idea cannot be a total failure—at least not for those with some creative imagination and courage to be original and think *functionally.*

## YOU NEED THE RIGHT TOOLS FOR THE JOB

What you must overcome first is any prejudices you now have about résumé formats, styles, content, or other characteristics. Regard the résumé as a functional tool which must be designed for a specific task, and sometimes even individualized for a specific application. One talented and versatile fellow who was in the habit of hiring himself out as a consultant specialist on short-term assignments (a few months each usually) as a technical/professional temporary, had over a dozen different résumés. Each résumé was designed for a different kind of job—since Mike hired out as an engineer, as a technical writer, as a data analyst, and as a qualified specialist in a number of other areas in which he knew he could function well. Of course, he could have had a single résumé that would have reported and documented all these specialist skills, but he would not have worked regularly because of that prejudice about specialization. He found it necessary to orient each résumé specifically to the type of job for which he was applying.

There are variants of that system. One is a standard résumé

made of modules which can be assembled in various patterns for easy and rapid duplicating. Kept brief, using the same head data, but with several *Summary* modules and each kind of experience written up as a separate module, such a résumé is easily taken apart and reassembled to match requirements.

Bear in mind that Mike, along with a great many others who were doing the same thing, was using specially designed and adapted résumés for short-term jobs, and he found it not only practical, but necessary to do so. How much more practical and necessary it must be, then, to use specially designed and adapted résumés when you are questing for a permanent, career job. How likely is it that any standard résumé you devise (or anyone devises for you) is going to be exactly right for each and every acquaintance you hand it to?

Perhaps the ultimate irony of using a standard résumé is that by avoiding that extra labor and expense of tailoring your résumé to different situations—even to the extent of tailoring a different résumé for each and every application—you are actually adding infinitely more labor and expense to the task of finding a new position. Finding a position, especially for the individual who has been holding high-level jobs and is seeking a high-level job, is usually a major undertaking. It certainly justifies a great deal of extra and special effort, but, more significantly, it *requires* that extra effort.

Most people learn that through practical experience. Even those who find jobs easily because they are in such professions as engineering and computers sometimes reach levels where they earn relatively high salaries as managers or top-level scientists. Suddenly they discover that it's not as easy to change jobs—not at the salaries they now command, in any case. Suddenly it's no longer enough to be a competent professional because the competition has become much tougher; there are hordes of other competent professionals seeking those higher level positions. They are one-of-a-kind positions, carrying heavy responsibilities, and employers understandably scrutinize candidates closely before deciding which to entrust with so much responsibility for the company's welfare. For it's the sensitivity of the position, with its possible effect on the company overall more than the salary, that gives the employer pause in deciding which individual to hire.

Now the competition becomes a battle of marketing and merchandising more than proving one's capability. In fact, working hard at demonstrating that qualification may prove to be defeating. It distracts the attention of the reader from the real issue, the factors that really count—not technical/professional abilities, but what one can do for the employer. That's worthy of some exploration.

One company which was expanding rapidly and operating a growing number of branch offices had traditionally been in the engineering-support industry, primarily in technical writing. The major activity of the branch office in suburban Washington, DC had problems with its principal customer, NASA (National Aeronautics and Space Administration), for whom their major work was done in the company's traditional field of technical publications. A new manager did correct that situation, and that alone justified his hire. However, he managed to make much greater contributions to the company by winning many other contracts which in sum represented even more business than did the NASA contract. Suddenly his abilities as the *marketer* of the services was much more important to the company than his technical and professional skills as a technical publications specialist and manager of such work.

It's not an unusual phenomenon. Again and again people find themselves progressing into activities and areas of their field for which they never prepared themselves formally in their education and early employment, but for which capabilities evolved eventually through experience and chance. When you are faced with a job search and preparing to document your credentials in a résumé, it is necessary to take stock without the irrational prejudice of your early ideals and aspirations. Again and again, young people get their law degrees and become financial vice-presidents or executive directors. They get an education in business administration and become production supervisors. They school themselves to become scientists and wind up teaching in colleges. Sometimes they never do practice the profession for which they were educated. Quite often they do start out in their chosen field and wander from it, either through choice or through circumstance. Lawyer Jones loves private practice and does it the rest of his life. Lawyer Smith prefers being on the legal staff of a large corporation, but advances into the ranks of corporate hierarchy and eventually occupies an office on "mahogany row," having long since given up thinking about torts and contracts. And Lawyer Green finds he has a great affinity for marketing and becomes marketing director, never getting near a brief or courtroom.

The point is that you must take into account not only that field for which you originally trained and perhaps worked in capably, but other capabilities you have acquired and developed which may or may not have any relationship to your original field. But, of course, the important thing is not you and what you are capable of doing per se, but what you can do that benefits the employer; you must always study your capabilities in those terms. You can bet, for example, that if you can demonstrate an ability to win large contracts—and win a great many of them—that you will do well to feature this ability prominently in your résumé as near the top as possible. And you will want to work this information into your résumé in a prominent position no matter what kind of position you are pursuing, for it is going to be far more attractive to most employers than almost any other skills or abilities you can offer. It will pay you, in such circumstances, to be as ingenious as possible in working that information into your résumé somehow; the ability to win business is never unimportant or irrelevant.

## SPECIALISTS BECOME GENERALISTS

In a great many jobs, and especially in jobs in the more rarefied atmospheres of management, you are a specialist only until you have been hired. Then you become a generalist. Had you offered yourself as a generalist and presented generalist credentials, you would not have been considered for even thirty seconds. Only specialists were considered. But having been hired and settled into your office or behind a desk in the office bull pen, you now discover that only occasionally and perhaps never will you really practice your specialty. You will be asked to handle it all. You will be hired as a specialist and utilized as a generalist.

If you are in management, it's inevitable. Every manager needs to know a little bit about a lot of things. You can't get along in a managerial slot without at least a recognition acquaintance with accounting, inventory, marketing, sales, advertising, personnel, and many other functions in the organization. And the higher the level of management you are in, the more you need to know about these other functions, no matter what department you are employed by.

If you are in a small company, you will be a generalist to some degree, no matter what job you were hired for. If you are a parts inspector, there will be many times when there are no parts available for you to inspect, and you will be handling shipments, writing a quality-control plan, interviewing a stock clerk, and otherwise helping wherever help is needed.

The point is that in a great many cases it hardly matters what job you were hired for; you will do whatever needs to be done, and what is important is not the job description or title, but the salary and opportunities. Again and again, individuals foreclose good opportunities because they envision a prospective job as being out of their field and not a match for their capabilities. So they stubbornly structure their résumés to represent themselves as specialists with specialist capabilities, when they are, in fact, entirely capable of handling a wide variety of good positions.

Take the profession of technical writer as an example. When I needed to recruit writers to develop training materials, I discovered, after a number of disastrous experiences, that technical writers usually turned out better at writing training materials than did any other writers I could recruit. I tried journalists, general "creative" writers, and even people who alluded to themselves as "educational technologists." Few of these worked out well, but as a class, I found technical writers far more satisfactory and capable of doing what I wanted done.

Technical writers are usually adaptable to proposal writing, another somewhat specialized field, and to report writing also. On the other hand, there is a specialized class of technical writer, the medical writers, for which technical writers usually do not qualify well. The point is that many technical writers perceive themselves as capable only in writing the traditional manuals for equipment theory, installation, and maintenance, when they can and should respond to other opportunities.

By the time you have had a few years' working experience and worked at a few different jobs for different employers, you have acquired several capabilities you had not originally anticipated. Probably no one starts out to become a technical writer, much less a proposal writer, marketing specialist, or expert in government procurement. Yet, many have wandered into these fields and can write at least a dozen different résumés, each valid and a solid presentation of a different kind of specialist. And so can many in other fields prepare many résumés, all legitimate representations of skills in specific fields and functions. Unless you have your eye fixed rigidly on some highly specialized target, you may want to think about having more than one résumé.

## HOW VALID IS THE IDEA OF SPECIALIZATION?

Specialization is a valid idea, but too often it has been permitted to run wild to the point where it has become absurd in practice. There is no question that our world has become so complex, particularly in the various sciences and technologies, that there is a need for specialization. (We can no longer permit barbers to perform surgery too, as they once did.) But if we examine some of the logical consequences of the idea as practiced, we arrive at a few absurdities:

1. One notion that has resulted from this insane frenzy to make everything a specialty is that everyone can be good at something, if the something is made narrow enough and the individual's training concentrated enough.
2. Everyone needs to be a specialist and would otherwise not be very good at anything.
3. Most of us are capable of being really good at only one thing.

Most of that is nonsense, of course. There are those who are incapable of being really good at anything. We deceive ourselves to think otherwise.

We do not really need to be specialists. Many of us are quite happy as generalists and quite good at many things. In fact, it is nonsensical to think that anyone who is really good at any one thing is not certain to be good at many other things.

Still, we must deal with perceptions in the real world of marketing, whether we are selling shoes, aspirin tablets, or our own services. If the prospect to whom we address our offer insists on believing in and pursuing a false image, it would be quixotic to try to disabuse the prospect, and that would be self-defeating. It is absolutely necessary to adapt the presentation to the perception. But it is not necessary to practice self-deceit; that is also self-defeating. Structure the presentation that you call a résumé to the perception, even if you must create a dozen, two dozen, or a hundred different presentations to sell the same item. The item—you—does not change; only the presentation does.

Again and again résumés are discarded after the merest glance because the résumés appear to offer something totally different from that which is wanted. Perhaps the writers of most of those résumés are entirely fit and suitable for the needs, but no one will take time to *study* those résumés, only to screen those which appear worth the time to read.

Unless you insist on accepting only a narrowly defined job, you will do well to study your skills and experience from the viewpoint of how you can qualify as a specialist in more than one field. And prepare a draft résumé for each specialty. Then use that draft as a guide to prepare a specific résumé for specific applications.

## THE "TRADITIONAL" FORMAT

Perhaps 99 percent of all résumés are designed along the general lines of the format shown in Figure 9. This approach to résumé design has been accepted widely, is rarely challenged by anyone, and appears in a thousand variations—none of them bears any significant differences or alternatives to the basic organization shown here.

## HEADLINES

Most advertisements begin with a headline and résumés ought to also. The headline in both cases ought to get attention, sum up the main benefit offered, and give the reader a good reason to read on and get the rest of the message. In a current magazine, for example, a full-page advertisement says this: SMITH-CORONA INTRODUCES THE ONLY DAISY WHEEL PRINTER FOR UNDER $900. That headline sums up the advertiser's entire story, although there is a photograph of the item and about a half-page of body copy supporting and expanding on the headline. Obviously, what Smith-Corona is saying is that here is a bargain: *we will save money for you.* That is the offer. The body copy

RÉSUMÉ

Name                    Address         Telephone number

Education:    Colleges, degree(s), dates
              Special schools, diplomas, certificates

Work experience:
       Present or most recent job: Employer, title, dates,
       duties, responsibilities, achievements.

       Previous job—same information.

       Previous job—same information.

       Etc.

       References

       Remarks, miscellaneous items, such as honors and
       awards.

FIGURE 9. Typical "traditional" layout/format of résumé.

sets out to furnish the proofs that it is indeed a bargain, that the prospect can save money without sacrificing performance or quality, and even invites the reader to fill out and send in the coupon in the advertisement to get more information. (You can bet that sending in the coupon will bring a telephone call from a salesperson!)

An advertisement in another magazine headlines: *Nead a littel hilp with yur speling?* It's an IBM advertisement for their word processing equipment and the message is plain enough, even before you read the body copy which explains how quickly and easily the advertised equipment enables one to make corrections.

A really good headline does two things: It gets attention, and it makes the principal benefit of the offer apparent. In fact, many headlines manage to do neither, and a very common failing of headlines is that they are often designed only to get attention, and provide little or no information about what is being offered, much less what the main benefit is.

The best headlines are those which get attention by making the main benefit offered quite clear. The Smith-Corona advertisement is a good example. It is clear about what is being offered—a daisy wheel printer—and what the benefit is—a bargain price. (An alleged bargain price, at any rate.)

Good headlines do not have to be inspired. They do not have to be clever. In fact, far too often advertisements fall on their faces completely because the copy writer got too clever and forgot to sell the product. Such stories are legion; it leads me to believe it is hazardous to be clever when writing copy. It's far better to remember who you are, what you are, and what you are trying to do.

## THE HEADLINE ON YOUR RÉSUMÉ

In that résumé format delineated in Figure 9, the headline space was allotted to presenting the subject's educational background. By implication, at least, that was what was supposed to get attention and explain in abstract the benefits offered the employer!

Looked at in that light, the format appears somewhat ridiculous. What employer finds his or her pulse quickening at the prospect of hiring this MBA from Mediocre University?

Another use of that space made by many résumé writers is to present an "objective" as in Figure 2, and sometimes even those things represented as "personal" data. This is perhaps an even worse waste of the most valuable space on your résumé. This is where you have what may be your only opportunity to get that moment's attention that will make the big difference to which stack your résumé gets consigned. And if really well done, the headline on your résumé may induce the reader to stop everything and reach for the telephone before this paragon is snapped up by some hungry competitor. How can you possibly waste the space on trivia?

Figure 10 offers another idea on how to head up a résumé. This is a format that is fairly popular and not without its merits, particularly if that boxed abstract is well designed and hits hard enough, as this one obviously does. Note that even the abstract has its own headline, and the headline makes the message clear enough. Aside from the fact that Joe Smith laconically announces in his head data that he is

Joe Smith                          Insurance salesman
Happenstance Lane
Citrustown, FL 32301

---

**MILLION-DOLLAR-ROUNDTABLE
MEMBER AVAILABLE**

I have sold not merely $1 million/
year in insurance, but over $6
million/year before retiring two years
ago. Bored with doing nothing now, I
am looking for a part-time
arrangement with any major
company.

---

FIGURE 10. Using an abstract as a résumé headline.

an insurance salesman, he boldly makes his offer to sell insurance, with the benefit plain enough—a salesman who belongs to that famed roundtable (every insurance company executive will know what that means), which means a very able salesman indeed.

Think about headlines of this type for your own résumé. What can you come up with? Could you write one for yourself reporting that proposals you have written have produced some $120 million in government contracts, if you were pursuing a job as a proposal writer? Or, if you were pursuing a job as a marketing director, you would simply state that your marketing had produced some $150 million in business. But that would also be a good headline for a résumé written to pursue a job as a general manager.

That does not mean that the headline on your résumé must make you a hero or heroine. Many more modest achievements are also suitable for good headlines. Here are a few examples to illustrate the point:

HOW I RESCUED THREE PROJECTS FROM DISASTER
I DESIGN BETTER ACCOUNTING SYSTEMS FOR MY EMPLOYERS
I HELPED MY PREVIOUS EMPLOYER FINANCE A 100% EXPANSION
I MANAGE ACQUISITIONS AND DIVESTITURES
I AM THE FASTEST FILE CLERK IN THE COMPANY
I AM THE FASTEST INSTALLER IN THE COMPANY
PER UNIT, I AM THE CHEAPEST INSTALLER IN THE COMPANY
I CUT INSTALLATION COSTS
I RAISED SHIPPING ROOM EFFICIENCY 20%
I CUT ASSEMBLY-LINE REJECTS 10%

I OUTSOLD THE SENIOR SALESMEN IN THE COMPANY
MY ADVERTISING COPY PULLED 23% MORE ORDERS
MAILROOM COSTS ARE DOWN 12% SINCE I TOOK OVER
I PERSONALLY HANDLE CORRESPONDENCE AND TELEPHONE FOR
  4 EXECUTIVES

Note that some of these headlines are for such relatively humble jobs as file clerks and installers, but all appeal to one of those employer ideals of cutting costs, raising efficiency, making more sales, making profits, and so forth. Note too that all of these headlines are about what the writer *did* or *does*, not about what the writer *is* or *wants to be*. The résumé is never about you; it's about what you do, can do, promise to do—about what results you produce. If you are more efficient than your predecessor was, try to translate that into something *quantitative* in the manner of some of the above headlines. I CUT COSTS 12% is better than I REDUCED COSTS, and I CUT COSTS 12% BY REDUCING ASSEMBLY-LINE REJECTS is better yet because it is far more specific.

## How to Find Your Headlines

The way to find headlines is to draft your complete résumé in detail first, writing out all those job descriptions—what you did, for whom, how, with what results. For each of those try to recall anything you did which you might count as an outstanding achievement *from the employer's point of view*—solving problems, cutting costs, and other such benefits. To the best of your ability, translate each of those achievements into some quantitative terms: dollars, hours, percentages. Work at this; it's important.

Go back over the completed draft and try to select the most important achievement, particularly as it relates to what you are after. If you reorganized someone's mailroom when you were still a youngster going to school but it happens to be one of your greatest achievements in terms of benefits delivered to an employer, try to adapt it to your present need. Suppose, for example, that you are now an accountant and you are in pursuit of a comptroller's job with some substantial firm. When you use that mailroom reorganization, don't stress the fact of being a mailroom or that it was some years ago, in your youth; those are irrelevant facts. Instead, express it in terms that might relate to a comptroller's responsibilities and capabilities. Be sure, for example, that you express the achievement in terms of costs, preferably actual dollars and cents. Your headline and abstract might read:

> **MY STUDY AND REORGANIZATION OF A DEPARTMENT CUT ANNUAL OPERATING COSTS BY $47,500.**
>
> It was a minor department, but I thought it a highly inefficient operation. After studying it, I installed a number of changes, including cost-control measures, with results stated.

Not in the abstract, of course, but somewhere you should identify the kind of job you are after, perhaps along with the head data as shown in Figure 3. However, if you wanted to include it in the abstract, it is possible to do that, too, with a little resourcefulness. You might bring this off by the simple expedient of adding this line in the abstract paragraph.

> And I was not even an accountant and candidate
> for a comptroller position then, as I am now.

Some who use this general format of a boxed abstract in the headline space of the résumé make the mistake of trying to present a résumé of the résumé in this space—an abstract of their total experience. That's almost as serious an error as saying too much. This space is not best used as an abstract of your whole résumé, but as an abstract of what you have to offer, almost as a subtitle of your headline.

### HEADLINES AND SUBHEADS

Frequently an advertiser finds it difficult or impossible to say everything that needs to be said in a single headline without making the headline impossibly long. One way out of the dilemma is to run the head with a subhead, the way newspapers often run heads on front pages. For example, here is the head and subhead of an advertisement run by the State of Texas:

> DON'T GAMBLE WITH YOUR COMPANY'S FUTURE
>
> The name of the game is profits, and in
> Texas you'll win every time.

The main head, which is in the larger type, of course, is intended to be the attention getter, and the subhead, in smaller type, explains the main head by expanding on it in an effort to lure businesses to Texas. The brief paragraph which follows the headline on your résumé should serve the same function as an explanation or elaboration of the headline, explaining in abstract what your main offering of benefit is.

Your headline is an implied promise, if not a direct one. If it proclaims that you have rescued three projects from disaster, it implies that you are a capable project manager who can help any prospective employer by rescuing projects in trouble and/or by preventing projects from getting into trouble. The promise, whether direct or implied, will get attention, but it won't hold it if you don't follow up. To turn that attention into interest, or to sustain the interest aroused by the headline, it is necessary to begin following up immediately with some amplifying details to lend the promise some credibility.

## CREDIBILITY: WHAT IT IS, HOW IT IS ACHIEVED

During World War II, when the training of millions of American soldiers was the subject of billions of words in newspapers and magazines, a great deal of attention was paid to something called *morale*, and a great many people took a swing at trying to define this elusive term. One of the best definitions heard, in my opinion, was that uttered by a green recruit who was asked by a newspaper reporter to try to define it. "Morale," said this young man, "is what makes your feet do what your head knows is impossible."

The rationale of advertising is analogous to that idea. In one sense, the true aim of advertising is to bring about the suspension of skepticism, to make the heart believe what the head does not want to believe. As modern sophisticates we tend to automatically raise the barrier of skepticism against anything we see printed and particularly anything that appears to be advertising. We have been conditioned to expect all advertising to be inflated and misleading, so we read such copy with a figurative arms-folded-across-our-chests, show-me attitude.

Basic rules for achieving credibility have been given before in these pages. Here they are repeated, briefly, to refresh your memory:

1. AVOID ALL HYPERBOLE—AVOID, IN FACT, ADJECTIVES AND
   ADVERBS AS MUCH AS POSSIBLE, AND STICK WITH THE SIMPLE
   NOUNS AND VERBS.
2. PROVIDE AS MUCH DETAIL AS POSSIBLE
3. QUANTIFY AND DON'T ROUND OFF NUMBERS; REPORT THEM
   EXACTLY.

Following is a brief example of the difference between using adjectives, and using simple nouns and verbs, to achieve a general effect of quiet self-confidence:

   a. I managed hundreds of contracts, worth huge sums of money,
      in the several decades I was general manager of Excelsior Tool
      & Die.
   b. In nineteen years with Excelsior Tool & Die I was entrusted
      with management of 125 projects, representing approximately
      $16 million.

Which of these, (a) or (b), is more impressive? Which more believable?

The tone of your résumé ought to be reportorial and objective. It will be objective and be accepted as reportorial if you follow these guidelines. Do not make the mistake of believing that the art of writing advertising copy is beating your own chest and lauding your virtues. It must not *appear* to be self-laudatory. It should achieve stress, emphasis, and drama by the indirect means of presenting emphatic or dramatic information. Find impressive numbers, for example; make them easy to grasp. It was my fortune to have been responsible for something in excess of $120 million in contract awards, but that number is usually considerably more impressive when written as $120,000,000 than when written as $120 million. But it also represents the writing of 260 proposals, totaling some 38,000 pages, and those figures might be useful to demonstrate something else, depending on what the strategy of the proposal happens to be, and for what the proposal is attempting to establish qualifications.

## ACHIEVING IMPACT

Numbers can be enormously impressive in a society which tends to judge everything by size, number, and other quantitative measures, rather than by qualitative measures; or to equate the two and judge merit by size, weight, or numbers. If you want to impress, try to find the numbers that you can use truthfully, but in such a way that they dramatize you and what you can offer.

Look at some of those other hypothetical headlines offered as examples, and consider what you could do with quantitative follow-up subheads or blurbs. (A blurb is a small block of text following a headline, serving the same purpose as a subhead.) Suppose you could turn that claimed "100% expansion" into specific numbers, or that outselling of senior salesmen into numbers of sales or their dollar equivalent.

The effect of minimizing your use of adjectives and adverbs is that of quiet self-confidence, rather than shrill huckstering, an effect to be desired.

## SEMANTICS

The word *semantics* refers to the meanings of words. Sometimes, to shrug off differences in meanings or the implications of selecting one word over another to express a thought, we remark that "it's just a matter of semantics," as though that didn't matter at all. But it does. It often "matters" a great deal. It matters so much that there is a field of study known as *general semantics*, which studies the relationships between words, and other symbols, and human behavior. It is therefore of concern to you how readers behave, in reacting to the words in your résumé. The complexities of semantics, or general semantics, and the subject in general will be discussed here.

Everyone knows that people react differently to different words, even though the words are synonyms. For example, people like to believe that they are persevering and determined and that they do not flinch from difficulties. But they are not exactly pleased to be thought of as stubborn or bullheaded. They want to believe that they are positive in their thinking and firm in their opinions, but they are likely to be offended if they are told that they are dogmatic and unreasonable. To call people courageous in pursuing what they aspire to is to suggest a certain nobility, but to tag them as being belligerent is almost insulting.

People do react to words and react differently to different synonyms for the same word. That's because when it comes to definitions—meanings—words have both *denotation* and *connotation*. A denotative meaning is intended to be an objective and unemotional explanation, often by offering several synonyms. A connotative meaning, however, is the implicit *shade* of meaning or *nuance*, which generally has the emotional content that causes the behavioral reaction.

Denotation and connotation, however, are also attached to expressions, as they are to single words, and must be considered as part of the *context* in which words and expressions are used. It is possible to use a four-letter word to describe a close friend, if the word is accompanied by a grin, an affectionate thump on the back, or some other gesture that shows the word to be used affectionately and without intent to insult. It is, therefore, the implicit intent behind the usage that affects connotation—connotation that the word generally carries with it as normal baggage. It is possible to tell someone that he is a "stubborn old son of a gun" in such a way that it is interpreted as admiration, actually a compliment. On the other hand, were you to tell someone that he's a "stubborn old man" and say it grim-faced and obviously without humor, it will be taken as an intended insult.

Unfortunately, there are few "rules" or established guidelines to help you judge which are and which are not words that generally offend, and which are the words that are either complimentary or at least neutral in emotional content. It is nearly impossible to compile more than a handful of "safe" words and terms because connotation so often depends on and changes with specific applications. If you are unsure as to connotation, the best thing to do is to have others read your drafts and render opinions as to whether any of the words and expressions you use are in bad taste, offensive, or unwise. A single word can undo you—undo a thousand good words, in fact—and a surprisingly large number of well-educated and well-read people are almost totally unaware of the nuances which distinguish one synonym from another.

## PLATITUDES AND CLICHÉS

*Platitude* and *cliché* are synonyms, although there are connotative differences. Both refer to trite, stale, too-often-used words, terms, expressions, or remarks. A platitude, however, is generally a statement, often a philosophical one, but trite. *Expertise* and *bottom-line* are regarded by many today as clichés. *Don't count your chickens* is a platitude.

Here again, many well-read and well-educated people use clichés and platitudes almost unconsciously, evidently unaware that they are dreadfully trite and that many people groan in agony at hearing those trite expressions. Some weary managers have been known to swear that they will immediately scrap the next résumé which claims "expertise" or claims a right to be "challenged" by a job. One individual used the word *adept* so often that it became known as a cliché by those who were compelled to read his proposals.

If you are unfamiliar with whether any given term, word, or expression you use is trite, play safe and avoid using any term or expression you have heard used often, unless it is an ordinary word. Here, too, it is difficult to provide rules, but some guidelines are possible:

A word such as *experience* doesn't "wear out" and become trite largely because it is emotionally neutral and is a common noun, useful only as a noun. On the other hand, *expert*, while used as a noun, is more widely used as an adjective (and sometimes even as an adverb) and therefore has a measure of emotional content. There is really no specific means for determining what is and what is not worthy of being judged to be expert; therefore, the term is one that reflects opinion or judgment and that makes it subject to emotional reaction. It's best to avoid such words because while they may not be considered by all to be trite, they have the same effect.

Even a perfectly good word or expression—an original expression, for that matter—can become trite in short order if used over and over. That fellow who was so fond of *adept* used it so many times in every document he wrote that mere sight of it set one's teeth on edge: He *made* a cliché out of the word, and in a very short time. But suppose you coin a word or a phrase, such as "front-end study." It's a perfectly sound term, has a good degree of freshness, is quite lucid and even imaginative—if you use it once, twice, perhaps three times. But some writers coin a phrase or a term and fall in love with it so deeply (with their own cleverness, that is) that they use it over and over. They want to be sure that the reader appreciates their cleverness. They thereby destroy the term and their own credibility. Or, at least, their acceptability. Moral: Don't be clever; it's dangerous.

There is another hazard in employing platitudes, even if they are epigrams or other expressions which are so time-honored or fresh that they do not come across as platitudes or clichés: It is essential that you quote these precisely. If you misquote or misuse, you will probably commit one of those humorous misuses of language which have become known as Malapropisms or Spoonerisms and you risk making yourself appear ridiculous. In that case, you will probably not be taken seriously. Unless you are sure that you have the expression correctly, it is safer not to use it. And there is this to consider: There is the twin hazard of misusing common expressions so readily that you are guilty of logical or grammatical errata, another way to risk appearing foolish and not being taken seriously. Legion are those, for example, who make the mistake of saying something about a "consensus of opinion" or "neither fish nor fowl, nor good red herring."

There are a few other, related problems, such as managing somehow to be gauche or banal. Banality is closely related to triteness, and yet there is a distinct shade of difference. Banal expressions are ludicrous ones, expressions reflecting naivete, lack of a veneer of sophistication, statements to which it is difficult to respond without offering insult, expressions so absurd that you may feel a bit embarrassed or awkward at hearing them.

To be gauche is to do or use language that could be characterized tactless, unsophisticated, ludicrous. Again, it is wise to seek an opinion from others, reacting to a draft, to see if anyone perceives the suggestion of any of these faults in what you have written.

Do also try to overcome any temptation to invent puns to display your wit and cleverness as a writer. At least as far as I am concerned, that fellow who wrote copy for a motel chain which urged everyone to "turn in" at the establishments of this chain missed the mark. Perhaps it *was* clever, and perhaps that copywriter was witty and even ingenious, but the copy did not do the job because it didn't offer a single inducement to patronize this advertiser. It offered no *reason* to do business with this motel chain. On the other hand, it did prove at least slightly offensive because it seemed to assume that I would be or should be so impressed with cleverness that I would overlook the fact that cleverness was not a reason for spending my money with this advertiser. But even for other reasons, such as the fact that many people think all puns to be in bad taste, do avoid the use of puns, no matter how clever.

## COMMUNICATION: WHAT IS IT?

When individuals try to explain problems linked somehow to interpersonal relationships, they often say something along the lines of, "It's just a breakdown in communications." Sometimes what they really mean is that the other party won't do what they want, won't agree with them, or otherwise refuses to see things their way. This line of argument says their differences would disappear if only the other party would listen carefully and understand. They can get so caught up in their logic and so convinced that their position is the right one that they are sure the other party will see the logical rightness of their position if only the other party will take the time to understand the issue.

It's a vain hope for more than one reason. For one thing, logic and conviction are not necessarily connected. Few of us think syllogistically, and fewer of us subject our basic beliefs—the notions we will accept as premises—to intensive scrutiny to ensure that they are worthy of being accepted as premises.

In short, a great many of us do not really mean communication when we complain of a breakdown in communication; we mean that our persuasive efforts have failed and that the other individual must be a boob to refuse to accept our arguments. If you believe for a moment that any logical arguments—even the most syllogistically valid arguments or the most scientific evidence—will prevail against prejudice, you deceive yourself.

Communication takes place when someone receives the same message as the one that was sent. When a receiver gets a different message than the one sent, communication can be said to have broken down. But the breakdown is not necessarily the result of a failure to use clear language, unambiguous statements, and uncomplicated sentence structure; it is often the result of a listener who prefers or *chooses* to get a different message than the one sent. It is often the result of either party (or both parties) consciously or unconsciously indulging in his or her own prejudicial beliefs. Example:

George says to Ira, "You don't understand *habeas corpus* because they really don't teach it properly at Yale." Ira hears: "They don't really know how to teach law at Yale." Ira accuses George of putting Yale down because he (George) went to Harvard. George

accuses Ira of an inability to be objective and admit what he knows
to be true. Both report to the outside world that they are having
a problem communicating with each other.

The question is not whether George is right or not, but whether
he really intended to express some contempt for Yale as a law school
and whether he did, in effect, so imply in his statement. Of course,
he didn't *say* that Yale had any deficiencies as a law school, but Ira,
who may be somewhat defensive because he knows that Harvard is
more prestigious than Yale, reacts predictably.

In common usage—and without regard to strict dictionary definitions—communication is more than absolute clarity of language
in exchanging or transmitting information. It involves being believed
and accepted, as well as being understood. And the reason is that it
is quite difficult, philosophically, to distinguish between believing and
understanding.

Where the common conception is that belief follows understanding—e.g., it is easy to believe that the Earth orbits the sun, rather
than vice versa (as once believed), after you understand the basic
scientific evidence—it is easy to argue that the opposite is true: first
comes belief, and then comes understanding. Or maybe there isn't
even a cause-and-effect relationship; perhaps they are the same thing.
Witness:

Many of us who have had a bit of scientific education "understand" atomic structure, with basic particles, such as electrons, protons, and neutrons. We "understand" how the atom is structured,
how electrons orbit the nucleus at various energy levels, how chemical
combinations take place, and other related matters. But how have we
come to that "understanding"? Have we ever actually seen an atom,
much less one of its component particles, through even the most
powerful microscope? Have we witnessed with our own eyes the quan-
tum leaps of electrons from one energy shell to another? Have we
watched different atoms join forces to create molecules of a new sub-
stance? Have we actually observed electrons speeding along a con-
ductor from the negative pole to the positve one?

Of course not. So far, although we have managed to actually see
a few of the largest molecules through the most powerful electron
microscopes, we have not yet been able to devise a magnification great

enough to see an atom. So what we understand is not atomic structure *per se*, but the *theory* of atomic structure. And to "understand" that theory, we must accept certain premises, such as the fact of electrons, protons, and neutrons. That is, we *believe* that such particles exist and that they are combined to form the basic building block of matter, the atom. So a great deal of our scientific understanding is at least based on beliefs.

There are individuals today who firmly believe that American astronauts and journeys to the moon are a hoax, that our government faked the entire thing. There have been books written and published, which work at "proving" that men never went to the moon at all. There is no evidence that will convince these individuals: they have decided what they will and will not believe and what they will and will not "understand."

There are those who maintain that the Earth is flat, and anything that purports to prove otherwise is fraudulent. But there are also those who deal in various metaphysical phenomena and allegations of phenomena, in black magic, in cultist beliefs, and in many other specialized fields that require a great deal of belief to substantiate what the aficionados like to offer as understanding.

If you wish to communicate with others effectively—if you wish the receiver of the information to receive what you're sending—you must take into account and allow for bias and prejudice. You must avoid saying things that bring about almost instant polarization, the way George polarized his and Ira's positions in the example. Just as emotional appeals are of critical importance in advertising or in any persuasion, so is emotion critical to any communication, for bias and prejudice are always emotion-based. People are prejudiced to believe what they dearly *want* to believe, just as they firmly reject whatever they do not wish to believe.

It is difficult to overcome any emotional bias, and inadvisable to try, because you are not likely to succeed. Do not try to overcome emotional bias with logic, for you only make the polarization even more extreme or you bring about a polarization where none existed before. And if you manage to present such forceful and overpowering logical arguments that you make it impossible for your opponent to put up a reasonable defense or counter-argument, the result is invariably unreasoning hostility.

## COPING WITH BIAS

In preparing résumés and pursuing a job, you will encounter bias. You may encounter an employer who thinks that an applicant without a college degree is unworthy of consideration for any job but that of floor sweeper. You may encounter an employer with the opposite opinion—that anyone with a college degree is suspect of being an impractical theorist. Or you may encounter an employer who believes that women can do nothing of value but type, file, and fetch coffee. There are all kinds of bias, against things as well as against people.

There are also biases for an MIT or Harvard degree, for an employee of a given religious or racial persuasion, for a youngster or an oldster, for one specific kind of experience, for the employees or former employees of some leading corporation in the industry, for people whose names are euphonius, and for a variety of characteristics which may or may not have any logical basis or appear in any way linked to one's merits and assets as potential employees.

The best way to cope with biases, then, is to do everything you can to avoid coming in contact with them. For that reason, as well as for other equally valid reasons, make the following items taboo on your list and do not include them or refer to them, either directly or indirectly:

Your age, date of birth, place of birth, citizenship.

Your race, religion, color, ancestry.

Personal hobbies (unless they relate directly to your work and are assets).

Data about family—children's names, wife's name, number of children, etc.

Extra-curricular activities in school.

References (especially those of other than former employers).

You may, of course, eventually have to supply some of this information, but wait until the time comes and cope with it then. By then you will be in a different position. Anyhow, there is nothing to be gained by including any of this in your résumé, for it has no bearing on your qualifications or their appeal to an employer. This kind of data can't help you and it can harm you.

Following advice given earlier—minimizing your use of adjectives and adverbs and sticking to nouns and verbs—will also help avoid setting off alarms unnecessarily, for it is often the modifiers that carry the emotional baggage in their meanings.

Avoid slang and jargon, too. Much of our colloquial language carries emotional content, and if you use formal language, rather than slang words, you reduce the risk of projecting an emotional message. Those who buy and sell stocks and bonds, for example, will not take offense at being regarded or referred to as *investors*, but some will be offended at being described by the word *speculator*, and few would like to be thought of as *gamblers*, even though these are proper enough words. But investment is thoroughly respectable, speculating is somewhat less so, and gambling is something society frowns on. If you told a prospective employer that you gamble in the market, the employer might consider you less than the solid citizen he or she would prefer to hire, and admitting to speculating in the market might suggest that you are a somewhat risky employee. But who could fault you for making sound investments in respectable stocks and bonds?

## USING FORMATS TO HELP

The typical résumé is typed, although a few are typeset, on an $8^1/_2$ x 11 inch sheet of white paper, the standard size of paper for general correspondence and other business uses. When you have it duplicated, whether by office copier or by offset printing, it is generally reproduced similarly. So in addition to sharing the same basic layout ideas with almost everyone else, your résumé resembles all the rest because it is printed or copied on the same size white paper.

There are things you can do about this. Here are some ways to break the pattern so that your résumé does not resemble all the others:

Use colored paper.
Use colored ink or print it in more than one color.
Use paper of a different size.
Use artwork—drawings and other graphic devices—in your
    résumé.
Use a combination of the above ideas.

These ideas are helpful in making your résumé stand out from the rest of them—in making your résumé distinctive. Cautions:

1. Don't go overboard and produce something garish, bizarre, or so badly overdone that it backfires on you by making you appear to be some kind of eccentric. Be different, distinctive, *but in good taste.*

2. Don't expect the distinctiveness to do anything more for you than get you a moment's extra attention. Your résumé must still be powerful. If you have a good résumé, and it is also distinctive, you have an excellent chance of winning an interview. If your résumé is distinctive, in exquisite taste, beautifully done, but the content is only mediocre, you've wasted your money and your time: the beautiful presentation will not have brought you anything.

Some individuals choose to have their photograph printed on their résumé, and some self-styled experts advocate doing this. Don't. It's risky. An employer might just decide not to like your looks. Or your beard. Or your hair style. You lose nothing by not having your photo on the résumé, and you run a risk by having it there. Why tempt fate?

Of course, the same thing may be said for any illustration. Suppose you use a drawing of some sort, such as any of those "clip art" illustrations, which can be purchased in most art-supply stores and may be used for whatever purposes you wish to use them. Of course, you can never tell how any individual will react. On one occasion I happened to use a simple drawing of a cocktail waitress in a short skirt to liven up a little sales brochure. To my astonishment I received a sharp note from one of my respondents, calling me down for stooping to such low tactics in selling. It is a good idea to think carefully and use a great deal of discretion in choosing graphics.

There are many graphic devices and symbols available, especially in decal form, at any well-stocked art-supply store such as *Zipatone* and *Chartpak*. A representative selection of these is shown in Figure 11.

Use judgment in selecting colored inks and papers. I received one résumé printed in dark red ink on dark brown paper. I refused to even try to read it, as I imagine a great many other employers must have. Be sure that your résumé is legible. One of the standard operating principles of sales and advertising tactics is to make it as easy as possible for the prospect to say yes or place an order. Every difficulty you create in the path of this hinders the sale and may very

FIGURE 11. Various graphic symbols available as decals.

well kill it entirely. If you use any of the graphics suggested, use them to help the reader grasp the main messages in your résumé quickly, and be careful that you do not *overdo* the use of graphics. Some people get carried away with a good idea and go to extremes. In this case, if you overuse graphics you will distract attention from the message that your résumé is trying to deliver, whereas you should be trying to accomplish the exact opposite of that. Use illustrations, borders, arrows, or other graphics to point to specific items, to highlight certain items, or to focus attention on one main message. Never use graphics to "dress up" a résumé, but only to accomplish some specific purpose. For example, putting a nice border around the entire résumé may provide a pleasing effect and make your résumé distinctive—get attention—but like the headline of a print advertisement, it should do more than get attention: it should also send a message. Putting a distinctive border around the abstract in the headline space, for example, will get attention while it also directs the reader to the main message.

Above all, do not make your résumé appear "busy" with a plethora of tricks and devices. The general appearance of your résumé is important; and that general appearance—the image that strikes the eye before the reader has focused on or digested a single word—ought to be one of trim, neat, and businesslike efficiency. Leave generous margins and white space between items, use short sentences, even telegraphic style (omission of articles, conjunctions, other words that do not add meaning).

. An easy way to make your résumé into a brochure is to type up the information to fit into two to four panels 4-$\frac{1}{4}$ inches wide by 5-$\frac{1}{2}$ inches long. This is the size of each panel you get when you fold an ordinary typewriter sheet into halves. Of course, you do not have to use all four panels, if you can get all your information into fewer than four. However, to get the full advantage of this format, it is often helpful to space your information out so as to use at least three of the panels, making each panel open and uncluttered. But there are a few other advantages in this format:

One effective use of this résumé brochure is to allot each of the panels a communication mission of its own. For example, you might use the first or outside panel for your "head data" (name, address, telephone number) and headline plus abstract or blurb. Place the head data at the top of the panel, use a proper headline and blurb and position that in the approximate center of the panel, surrounded by a neat border. You may then use the other panels for whatever missions you find suitable—perhaps the inside panels to list your experience, and the last panel to describe your education and any miscellaneous data you believe useful.

This, of course, helps greatly in focusing attention where you want it focused, while it costs you no more except a minor cost for folding, when you have it printed.

If you wish to go to the expense of being really different, you may be attracted to the idea of either a large brochure—four or more panels, each 8-$\frac{1}{2}$ x 11 inches (must be printed on an 11 x 17 inch sheet) or a very small one of six panels, achieved by folding a standard typewriter sheet into thirds. The hazard with the large one is that it is not really different in outward appearance, unless you go to great expense over costly papers and typesetting. The trouble with the small one is that it is almost inescapable that you must have this typeset— it is most difficult to use typewriter composition with this size brochure. And there is the even more serious problem that a great many readers will not recognize it as a résumé immediately and may discard it without more than a casual glance. All in all, it appears that the

John Henry Jones
3722 N. Oak Drive
Puscatawket, NH
336–7707

EDUCATION:

BBA, major in Accounting, 1965, PDQ University
MBA, major Financial Management, 1967, XYZ University

EXPERIENCE:

1970 – Present. J.K. Smith Tool & Die Manufacturers, Inc.
Office Manager, responsible for payroll, purchasing, accounting, supervising three clerks and secretary.

1968 – 70 Brown Shoe Company, shoe wholesalers. Made up payroll for 12 people, keep inventory, records, processing, payables and receivables.

1967 – 68 Association for Business Development, Director of Public Relations. Wrote news releases, brochures, newsletters and handled membership correspondence.

HOBBIES:

Skiing, swimming, reading Civil War History, chess, gardening

MEMBERSHIPS:

Podunk Men's Club, Baptist Christian Association, Young Republican's Club

PERSONAL:

Age: 31. Married, two children: Brian, age 8 and Marilyn age 4. Own home

FIGURE 12. A standard sheet of paper folded over to create a résumé brochure.

4-$^1/_4$ x 5-$^1/_2$ inch brochure is the most suitable size and most adaptable generally to use as a résumé presentation.

Note that everything is geared towards marketing and selling—*everything*. The format considerations, like the rhetorical, semantic, and other considerations are all marketing considerations. Decisions regarding them should be taken strictly on the basis of what is most conducive to getting an order—being asked to come in for interview, in this case. That's the ball you must keep your eye on.

# 8

# Enter the "Super-Résumé"

*It's time now to finally discard all those reactionary ideas about what a résumé is or ought to be, and begin to do some truly independent, results-oriented thinking.*

## A FUNCTIONAL AND LOGICAL APPROACH

**I**F we are in agreement now that what is important is not what a résumé *is* but what it *does*, we can divorce ourselves from all those prejudices of what a résumé ought to look like. We talked earlier about the importance of the prospect's *perceptions* because prospects are motivated, not by what things are, but by whatever they happen to *think* things are—by how they perceive things. We also talked about the problem of getting your résumé past the personnel department, which often accepts it as a solemn duty to accomplish 100-percent screening of incoming résumés, thereby saving the line managers and executives the trouble of reading any résumés. Still another related problem is having line managers and executives to whom your résumé has been addressed recognize the contents of the envelope as a résumé, and immediately consign it to the personnel department to screen it.

In short, whether your résumé arrives addressed to "personnel," unaddressed and therefore opened in the mailroom or by a secretary, or addressed directly to a manager or executive, if its very appearance betrays the fact that it is a résumé, it is likely to be consigned to oblivion without consideration. Sad but true: Instant death for anything that remotely resembles a résumé, or what a résumé ought to appear to be.

One way out of this dilemma might be to disguise the résumé so that it does not appear to be one. Perhaps if it appeared to be a letter, it would be treated like a letter, especially if it were addressed like a letter to some specific individual. Yet, would a letter get a serious reading, if it appeared to be a letter from someone unknown to whomever it is addressed?

These are problems to be solved. And if we do objective functional analysis, we come up with two basic considerations of what we need to do and want to achieve:

1. We want to boil down that presentation of our qualifications we call a résumé to the essentials—to the most compelling attributes or promises we can offer as our *bona fides* for seeking an interview with the goal of winning a job offer.

2. We want a résumé that does not look like a résumé, but yet somehow persuades the addressee to read what we have to say.

When analyzed logically, both considerations lead inevitably to the briefest possible presentation. On the one hand, it is important to select the most compelling reasons for asking you in for an interview. On the other hand, you must somehow induce the addressee to read and digest that presentation. One way to do this is to make it so short that the addressee need hardly read it all, but may take it in almost at first glance.

The fact is that this works in your favor in more than one way: On the one hand, it achieves a sharp focus, something that has been stressed repeatedly here as a decided asset in any presentation. On the other hand, almost anyone will take a moment to read a *short* letter.

Consider the example of Figure 13, to illustrate the point. If you study it carefully, you will find that it has all the important elements of any résumé:

Head data—name, address, telephone number.
Promise—a multi-million-dollar producer.
Evidence—a seventeen-year record of doing what the promise says.
Experience—summarized neatly and emphatically.
What is wanted—a part-time job as an insurance salesman.
Call for action—invitation to call or write for interview/discussion.

Joseph T. Smith
Happenstance Lane
Citrustown, FL 32301
(305) 555–3333

November 27, 1985

George S. McReady
Vice-President
LIFE Underwriters, Ltd.
37 Oldtown Road
Gerrymander, GA 30344

Dear Mr. McReady:

For the last 17 years of my career as an insurance salesman my annual sales were never less than $1 million, and usually were closer to my high annual figure of $6 million. I am now nominally in retirement, but am still in good health and bored to death. I would like to return to my profession on a parttime basis.

Please call or write me at your convenience to discuss this further.

Cordially,

Joseph T. Smith

FIGURE 13. A "super-résumé"—actually a brief letter.

Of course, I hear your complaint already that Joe Smith's résumé—especially his abstract (see Figure 10) fits neatly into this brief-letter format, and your résumé does not. Yours, in fact, does not fit at all, for one reason or another. Never fear; there are ways to cope with all these problems. Few résumés fit precisely and neatly. But that does not invalidate the idea.

## A FEW TIPS FOR COPING

Even if your résumé is not a "natural" fit, which is irrelevant, the super-résumé (calling it that for lack of a better name) will work for you too. In fact, it may very well be the *only* way you can make a strong case for yourself; that has proved true for many people already.

Let us suppose that you have had an assortment of jobs, none of which you consider a true career position, and you are still trying to find that job which will start you on your way to a real career. Search back in memory for whatever it was you did in any job that was truly valuable for your employer. Did you produce an idea that helped move off surplus inventory? Find a good buy in something or other? Discover a way to reduce rejects? Improve production? Speed up parts inspection? Salvage a project in trouble?

Think in terms of accomplishment that benefited the employer. Try particularly to think in quantitative terms; numbers are always more credible and impressive than are qualitative statements. But there are right and wrong ways to present quantitative information— some ways are far more dramatic and, therefore, more impressive, than others. Here are a few basic rules for presenting quantitative data:

1. Use arabic numerals, rather than nouns and adjectives; that is, not *twenty-two million*, but *22,000,000*.

2. Do not round the numbers off: not *over four thousand* or *nearly five thousand*, but *4,765*. (If estimating, not guessing, use a formula and report the *exact* number your formula yields.)

3. If you are reporting rates, choose the units that are most easily grasped and appreciated. Example: If you are an incoming parts inspector and you wish to report your typical rate of production, you have several choices. You can express it in parts per day and/or parts per year (it is often beneficial to report both rates), cost per part, percentage of each batch sampled (and therefore total number of parts accepted and approved), or other such adaptation. Work with a calculator and see what numbers are most impressive. Of course, numbers relating to cost are most appealing to an employer, if the cost figures are favorable ones.

In writing your super-résumé, it is more important to use active voice and action verbs than it is in writing a résumé. The pace and tone of the super-résumé must be brisk and businesslike, moving swiftly to the point and making sure that you are "coming in loud and clear" in making that point. Suppose you wish to make the single point that a sales department you managed went from $14 million in sales per year to $33 million in sales per year while under your management, over a period of seven years. Here is how NOT to do it:

NO-NO:         Annual sales went from $14 million to $33 million a year during the seven years the department was under my management.

BETTER:         My department raised sales from $14,000,000 per year to $33,000,000 per year.

BETTER YET:      I raised sales from $14,000,000 to $33,000,000 per year.

STILL BETTER:    I raised sales an average of $2,714,000 per year, from $14,000,000 to $33,000,000.

If you managed the department, you *were* the department. Whatever the department did was *your* accomplishment. Take credit for it. And do it in that active voice. Note, too, that there are no adjectives or adverbs, just nouns and verbs—just *factual reporting*. And the seven years noted carefully, of itself, adds nothing, but the average annual increase in sales means a great deal and will warm any employer's heart.

There is no room for modesty in a résumé, and even less room for it in a super-résumé. And yet you don't have to appear to be bragging, and you won't be if you stick to factual reporting.

*Aha!* you are saying, *this guy keeps throwing me a curve. He keeps picking out ideal cases of people who sell and can brag without appearing to brag about their accomplishments. How about me? I've never sold anything in my life. I'm just a TV repairman looking for a job.*

Okay, let's see what a TV repairman could say about his abilities and accomplishments:

Out of approximately 1,300 service calls, I have managed to repair nearly 87 percent—1,125 of those 1,300 sets—in the customer's home, at an average billing of $49 per receiver. This produced $55,125 in gross income for my company in 12 months. Together with antenna work and shop repairs I brought in from service calls, I produced over $93,500 during the past year.

I believe any TV shop with an opening for a repairman would be pleased to add this producer of income to their staff of service people. And some would create an opening, if possible, for someone who can produce this way.

Here are a few other ideas of how super-résumés could be based for different backgrounds:

I installed 17 shower-stall units a day, nearly twice the norm and required minimum production rate.

I cut the time required to deliver the mail in the building from three hours to two and one-half hours, despite an increase of 22 percent in offices, employees, and mail volume during my 2 years in the job of mail clerk.

I cut the cost of answering queries 33 percent by developing seven standard responses and a system for coding each query for the proper response.

My assembly-line inspection reduced the reject rate by seven percent.

I reduced the costs of parts an average of 13 percent by requiring competitive bids on every purchase over $100, and seeking out new suppliers who were more competitive generally than the ones the company had been using.

I cut postage expenses for the year by $11,675 by initiating the use of pre-sorted first-class mail and taking advantage of the lower rates offered by the Postal Service.

Of course, there is the problem of your most notable accomplishment having no relationship to your career jobs you are most interested in landing now. If you were that mail clerk who reduced the delivery time in your office building, it may have been years ago, while you were going to night school to become an accountant. Now you are an accountant and are seeking a more senior position in accounting than the one you have now. So why bring up that old accomplishment of years ago?

First of all, you should certainly try to find something in your more recent, career experience to report—something you have been able to accomplish as an accountant. But whether you are or are not able to point to some fine achievements as a "number cruncher," that mail-clerk experience helps demonstrate your energy and efficiency, and may be used to support that image. You might be saying, for example, something along these lines, as part of your super-résumé:

Even as a mail clerk, while attending night school. . . .

## SPECIAL CASES

That example of the hypothetical individual who developed standard letters to cut the cost of answering queries, incidentally, was inspired by the actual case of a consultant who was retained by the Energy Research and Development Administration, the U.S. Department of Energy's predecessor organization, to help one of their offices catch up with its correspondence. The office in question was unable to keep up with their mail—understaffed, which is not an unusual situation in government agencies—and had some mail that was two years old and still unanswered. And the office had a chief who insisted that every inquiry merited an individual response, and not a preprinted form letter. So in their desperation the staff went in quest of a consultant to help them get out and stay out of trouble. That consultant did manage to help them catch up their backlog of some 200 unanswered letters, while designing a system for them to handle the problem in the future. Had he done this as an employee, it would have been quite a thing to brag about. But as a contractor or consultant, such results were to be expected, and no special congratulations or plaudits were in order.

Nevertheless, if you have such an accomplishment in your background and are looking for a job, don't hesitate to use it. Your accomplishments may have been for a client or customer; they do not necessarily have to be for a former employer *per se*. What is important is not whether or not you were on the payroll when you accomplished whatever feat you accomplished, but the fact that there was a substantial benefit to someone else for whom you did what you did—providing the benefit bears on your qualifications as a potential employee. Your prowess as a mountain climber or golfer is relevant if your career work relates to these and your prowess is an asset to a prospective employer.

One of my colleagues has had considerable success in selling to foreign governments and, additionally, his travel to and familiarity with a number of foreign countries is his chief asset today. And the more foreign countries he becomes familiar with, the greater that asset becomes. Originally, he was sent abroad to handle technical-writing assignments in Europe for an American firm, but soon gravitated to foreign marketing and then to guiding foreign marketing for others. And he turned that accidentally stumbled on asset into an entirely different career. (A most profitable career, too.)

Another man had joined a firm which had an unbroken record in one of its divisions for laying an egg on every project—bringing projects in behind schedule and over-budget again and again. By long, arduous effort this man designed a system to overcome the problems and begin bringing the projects in on schedule and within their budgets. That record has led him on to much more rewarding positions than the one in which he developed his methods.

Many individuals discover within themselves capabilities they did not even suspect existed, and some are wise enough to take advantage of these newly found abilities and benefit from them. In one case where an accountant in a small firm was found inept and dismissed, his chief posting clerk was given the accountant's job, although she had never had formal training as an accountant. But she had shown an ability to do careful work and had learned the company's methods and accounting needs, so she was a competent accountant for that company and qualified for the job at a considerable increase in salary and position. Obviously, this is an asset in any subsequent effort to seek out a better job, if she uses it properly. (She was not only a better accountant for that small company, but a much less expensive one.)

A young man hired as a technical writer by a small New York engineering- services firm proved to be so engaging a personality and sales-oriented that he soon moved over to the sales department, met great success at that, moved on to become a marketing vice-president for another company, and eventually departed there to establish his own successful business as a marketing-services contractor. In that same company, however, another man who had moved from technical writing into sales remained with the company, experienced almost as rapid a growth pattern as the company itself did, advancing from technical writer to salesman to vice-president sales, as the company progressed to a $250 million per year size

As auctioneers sometimes put it when the opening bid for an

item is shockingly low, it's not where you begin that counts, but where you finish. All experience is good experience, if you search out the most positive aspects of it. Keep records, even an informal diary, so that you will have the right ammunition for future résumés and, especially, super-résumés. Note everything you are able to accomplish, especially in quantitative terms. Keep a record of the people who are in a position to provide reference data on your performance. And, especially, start and maintain a network. (More on this in a subsequent chapter.)

## WHY "SUPER-RÉSUMÉ"?

The term *super-résumé* is an arbitrary one. In one sense, the type of letter recommended here *is* a super résumé because it is the ultimate in boiling down and condensing your credentials and qualifications into the shortest presentation possible, selecting the most compelling items. That is, calling such a brief letter a résumé is carrying the résumé idea to its logical extreme. That, in my opinion, justifies the term.

It does not mean, however, that you do not and will not need a more conventional résumé, one that gives a more complete accounting of your educational and working background. At some point in the process and for some purposes, you do need one because employers require it in many, if not most, cases. The concept of the super-résumé, however, is that it should be the initial approach, a door opener. And it is also most useful as a means for solving some of the more vexing problems we encounter when we are trying to create a helpful conventional résumé.

# 9

# How Super-Résumés Solve Related Problems

*One of the best reasons for using super-résumés is that the method helps you overcome many of the problems and drawbacks of conventional résumés. It might very well be called the "bottom-line résumé."*

## CLASSIC RÉSUMÉ PROBLEMS

**E**VERYONE who has ever written a résumé knows that résumé writing involves some problem-solving. The young person has the characteristic problem of not having enough experience to present; the older person has the problem of having too much information and therefore confronts a typical résumé dilemma—a résumé that is too long, and difficulty in deciding what's most important. But these are only the beginning of the problems; there are many others:

The working experience and accomplishments you'd most like to talk about happened ten years ago, about midway through your working career, to date. No matter which chronology you use, that experience will wind up buried in the middle of your biographical account.

There are a few things you'd rather not include in your résumé— perhaps a job you took when things were tough, which you think is rather demeaning. At least, it makes you look like a loser, which is hardly the image you want to present. (You worked one summer as a table waiter or you set pins in a bowling alley—honest work, but hardly in keeping with your professional status as an engineer.) How can you leave it out without an obvious, yawning gap in the record?

There was also that job which lasted for only a few months because you could not possibly get along with that surly supervisor. How can you skip over that one? (You would hate to have anyone call *that* place for a reference.)

There was also the employer who fired you for habitual lateness. He didn't know (or care) that you worked a second job at night to keep up with the cost of everything, and just had trouble getting up in the mornings.

There are weaknesses in your educational qualifications, too. You've had some fine jobs, and you've won them the hard way—by overcoming the lack of what many consider to be the necessary educational background—college degrees. But every time you want to make a change and try to get a step up by doing so, you run into this problem.

None of these problems are unique. In fact, they are the common, even classic, problems that are characteristic of the résumé-preparation process. Most young people have that familiar problem of not having enough work experience to talk about, and little or no work experience directly related to the career goals. Most older people have the problem of certain matters and former jobs they'd rather not mention, for one reason or another. And many older people have had much working experience, but have made a career switch which is quite common, and are in the same situation as are the young, recent graduates: they have little or no working experience relevant to the jobs they are pursuing. Let's consider the super-résumé in this light—how it helps solve some of these problems.


## THE AUTOMATIC SOLUTION

To a large degree, these problems exist simply because it has always been taken for granted that a résumé must be a complete accounting of everything you did since leaving high school, as far as education, work, and anything related to these are concerned. And under that concept, anything left out—apparent gaps in the record—automatically become causes for suspicion. The employer is immediately convinced that you are covering something up. (Maybe you did a little stretch in Folsom or Leavenworth?)

There are ways this problem can be resolved in a conventional résumé—as in Figure 5, make it a functional résumé, which obviously does not list events in chronological order. One problem with that approach, however, is that such a résumé almost automatically brings a request for missing information, if the employer is interested at all. So you might just as well use a super-résumé; you'll do as well, in terms of solving basic problems, and have more powerful appeal. Why bother with a functional résumé?

There are other ways to handle the problems in conventional résumé formats. For instance, the problem of the work experience and accomplishments you'd like most to feature, but they are part of a job of ten years ago. One way to handle that problem in a conventional résumé is to feature it in the headline space of the résumé. But you are beginning to approach the idea of the super-résumé, then why not the far greater impact of the super-résumé itself?

The basic advantage of the super-résumé, as a résumé-problem solver, is that it does not appear to be a résumé so the respondent does not expect it to conform to those conventional ideas of what a résumé is or ought to be. And even if the reader does assume that it is a résumé, it is obviously not the conventional résumé and could in no way attempt to be a complete accounting of the writer's educational and career-experience background.

In short, the very approach frees you to do whatever you believe is in your best interests to do. Let's consider, for example, some characteristic drawbacks which are inherent in using résumés at all, without regard to the problems that arise in specific cases.

## SEVERAL BUILT-IN PROBLEMS WITH RÉSUMÉS

One of the worst aspects of the résumé is that it is a dull and dreary document; at best, about as fascinating to read as a stock prospectus. It is inconceivable that anyone who must read résumés approaches the task with anything resembling enthusiasm. That's hardly the attitude you would like a prospective employer to have before picking up your résumé to read it. But these characteristics are truly inherent in the résumé, almost impossible to avoid or overcome, and still make your résumé appear to be what it is intended to be. (Not even Ernest Hemingway could have enlivened a résumé.)

A second problem with the conventional résumé is that it inevitably compels you to include a great deal of information that is largely irrelevant. In fact, it is likely that 75 percent of the information in most résumés is of doubtful relevance—much less usefulness to the employer. It can hardly cheer the individual condemned to read résumés to know that he or she is probably wasting about 75 percent of the time so spent.

Still another disagreeable characteristic of the résumé idea is that matter mentioned earlier of most résumés—probably more than 90 percent—looking very much like each other so that when dozens or even hundreds are neatly stacked on a desk, few, if any, stand out. Moreover, a typical conventional résumé announces or identifies itself as such instantly, by that very standardized general appearance, which means that it almost invariably is directed to the personnel office by any individual who opens the envelope containing the résumé. And we all know what happens to 99 percent of the résumés directed to any personnel office.

Another unfortunate consequence of the résumé idea is that it is based on the concept of playing the percentages by distributing enough copies so that mathematical probability will—presumably—work in one's favor. That idea leads inevitably to structuring the résumé so as to be as general as possible, in the hope that it will be a reasonable match for the maximum number of openings, with their various sets of qualification requirements. That leads directly to diluting and weakening any special impact, because it is a most rare occasion on which a preprinted résumé happens to be a good match for any given opening. It's very much like the proposition of trying to please everyone and, therefore, managing to please no one. It is all but impossible to create a standardized résumé that is really responsive to all the job possibilities you will think suitable for you and therefore opt to pursue. The jobs and their requirements may all be good prospects for you and your capabilities, but rarely will your standardized résumé be a good match for those jobs and their qualification requirements. In most cases—and "most" is only a theoretical or philosophical truth; in the actual, practical case, substitute "all" for "most"—to make the strongest possible case for your pursuit of a given job opportunity, you need a custom-tailored résumé, which focuses on those qualifications of yours which are most suitable to the job in question and most likely to produce solid benefits for the employer. That "boiler-plate" résumé simply will not do the job, even if it is exceptionally well written, because it *is* standardized and boilerplated.

You need to prepare a separate, custom résumé for each application. Of course, it is most difficult to do so, for a variety of reasons; but at least for these two:

1. It's a great deal of work, even for a one-page résumé, when you are going to send out and distribute dozens of résumés. The typing itself is not that big a job, if you are a good typist and have access to an adequate machine, but writing all those individual résumés is a big job, even for a writer. And it's a frustrating job, too, because you know in advance that by far the majority of those résumés are not going to draw a response.

2. Rarely will you know what to put in that custom résumé—precisely what the prospect really wants in the way of qualifications. What you can learn about most jobs from their listings in newspaper advertisements and notices in personnel offices, on bulletin boards, and elsewhere—even by direct conversation with personnel people—is so general as to be useless. They describe the basic duties and functions, and the most basic qualification requirements—college degrees and experience—but they don't tell you what those specific hiring criteria are going to be because they don't know. Not even the manager who does the interviewing and makes the hiring decision really knows in advance on what he or she will finally base a decision.

There is still one other, quite serious problem with a résumé: The résumé that is quite detailed has the serious drawback—it leads the reader into believing that he or she knows enough about the writer of the résumé, the applicant for the job, to make a decision. There is (the reader usually reasons) enough information to make an evaluation and decision on at least a preliminary basis. And if the résumé is exceptionally detailed, there is probably enough information to make a final decision.

That is, of course, absolutely opposed to what you want your résumé to do; your résumé should have the opposite effect—to lead the reader to the idea that it is necessary to interview you to learn more about you. You want your résumé to bring about something in the order of the following thought process: *Hey, this is an interesting individual who appears to have real possibilities. I think I simply must talk to this one and find out more, because somebody is going to grab this one up.*

The idea behind the résumé is, therefore, that it ought to be a teaser. How can you do that with two or three pages of information? Or even with one page, if it purports to be a summation of a complete career?

Obviously, you cannot. It would be a contradiction in terms to offer what purports to be a complete history, even in the briefest abstract, and hope that it serves well as a teaser item.

There are linkages between the super-résumé idea and these problems with the conventional résumé. The super-résumé is not just another way to do things, it is a way to do what conventional résumés cannot do. In fact, it does not replace conventional résumés, but supplements them and enables you to create more-effective conventional résumés. It does not do away with conventional résumés, although it replaces conventional résumés as the best way to open each effort to market yourself—to win a job you have decided to pursue. And the idea works well to solve a variety of problems, even that of satisfying the need for those individually designed résumés, prepared specifically for every job pursued, and the difficulty of doing this, can be solved by the super-résumé, coupled with proper methods for using that super-résumé. For the super-résumé is useful by its very format, and the greatest benefit is realized by the ways in which it is used.

The super-résumé, by its nature, overcomes some of the résumé problems we have discussed here. The basic concept allows you to select from your total experience history those items and elements you believe most helpful to your cause and use them as the focal points of your super-résumé. You need not introduce extraneous data, unrelated trivia, irrelevant filler, and other items which most résumés include only because that seems to be obligatory by tradition or by what we like to believe is conventional wisdom. You need not make your reader's eyelids heavy with accounts of the thirty-three special classes and certificate courses you took in the military and civil service. You need not provoke yawns with dull recitals of your duties in a job of eighteen years ago. Instead, you can come directly to the point of why your presence on the staff will be a boon of such unprecedented magnitude that immediate action would be wise. Your reader will not have time to be bored, and there isn't enough information to base a decision on.

That latter consideration is an important one. Remember that idea I stressed more than once (because it needs to be stressed more than once) that people act out of what they *perceive* to be fact, so we have to worry about what our prospects think things are, not what they really are. We must never—NEVER—let a prospect think that he or she knows enough about us to make a decision without an interview. And a super-résumé does that job admirably. Anyone who gets from you a half-page letter can have no doubts that this is merely the topping; it will require a meeting and discussion to get down to the cake. In fact, your super-résumé ought to make that clear by specific language, and not rely entirely on the reader's wisdom. Joe Smith (Figure 13) specifically suggested to his addressee that a meeting and discussion were clearly called for. And at this point let me digress for a moment to dwell on a most important point in selling, which is relevant to our discussion here.

## CLOSING

A friend of mine, Nido Qubein, a most successful entrepreneur (largely because he is a great salesman), says:

1. I have never seen a successful professional who could not close (wrap up) a sale effectively.
2. I have never seen an effective closer who was not successful.
3. I have never seen an effective closer who could not improve his or her closing techniques.
4. I have never seen an effective closer who was not looking for ways to become more effective.

*Closing*, contrary to the impression gathered by those not totally familiar with the full art of selling, is not getting the order, but is *asking* for the order. And there are many ways of closing or asking for the order. (Nido Qubein lists twelve ways; others think there are more than twelve ways.) What is important here is, not that there are many ways to ask for the order, the fact that successful salespeople are always good closers: They are good at asking for the order. And equally important to note is that it is always *necessary* to ask for the order, if you wish to be successful in selling.

Nido Qubein makes one other excellent point worth considering here: He points out that every successful professional is someone who has learned how to sell. That does not mean that every successful person is one who conforms to the stereotype of salespeople. But we all sell, to some extent, if we are to succeed at anything. And there are right and wrong ways to sell, as there are right and wrong ways to do anything. So that term *salesman* or *salesperson* is not derogatory; it is simple recognition of an important fact of life.

That's another fault with the traditional résumé: It does not lend itself well to closing—to asking for the interview. (In this case, *selling* means getting the interview, for that is what you are after.) The best you can do in résumés to close is to suggest your availability for interview and furnish addresses and telephone numbers. But the super-résumé, because it is different and because it is a letter, or in a letter format, which is *addressed directly to an individual* and may therefore specifically request an interview—*close*. That is a most important part of the super-résumé, and the example in Figure 13 is only one way to close. There are other ways, some very effective.

## USING THE SUPER-RÉSUMÉ TO LEAD TO THE CUSTOM RÉSUMÉ

The purpose of the super-résumé is to get an interview set up as a first goal. A legitimate immediate goal of the super-résumé is to draw attention and to arouse enough interest to draw from the respondent an inquiry, and using that inquiry to induce an interview. Then, as a result of that interview, draft a custom-tailored résumé, detailed to fit the specific requirement, as determined by you during the interview—using the interview as a guide to determine what will make the employer decide in your favor (assuming that the interview does not of itself result in a direct job offer). You have gathered the information, so you should not have a problem deciding what belongs in that résumé and what does not. You will not have the problem of creating a large number of individual résumés because you do one only after winning an interview. And you may decide after the interview, that you are not interested in the job; in that case, there is no need for an individual résumé. Why bother with a detailed, custom-tailored résumé before you know that you are interested in the job and have a reasonable chance of winning it?

## ASSOCIATED PROBLEMS AND OPPORTUNITIES

There are some problems associated with using super-résumés. All the problems can be handled, of course; but significantly, most of these so-called problems are opportunities; they are really what you should want to appear, once you decide to abandon the conventional and unproductive résumé route and use this different way of pursuing a job. There will be those who learn what you are doing and sneer at your methods; there will be puzzled employers who call and ask you to submit a "regular résumé"; there will be skeptics who question your brief claims in your super-résumés; and there will be difficulties in learning the names and functions of those to whom your super-résumés should be addressed. There will be lots of problems of various kinds, but all have solutions and most you will eventually learn to greet with a smile and a mental rubbing of your hands, recognizing that these are the kinds of problems that rapidly become opportunities when you exploit them properly.

Let's go on to the next chapter and discuss these matters and how to conceive and carry out those exploitations.

# 10

# Using the Super-Résumé

*The super-résumé, like the résumé, must be used in a variety of situations. But unlike the conventional résumé, the super-résumé is readily adaptable to all situations.*

## HOW MUCH INFORMATION?

ASKING yourself how much information a super-résumé ought to offer is very much like asking how long a man's legs ought to be. Lincoln is alleged to have responded to such a question with, "Long enough to reach the ground." If so, it was an excellent response. How much information you should include in your super-résumé depends primarily on surrounding circumstances—what you wish to accomplish, what you are responding to (if you are, in fact, responding to something or someone), what kind of lead you are pursuing, what kind of individual you are approaching, and many other variables. In fact, it is because there are so many variables that the most effective way to respond to the variables is by being equally variable in your response. To do that, however, you have to employ something that is readily variable.

This does not mean that you may not have what might be considered to be your standard super-résumé—standard within these two limitations:

1. It is to be used only for situations where there are no known requirements or qualifications to be met—or possibly even no known job opening—so that it is necessary to operate strictly on assumptions and thrust out more or less blindly.

2. It is standardized only for this job hunt, not for all time, and/

or is one of several standardized forms used for this job hunt only, in conformance with the condition of (1) above.

Other than these situations, super-résumés should always be prepared individually and specifically tailored to known requirements. These factors will control how much information as well as what kind of information you will include in your super-résumé. Let's look at a few typical situations now, and how you might respond to each.

## HELP-WANTED ADVERTISEMENTS

There are many help-wanted advertisements, even in the most recessionary periods and periods of high unemployment. In fact, there does not appear to be any great reduction in the number of advertised openings when business conditions slow down, although there is definitely a marked increase in the competition for the openings. But there are many kinds of advertisements. There are the little three-to-six-line notices in the classified columns. There are the larger advertisements in the classified columns, some of them occupying a large portion of the page, dominating the page in many cases. There are display advertisements for help in the business sections of many newspapers, such as the *Washington Post*, the *New York Times*, and the *Wall Street Journal*. And these, too, may be prominent enough to dominate the pages they appear on. There are some that appear in the pages of technical, professional, and other trade journals.

Some of these advertisements are placed by the firms offering the jobs. Some are placed by middle people—brokers and agents—acting as recruiters. And some are placed by a special kind of middle-person broker, agencies for temporaries of various kinds, both office personnel and professionals. The latter hire the individuals on their own payrolls if and when the individuals have been interviewed and accepted by the broker's client, to which the individual will be assigned as a temporary. (In most cases, at least for professional temporaries, clients wish to interview candidates and approve them before assignment.)

For this latter class of employer—the broker becomes your employer and places you on his or her payroll, although you are hired specifically to work as a temporary employee of a client. It is rarely necessary to furnish a super-résumé, nor will most such brokers accept a super-résumé in place of the conventional résumé. This is because the situation is entirely different here: You have no need to persuade the broker to hire you. The broker is most eager to do so, but must usually get the client to approve you first. Therefore, what the broker wants is a conventional résumé to send on to the client for his or her approval of an interview.

Much the same considerations apply when dealing with any other kind of broker. Every broker wishes to place you, the employment agency or recruiter to earn a fee, the "job shop" or temporaries firm to earn a profit by billing you at a profit. Therefore, only those conventional résumés are in order in pursuing these avenues of employment.

However, when dealing directly with the employer, the super-résumé is very much in order, whether responding to a help-wanted advertisement or seeking out a prospective employer for any reason or via any other route. But let's look first at typical help-wanted advertisements and see what you are asked for.

## The Typical Requirements in the Help-Wanted Advertisement

Typically, when an employer invites you to respond to a help-wanted advertisement, you are given the briefest of descriptions of the job. One such advertisement which appeared recently in our newspaper called for a "Washington Editor" of a top business magazine (so they characterized themselves), and described the kind of writing expected. It's a "blind ad"—uses a box number for responses—and significantly enough says this:

> Send a résumé, but you'll make your best case with a letter that describes your background and interests and tells us why we should hire you.

Could the invitation be plainer? This employer specifically does not want to see the typical, traditional, conventional résumé, and anyone who responded to this advertisement with such a résumé obviously did not have a chance. But neither did anyone who wrote a long-winded, multi-page letter. This employer wanted a brief, to-the-point response. And since the job was for a Washington editor who was expected to write incisive, interpretive pieces (not reporting, the copy specified), that letter had better demonstrate the ability to be incisive and to the point.

This advertiser offered "a very competitive salary and excellent fringe benefits." Many others do not know precisely what salary they expect to pay, and it is quite a common practice to ask respondents to such advertisements to state the salary they wish or expect. Or, as a variant, to describe their "salary history." And a great many of these advertisements do specifically request a résumé. Many are blind advertisements, too, foreclosing the possibility of making a direct call on the employer. (Of course, it is specifically to prevent a horde of job seekers descending on them that they choose to run their advertisements under the anonymity of box numbers.)

How does one respond to such demands, stated as requirements, of course? How can you send a super-résumé to someone who has specifically demanded a "complete résumé" or a "detailed résumé"? Would it not be self-defeating to send a letter—even a super-résumé kind of letter—when the employer has made a regular résumé a requirement?

First you must recognize that in most cases yours will be only one of a large number of résumés that arrive in response to the advertisement. Even a small classified advertisement can draw fifty or more résumés in times of excessive unemployment, and large advertisements may easily draw as many as 200 responses, producing a large stack of résumés on someone's desk.

Second, bear in mind that these résumés are almost surely going to a personnel office, especially if the advertisement was a blind one. And you know your chances to survive that journey.

Third, keep in mind that this employer—who may be a clerk, personnel manager, secretary, or anyone who placed that help-wanted advertisement—is like most others and imitated other advertisements under the impression that what others do is the right way to do things. (Another case of accepting what passes for conventional wisdom or what "they say.") So, "requirements" may not be firm convictions that things must be done this way, but just imitative statements, with the employer receptive to deviations, if it appears promising enough.

Fourth, being different—novel and innovative—in itself gets you special attention. If you can follow up quickly with a sound-enough appeal, the employer may forget that you were a bit out of step with the rest of the sheep who responded.

Fifth, it's a calculated risk, which is far smaller than that of competing directly with dozens and dozens of other résumés, some of them probably stronger than yours.

When you analyze the situation in this logical manner, you realize that the risk you take of being rejected because you are different and didn't do precisely what the advertisement asked you to do is much smaller than the risk of being routinely rejected or overlooked as only one of many. Just being especially noteworthy is worth a great deal in this kind of competition.

There is point sixth, too; and it deserves special attention, which is why I choose to address it separately from the first five points.

All others responding to the advertisement are responding with their undistinguished, standard résumés, although a few might be responding with letters and résumés. (This is even worse, usually, because all the letter says is that a résumé is enclosed and the writer would very much like a job, thereby wasting still more of the employer's time, to no purpose.) Your response is different: Not only is it short, pithy, and to the point, but it is custom-tailored to the advertisement. Tailored not to what the advertisement said, but to what you believe will be most effective in striking a nerve.

Weigh all of this versus the possibility that your application will be cast out as "disqualified" because you did not comply with the advertiser's demand for a conventional résumé. Weigh being only one of many—perhaps hundreds—who is almost indistinguishable from the others versus getting—demanding—special attention by being different. But different in a most positive way—by being less demanding of the advertiser's time (you're sending a brief letter-résumé, instead of a lengthy conventional one). And you're actually being more responsive, not less so, because you are getting down to business without preliminaries.

## THE BOTTOM-LINE RÉSUMÉ

The term *bottom line* has come into wide usage in the last few years. My first experience with it was long before it became a popular colloquialism, when it did indeed refer to a bottom line—to the bottom line on the cost form we made up when submitting a proposal to a government agency in pursuit of a contract. The government's contracting officer would often say something such as, "What's the bottom line on this?" He meant by that question that we would discuss the various cost items later, including our markups or fees, but let's first find out what was the total amount of money we expected the government to pay for what we had proposed. And that was literally the bottom line on the estimate form.

Financial statements, such as those published in the Annual Report of public corporations, reveal, in general, the corporation's profit or loss on the bottom line of the financial statement. The bottom line reveals to anyone interested to know whether the corporation has made or lost money and how much. That's what a stockholder in a public corporation wishes to know when he or she asks for the bottom line.

In more popular usage, then, the term has come to refer to the essential or most important element in whatever matter is under discussion or referred to. In a court case, the bottom line might refer to the verdict, the judgment rendered in a civil case, or the sentence handed down by the judge in a criminal case. In any argument of dispute, the bottom line is how the dispute turned out. In any matter when you demand to know what the bottom line is, you are demanding to skip all the prologue, all the details, and reveal the final result or the essence of the matter.

So with this approach, the super-résumé might also have been called the *bottom-line résumé*. And it may be helpful to think of it in that way—that it is the essence of what you, as a potential employee, are all about. In effect, it is saying: *We can discuss the details later, if you are interested. Here, to save time, is what I and my offer are all about.*

That is the essential philosophy of the super-résumé. That because it is the bottom line, it automatically bestows on you the right to skip *all* the details, for the moment. *Time enough for those later, after we have established a basis of mutual interest,* your approach says. *Let's not worry about the details now, but only about whether what I offer is interesting enough in principle to get together and discuss it. Then we'll get to the details.*

That is why and how you can justify choosing to respond to the demands of the employer's advertisement in whatever way *you* believe is helpful. You do not refuse to supply whatever information is requested, but only to save your time and the advertiser's time by getting directly to the bottom line and finding out whether the two of you are interested enough in each other to invest the time for discussion of details.

## A BUSINESSLIKE APPROACH

One of the several advantages of this approach is that it is very much like the approach one businessperson would use to another were they considering some kind of business deal, such as a merger, a joint venture, a major sale, or some other proposition of such a magnitude that would necessarily involve person-to-person discussion. In such cases, two busy people rarely agree to invest the time—and often the out-of-pocket expense—involved in a personal discussion without first having some "bottom line" exchange to indicate whether there is enough mutual interest to justify the expense and time involved in detailed discussion. Employers are businesspeople, of course, and may be expected to grasp this concept readily and perceive that hiring someone is a business proposition and ought to be done in a businesslike manner. Sending an employer a brief summation of your offer is businesslike indeed, especially when it is in response to the employer's request for information.

## "SALARY DESIRED"

One of the problems you may have found most vexing in the past is how to handle that advertised demand for "salary expected" or "salary history." The latter, salary history, is bad enough, but naming salary desired or expected in your initial approach is likely to be instant-death for your chances, even if you otherwise may have had a good chance of winning an interview. Or, even worse, it may result in your being offered and accepting the job at substantially less than it should pay. Eventually, you would learn that you had sold yourself too cheaply, and from that time on you would never be happy in that job, even if you had liked it at first.

There are several reasons for not offering salary history or salary requested—especially not the latter. One is that you've no idea what the employer expects or is prepared to pay for the job. If your figure is too high, you will probably get no consideration at all, no matter what the rest of your *bona fides* happen to be. But being too low can have the same effect: True that being too low may result in an offer eventually (if your qualifications are acceptable) at a lower figure than you should have gotten. But being low by a large margin is likely to result in immediate rejection because it is taken to indicate that you do not know what the job is all about. Besides, it's premature—too soon to talk salary.

It is always a mistake to specify a desired salary in your initial approach or response, and it should require some unusual circumstances to persuade anyone to furnish a salary history in an initial approach. Doing so is practically never in your best interest, so why do it? And that ought to be always your first consideration: What is in your best interest? Do not be influenced by anyone's claim that what he or she wants is best for you. Make that decision independently.

When you respond to an advertised opening, simply ignore any request made for salary information or salary-expected figure. To supply one can never help you, of course; and the failure to supply it will not hurt you, either—if you have made your super-résumé strong enough. Remember always that when you are in pursuit of a job, you are not soliciting favors or patronage; you are making a business offer. No one hires you to do you a favor (except, perhaps, your father or father-in-law), and you are not going to win the job by apple-polishing tactics. You win a job by making a good enough offer. You say: *Here is what I can do for you. If this appeals to you, let's talk, and I'll tell you more.* You don't say it, but you should be also thinking: *And I'll see what you can or are willing to offer me, also.*

## TAILORING THE SUPER-RÉSUMÉ IN RESPONSES

Even if you are a specialist in some field, you are likely to be responding to a variety of solicitations which are different enough from each other to justify, if not absolutely demand, customized responses. Let us suppose, for example, that you are a computer specialist, highly trained and broadly experienced. There are few computer-related jobs you could not handle quite well. But look at just a few of the advertisements:

IBM/CICS COMMAND OR MACRO LEVEL. Two or more years experience with commercial or government applications.

PROGRAMMERS—MASTERS DEGREE REQUIRED. Experience includes: Simulation–Modeling–Data base mgmt–C31–

E-W–Artificial intelligence–PASCAL–LISP–INTERLISP-ROSIE–Army background–VAX–Color–graphics–Microprocessors.

PROGRAMMER, RPG 11. IBM S/3, Model 15D, CCP desired, minimum 2 years experience.

PROGRAMMERS—small consulting firm needs programmers to modify and run nuclear power forecasting models. JCL, TSO, FORTRAN, PL/1, SAS and some statistics essential.

Perhaps you are an individual who could handle any of these jobs. However, should you say so—should you make the brag that you can do anything in the computer field—your application won't get a second glance; it will be dismissed with a grimace and a snort. Truth doesn't matter, remember; only *perceptions* do. And although some of the qualifications demands made may appear unreasonable, the jobs are going to go to the individuals who manage somehow to satisfy the employers that they (the applicants) do meet those demands.

Obviously, to meet the demands, if you decide to apply for every one of these advertised openings, calls for somewhat different claimed or reported experience and knowledge. But let us suppose, for a moment, that you are so widely experienced that you can meet the qualifications demands of all these advertised openings. And let us suppose, further, that you could document and prove that you meet all these requirements. How should you approach the problem? Here are two possibilities:

1. Make that general claim of sweeping, all-encompassing experience in general enough terms to suit virtually any and all situations, with a spot of evidence and an offer to furnish full details in interview.

2. Offer all the evidence, in as brief a presentation as possible, but including specific mention of all languages, machines, and functions in which you claim capability.

Let us suppose, for purposes of discussion here, that you choose to use that first possibility and manage to develop a single super-résumé that is suitable for all these solicitations. Let us suppose further that you make your case in that super-résumé: You provide pretty good evidence, for a brief presentation, that your length and breadth of experience and your capabilities in general are far superior to those of any other candidate for any of the positions. What then? How are employers likely to respond to your super-résumé?

That's an easy question to answer. Even if no employer had a tendency to be skeptical of your possibly unprecedented capabilities and experience, there would be an almost automatic tendency to favor the application of someone who had far less general experience and capability than you, but could cite the *specific* experience called for in the advertisement. And there are several reasons for this tendency to weigh responses in this manner, tending always to favor some specific qualifications over general qualifications, even when the general qualifications are, in fact, superior to the specific qualifications:

1. There is always the tendency of employers to believe that the job they need filled is very special and requires very special abilities. Employers get so caught up in the intricacies of their own enterprises that they believe that theirs is a unique enterprise and their requirements are therefore unique. And such perceptions as these are particularly prevalent in technological enterprises and complex businesses, or businesses based on some new or clever idea.

2. There is today's prejudice about generalists and specialists. In many fields today, such as computer systems, the specialty has become so diverse and broad that one must be a specialist within the specialty. To claim capabilities throughout that field is the same as claiming to be a generalist, which is a no-no now and arouses suspicion and skepticism immediately. The more you specialize in today's world, the more credible, prestigious, valuable, and desirable you become.

3. Specific details are always far more credible—convincing and persuasive—than generalizations. Even when the advertiser is wrong about what is needed to do the job—and as an expert, you may be able to discern that the employer is wrong about the true requirements of the job—one way to be persuasive and convince the other party that you are very wise is to tell the other what he or she wants to hear. If the advertiser believes that you can't do the job properly without knowing all those computer languages and being experienced in those specific computers, you are not likely to convince that employer that the truth is otherwise. It is far more effective sales technique to go along and comply with the prospect's prejudices.

This is also true in other professions, even those which are not related to modern technology—the older, longer-established fields that are not changing rapidly, such as accounting. Here are what several advertisers say they want to qualify applicants for accounting positions:

> ACCOUNTANT—experienced accounting manager for government contractor in Northern Virginia. Familiarity with DAR [Defense Acquisition Regulations] essential.

> ACCOUNTANT, CPA FIRM—Senior or semi-senior with approximately 2–4 years experience with CPA firm needed in our expanding Northern Virginia practice.

> ACCOUNTING—Graduate accountant or full charge bookkeeper for Washington area NY based construction firm. Applicants must have construction accounting experience and be able to prepare cost reports, requisitions, certified payroll, in addition to general accounting duties.

> ACCOUNTANT—For small business oriented accounting firm.

None of these furnish any details of the job requirements beyond those reported here, and all request résumés. Except for the last one, which furnishes extremely little information, all give fairly good indications of what they consider to be necessary experience qualifications. So even though accounting is not exactly a rapidly changing professional field, as computers and many others are today, there are specialties within the field. It is interesting to note, however, that none of the listings mentions computers, although the accountant who has some computer knowledge and capability would usually do well to mention that in applying for a job—it's a definite major asset to an accountant, especially today, when even one-employee accounting offices are becoming computerized.

## DIFFICULT-TO-RESPOND-TO SOLICITATIONS

Sometimes the advertisement provides little or no detail, as the fourth of those accountant-wanted advertisements reveals. In that notice, all you can learn is that an accounting firm specializing in services to small businesses wants an accountant. (Without proper punctuation, that advertisement could be interpreted as a small accounting firm which is business-oriented, rather than an accounting firm which is oriented to small business, but since that would make little sense, the latter interpretation is inferred.) There is no suggestion as to the size of the firm or whether the accountant wanted will handle all the needs of a small office, head up a group of people, or specialize somewhere in a large accounting office. This makes it rather difficult to tailor your response, of course.

Here is another example of a difficult-to-interpret advertisement—difficult, to know exactly how to tailor your response:

> GRAPHIC ARTS PERSON—Aggressive individual to organize advertising for wholesale distributor with locations in MD, VA, and N. Carolina. Automotive parts background desirable.

That's a rather cryptic notice. Just what is a "graphic arts person"? An artist? An advertising copywriter who knows how to use graphic arts? (Remember, printing, engraving, and several other things are included in "graphic arts" as much as are illustrating and painting themselves.) Just what kind of individual is this advertiser really seeking? Or does the advertiser really know?

The latter question is not an idle one. There are cases where an employer wants something done, but does not really know what kind of individual to seek as an employee to handle the work, possibly because the work entails entering upon a new function for that employer; a function that is unfamiliar. The employer is, therefore, floundering a bit in the quest for an employee to carry out this new function, not really knowing what kinds of people handle such functions or what proper qualifying experience is. In the case of this "graphic arts person," for example, the advertiser may be making the all-too-typical mistake of confusing graphic arts and illustrating with advertising, as though the functions were synonymous. (This confusion has led more than one graphic-arts firm to disaster in trying to qualify automatically as an advertising agency.)

The confusion is understandable, in a way. Because so much of traditional advertising revolved around signs, posters, and print advertising, there was a continual need for graphic arts people. Even its more recent expansion into TV commercials has entailed a good share of graphic arts functions, so that those who are not familiar with the advertising field often tend to be unaware of all the other functions of copywriters, account executives, and others who do the daily work of creating advertising in its many forms. Since that advertisement cited here calls for an "aggressive individual to *organize* advertising" activities (emphasis added), it is likely that what Mr. Wholesale Distributor really needs is not an illustrator, but someone who would probably qualify as an account executive in an advertising agency.

Coping with these kinds of solicitations can be something of a problem. Sending these advertisers a standard résumé is an out-and-out gamble against long odds. The probability is great that the advertisers don't know just what they want or need, but plan to study the résumés drawn in by their advertisements and educate themselves thereby, finally selecting those résumés which appear promising (in retrospect) and inviting the writers in for interviews. And those interviews will provide further education for the advertiser, and help solidify decisions about what is properly qualifying and who appears best suited to the needs.

In short, employers do not always know what they want or need, and look to respondents to help them discover their own needs. It is important to understand this, of course, if you are to respond effectively. These cases are very much like some cases of organizations soliciting proposals from contracting firms: Often the organization does not know exactly what they need or want, but only that they have a problem of some sort. Soliciting proposals is, therefore, often more than providing an opportunity for some business; sometimes it is a way of saying to prospective contractors, *Here is my problem/general need. Tell me what you think I ought to do about it, and if I agree with you, I'll pay you* [issue a contract to you] *to help me by doing it for me.*

Of course, that's a golden opportunity for you to get in your best shot and almost guarantee that you will be invited in for an interview, at which you can do some heavy selling. But you must be sure that you have evaluated the situation correctly. It is possible that the employer knows exactly what he or she wants, but has either neglected to be as specific as he or she should have been or prefers to be general because it will thereby draw a great many more responses.

If the advertisement has included a telephone number or anything to identify the advertiser, a visit or telephone call may be most helpful. Asking a few questions judiciously—and it is perfectly proper to do so, explaining that you are doing so in order to respond most effectively and supply the most useful information—will probably help you get the information you need to prepare a response tailored to the requirement. That failing, as it may very well, you have only two options:

1. Prepare a generalized super-résumé and cross your fingers.

2. Say frankly in your letter/résumé that you do not have enough information for the response you would prefer to make, but will be happy to supply more information as soon as you've had the opportunity to get that information. *In the meanwhile*, you say, *here are a few facts about what I can offer*. And you then provide a choice selection of your accomplishments which you believe relate to the job advertised. And/or seek more information by methods to be described shortly.

## TAILORING A SUPER-RÉSUMÉ TO THE ORGANIZATION

The kinds of submittal we have been discussing are in response to specific job openings which have been advertised and for which applications are solicited. But you cannot afford to rely on advertised openings only; there are other opportunities, which you must seek out and exploit. Aside from the brokers—employment agencies, recruiters, and "job shop" or temporaries enterprises—there are at least these prospects and possibilities to be followed up:

1. Applications to organizations who appear to have activities which would be relevant to your own field.

2. "Contacts" you can make at such events as trade shows, conventions, conferences, and other such occurrences.

3. Leads you can get from such special placement offices as those of your former college or vocational school, professional or trade associations you belong to, friends and relatives, and strangers you happen to make casual contacts.

That last-named category, friends and relatives, ought to include also the network contacts mentioned earlier. You should, throughout your career, keep a file of all the individuals you encounter, especially those you have any sort of career, professional, or business relationships with. You should try to maintain those contacts in any way you can, such as by attending those special events and belonging to organizations. Such acquaintances are a rich source of leads for you to follow up. In many cases, you'll learn of a specific opening, which may not even have been advertised or listed with a broker yet, and you can pursue it with a super-résumé tailored to the position and its requirements. However, even when you have nothing more to go on, in the way of a lead, than the name of an organization, you can tailor your super-résumé to that organization.

For example, going back to look at some of those computer-field jobs that were advertised, look at what they say and what the advertisement tells you *between the lines*—by enabling you to *infer* certain things: The first advertiser actually specified that the experience qualification could be either commercial or government. The second one made it clear enough that a military background—Army—was favored, if not required. The third gave little hint of any special applications field required, but the fourth made it clear enough that the work concerned nuclear power. Too, for the computer expert, the cabalistic computer-language designations often provide clues to the applications field. The experienced computer expert knows, for example, that FORTRAN is used for mathematical manipulations, primarily in scientific applications, and all the other codes or acronyms have some meanings easily inferred by those experienced in the profession.

In fact, the advertiser often expects the respondent to understand the codes and jargon, and to respond specifically to them. That itself—the ability to respond to jargon—is a sign of proper qualifications. Once, when I instructed my personnel manager to insert an advertisement for writers and editors who were familiar with cold-type publications, the personnel manager demurred that maybe some of the readers would not know what "cold type" means. My answer was that the people I was looking for would know the term, and if they didn't, they were not the people I was looking for.

However, suppose you wish to send an application to Acme Information Systems, Inc. You don't know of any specific openings there, but you do know that they employ computer specialists of all kinds, so they ought to be a good prospect for you. Since you don't know of any specific requirements there—or if there are, in fact, any openings at the moment—how can you tailor your super-résumé to the need?

One thing you can do is determine what kinds of work the company does, beyond the mere fact that they are into computers. Here are just a few of the activities you might encounter in any "information systems" organization:

Computer programming in general.
Computer services in kind.
Computer systems design, such as hardware specifications.
Information-systems consulting.

Indexing and abstracting documents.
Designing library systems.
Scientific programming.
Commercial applications only.
Government applications, general.
Military applications only.
Facilities management (operating the client's system).
On-site services only.
In-house services only.

And even these are only a scratch on the surface of this field; there are dozens of ways in which an organization might specialize and hundreds of possible combinations of services an organization might offer. Without having some understanding of this, you are stabbing blindly in the dark. Your super-résumé might be terrific—enormously effective—but never get into the right hands.

You cannot go at the business of job-seeking blindly. It must be an organized, intelligent, directed effort, if you are to get results with any degree of efficiency. When you are approaching organizations in general, without aiming at a known opening, you must know two things about each and every one of your prospects:

1. What kinds of jobs the organization provides. And you must know what kind of work/services/products the organization produces, if you are to make reasonable inferences about the kinds of jobs that exist there.

2. The names of the individuals to whom you should address your super-résumés, preferably their personal names and job titles, but at the least their functional titles and departments.

If you do not have this information, what are the chances that your super-résumé will land in the right hands? The answer is *not very good*, of course. Addressed to the personnel department, a super-résumé will drive the personnel manager slightly mad with frustration: what do you do with this? It doesn't seem to be a résumé, and yet it isn't addressed to anyone especially. Therefore, what most personnel departments would do is either put your super-résumé in the in-basket or a dead file, never to emerge in the light of day again, or send you a form letter advising you that there are no openings and thanking you for your interest. Addressed to no one in particular, your envelope will be opened by the mail room or by a secretary, depending on the size of the organization, and from there it is likely to wander almost anywhere, quite possibly to the personnel office, where people tend to send anything they don't quite understand.

## HOW TO GET THE INFORMATION YOU NEED

There are several ways to get information about an organization. Let's take them in their proper order:

1. If your lead is from some personal contact, pump your contact for as much information as you can. Ask, also, if your contact can supply the names of anyone else who might have useful information to pass on.

2. Use the telephone to call the company. Try the personnel manager, but without tipping the personnel manager off that you intend to send your résumé directly to some manager. Use a ruse; tell the personnel manager that you are interested in the company, as a possible future employer. Of course, you'll be advised that there are no openings at present. That's okay; you're not looking for a job today, but checking for next year, when you get out of school. Better yet, you're doing a report [thesis, dissertation, magazine article] on the industry, want to write up that organization: who should you call and ask for appointments in the company? Who would be most knowledgeable? What are the various departments? Who heads each one up? What is the background of the company? Are there brochures or annual reports available?

3. The personnel manager is not the only one you can approach this way, and sometimes not the best one either. Some companies have public information offices and advertising departments who can supply lots of useful information. And sometimes you can get acquainted with the secretary of a high executive, who can be exceedingly helpful.

4. The public library is a big help. You can look up most companies in the *Thomas Register, Standard & Poor*, and *Dun & Bradstreet*. Those directories will not only furnish listings of various kinds of companies of interest in whatever geographic areas you wish to know about, but they furnish detailed information about the companies— organization, names of managers and executives, and many other

details. Ask your librarian, and you'll be surprised at how much help you will get.

5. Read the trade journals and the financial/business sections of your bigger newspapers. Read the advertisements of the companies to determine what businesses they are in. And they need not be in a business similar to the one you are now with or were last with. If you're a computer expert, you need not necessarily work for a computer company or a computer-services company; you may very well find an attractive job with any organization that uses a computer. If you are a copywriter, you may work for an advertising agency, but you may also work for the advertising department of any company. Broaden your perspective when you are seeking opportunity; it often exists in places you never thought about, perhaps places of whose very existence you did not know.

6. Go to every event that offers the possibility of making a useful contact. In my own case, I attended a meeting of the Society of Technical Writers and Publishers some years ago, because someone invited me to attend. (I had not joined the organization at the time.) There I listened to a Dr. Richard Walther explain his work with an educational-services firm, which intrigued me. After the meeting, during the coffee and cake social hour that followed, I sought the gentleman out and inquired further. He invited me to visit him at his office. I did so and eventually that led directly to a job offer, which I accepted, and which made rather substantial changes in my career—good changes. Oddly enough, I was not happy with my employment at that time, and was interested in a change. But a job was the furthest thing from my mind that evening—until I spoke with Dr. Walther and he suggested an interest in doing business together.

7. If possible, hire out as a temporary. Many good job offers are extended to individuals who have shown their potential as temporaries. Be aware, however, that you may be asked to sign an agreement that you will not accept such direct employment with any client of your agent before some specific time—perhaps three months or six months—after your employment on the client's premises as a temporary. Try to avoid signing such agreements, if you are hiring out as a temporary but plan to seek a permanent position. Or, if the agency selling you as a temporary (which agency is your actual employer, technically) insists on such an agreement, bargain and ne-

gotiate for the most favorable terms possible. You can probably get the terms softened, if you try and if you are fair—agree that the agency has a moral right to earn some money from your employment for a few months, at least. (My personal experience with such employers is that they are reasonable enough, if approached properly and negotiated with in a businesslike manner—with due regard for their interests and needs, as well as your own.)

8. If you choose to run *situations wanted* advertisements, as many people do, use the same philosophy that you do when writing your super-résumé: Focus your copy on the offer you are making—what you can do for the prospective employer, and not on what you expect the employer to do for you. Don't forget that you are the seller and the employer is the buyer: The burden of making the trade attractive is on you.

9. Create your special opportunities to meet new people in your own field or in fields related somehow to yours, and draw special attention to yourself by getting into one or both of two special activities: writing and speaking. Offer to speak about your specialty, whatever it may be, to interested groups of professionals and businesspeople—there are usually associations and groups who are glad to get new speakers, especially speakers who do not charge fees—and very much the same thing may be said for various publications, such as the newsletters and magazines associated with your own and related fields. Offer them articles about your own specialty, and you'll get many published, with the accompanying attention that will be helpful. Find out, also, about seminars and other such events and don't merely attend: participate. Organizations and individuals sponsoring such events are often delighted to find new speakers.

10. Offer consulting services in your specialty. You'll make many valuable contacts this way, and probably find yourself getting either excellent leads for jobs or being offered jobs spontaneously. And you'll be earning a bit of income too, while you're doing this. Note that *consulting* is a most flexible term, and technical/professional people hiring out as temporaries consider themselves to be consultants. That is, you do not necessarily have to become a temporary through the services of a broker or agent; it is possible to do it all yourself and keep all the profits, while you are in total control. You can use direct-mail, brochures, cards, advertisements, bulletin-board notices, and/

or super-résumés to offer your services and win assignments. Usually best, however, are speaking, writing, and those contact-making activities described because most consulting assignments come about through contacts and recommendations. And you may decide that you like this job—being your own employee—best of all.

# 11

## The Follow-Up

*Because it is part of an overall concept and not a gimmick, the super-résumé must be used properly, in concert with the whole theme.*

### TYPICAL FIRST-REACTIONS TO SUPER-RÉSUMÉS

**H**AVING mailed out your super-résumés, whether in response to advertised openings or those all-too-common invitations to "drop a résumé in the mail," you are going to get at least some responses. And they are going to be varied. The response you want is an invitation to come by for an interview—perhaps to "have a chat," as some respondents put it cautiously. You'll probably not get that as a first reaction very often. You're more likely to get a somewhat puzzled request for a résumé, perhaps by mail, perhaps by telephone. Should you then send off one of those conventional résumés, you will have probably nullified whatever your super-résumé accomplished, and you'll be back to square one.

The respondent will not have recognized, of course, that you have sent a résumé, albeit a super-condensed, super-focused one. The request for a résumé is a reliable indication that your super-résumé has touched a nerve: the employer is interested enough to want to know more. You've accomplished your immediate purpose, reached your first objective: To get attention and arouse enough interest to draw a response. The worst thing you can do now is to actually send a résumé; that will only lose for you what your super-résumé has already accomplished. Still, you can't very well simply refuse; that would also wipe out the gain you have already made and probably result in ending all efforts by the employer to get more information. Employers do generally operate on the premise that they are in total control, that any applicant is merely a supplicant, and that they are free to dictate all the terms. To some degree, you must pretend to go along with that premise, and yet manage somehow to operate on the basis of making a trade, not seeking favor. Therefore, you never polarize the situation by a direct refusal to supply a résumé immediately. Instead, you use dilatory tactics, in which you apparently comply, but actually maneuver.

## SAYING *YES, BUT*

You may—and probably will—have to supply a résumé at some point in your negotiations with every prospective employer. But it is not yet the time to do so. (If you study the art of negotiations, you'll find that timing is always a critically important factor, as it is in this situation.) You floated some attractive bait, and you've gotten a solid nibble—no more. You need to let out a bit more line next.

Smart salespeople know that you should never argue with a prospect, never say *no*, not even to a prospect's objections. Instead, you learn to always respond, when you wish to differ with a prospect, with *yes, but*. And that is the way you respond now to requests for a résumé. You agree to supply one, but you maneuver to supply a résumé on *your* terms, in *your* way. The most basic way to say *yes, but* in this situation is to explain that you don't really have a standard résumé, but will be most happy to prepare one and bring it along to the interview. Like any good salesperson, you are closing by assuming the order (interview, in this case). You can explain that you believe a preprinted or standard résumé does not do you justice nor help an employer very much because a prospective employer is entitled to know about a prospective employee those things most relevant to the job and the organization's needs and interests. Or, if you prefer, you may explain that your existing résumé is terribly out of date, but you are at work preparing an up-to-date one, which you will bring along to the interview. But whatever ploy you use to say *yes, but,* keep it short and be brisk about it. Don't give the other party too much time to push the matter, but attempt immediately to set a time and day for the interview. Ask, for example, when it would be convenient to see you, and if that doesn't bring a swift response, try suggesting times you have open.

The caller may attempt to counter by trying to interview you or get the equivalent of a résumé over the telephone. Refuse to be interviewed over the telephone. Take command and keep command. Being interviewed over the telephone—even answering questions spontaneously—is an even worse mistake than supplying a résumé at this point. Be evasive, repeat that you'll be happy to supply any information needed at the interview. In general, keep the telephone conversation as short as possible, with only one objective: to set a time and date for an interview. As soon as you have done that, terminate the conversation promptly. Even if you have not succeeded and you perceive that you are not going to be able to do so at the time, get off the telephone as quickly as possible. Make an excuse, if you have to: someone at the door, some intermediate emergency, your other telephone ringing, or some other ploy.

One thing you want to do definitely, however, is learn the name and title of your caller, and if the caller is a personnel manager or anyone who is obviously not the decision-maker who would normally interview candidates for the job, try to get the name of that individual. It will be useful for your next step, in the event you do not succeed in getting an appointment set up for an interview.

The same considerations apply if you hear from a prospective employer by mail. Perhaps you have received a form letter or even a personal letter requesting a résumé. You can respond by telephone or by letter. Here are some things to think about when deciding how to respond:

1. The request for a résumé or more information, even if a form letter, indicates strong interest on the part of the employer. You have now converted a lead into a solid prospect. It's now worth making some special effort.

2. A telephone response to the letter may be in order. If the letter was signed by a personnel manager (or administrator of some sort wearing the personnel manager's hat), one thing you want to do is learn the name of the individual who would interview you and make the decision. You may be able to do that in a telephone call. Or if the letter was signed by a manager who would probably be that person, a telephone call directly to that individual may enable you to get that interview set up.

3. You can do the same things in a response by letter, of course. Once again stress the major points made in your original super-résumé, perhaps add a point or two to strengthen the original (since obviously there is some interest now).

4. You might wish to consider preparing and sending a résumé of sorts. However, if you do so, do with great caution. Do not send anything that appears to be anything remotely resembling a full account of your educational and working history. Whatever you choose to send in response should be obviously far less than a full history and account. In fact, it probably should be little more than a slightly expanded super-résumé. And with it, explain clearly that you are still in the process of bringing your résumé up to date and will bring it with you to the interview, but here are a couple of items to expand a bit on your original letter. (Remember, that super-résumé purported to be merely a brief letter expressing interest in learning more about the opportunities to be had in this employer's organization.)

Whatever you do, never lose sight of your objective: To arrange an interview. And to do that, you must not give the store away prematurely. The employer wants more information about what you have to offer. You want an opportunity to be interviewed so that you can do some selling. It's a negotiation already—not for the job, but for the conditions and terms under which you'll supply that additional information. Obviously, you can't win the negotiation by surrendering to the other party's demands, which is what supplying more than a teaser of additional information would be.


## YOU MUST KEEP THE INITIATIVE

One thing salespeople learn is that there are many prospects who are induced to become customers only after several attempts to win their patronage. The field salesperson, for example, may call on a prospect a dozen times before landing a first order, and may then do business with that new customer for many years thereafter. Those selling by mail learn the same lesson: Many people will respond to sales appeals after the third, fourth, fifth, or even more appeals, but not to the first or second appeals.

There are many reasons for this. One of them is "name recognition." The first time the prospect hears from or about you, it usually doesn't register. After two or three exposures, the prospect begins to recognize your name. Subtly, your name begins to assume some importance, some aura of dependability, respectability, and other attributes that attach to anything that becomes familiar. (The American in London or Paris is absolutely delighted to discover "Joe's American Hot Dog Emporium," which must be absolutely great because it's American.)

It is not different in job finding. Employers are people too, and they have the same drives, motivations, reactions, impulses, and psychological influences that the rest of us do. Once, while working as a professional temporary in engineering work, I wanted to work at the General Electric Company's space department in Philadelphia. It was quite a while before I was finally invited in for an interview. When the interview was concluded and I was advised that I was to report for work the following Monday, the interviewer said to me, "Who are you working for?" That was a reference to which of the engineering "job shops" would have me on its payroll, while I actually spent my days working at the GE establishment. It seems that no less than five of these firms had sent GE my résumé, and the manager there decided he wanted me to work there, but it was a matter of indifference to him which firm was my employer of record. It was seeing so many copies of my résumé—and they were not all identical, having been written and placed in these several companies' files at different times—that made my name a familiar one there at the GE plant.

For this reason alone it is necessary to repeat your mailings. Making your name and what you offer familiar to your prospects is an excellent way to draw offers, whether you are sending your super-résumés out "cold turkey" (to firms who have not announced openings, but who appear to be good prospects for you) or in direct response to announced openings and invitations to submit résumés.

In this manner, you can manage to keep the initiative. It is entirely frustrating and unproductive to send out a batch of super-résumés and sit idly waiting for responses. You may get those responses, but then again you may not. Even if your offer is the most attractive one the employer has received, you may wait and lose out in the end. Here are a couple of rather typical situations that produce such disappointing results:

## PROCRASTINATION

Employers are human in their failings, as well as their virtues. The busy manager may keep postponing doing whatever must be done to set up interviews, conduct them, and make a hiring decision. There is always tomorrow. (It isn't only in Latin countries that *mañana* is an occupational disease.) In these situations, it can take an incredibly long time for final action, even when the organization has run large, expensive advertising in their quest for people.

## BUREAUCRACY

Large companies—and today, even small companies—suffer increasingly from the disease that afflicts governments: bureaucracy. In bureaucracy, the end is never as important as the means. Someone performs the personnel function, whether it is a full-time personnel manager or an administrator who wears more than one hat. There are forms and reports—paperwork—attached to all hiring. There is scheduling of interviews—no one gets hired with only one interview; there is always a series. In the tedious, time-consuming shuffle of all this, the applications of even the best qualified and most attractive candidates tend to get lost and somehow vanish from view.

## UNEXPECTED OCCURRENCES

Before the hiring originally planned is carried out something new and unexpected happens, and plans are changed. You may have even been slated on the calendar to have been called for interview, but before it was arranged, a nephew of the big boss was hired; someone decided that the job did not need to be filled; a reorganization wiped out the opening; the individual who was to do the hiring left the organization or was transferred somewhere; or any of dozens of other events shelved or terminated the process of hiring someone.

In general, the longer the process takes, the greater the possibility that something will come along to interrupt, delay, and possibly terminate the entire process. (Murphy's Law explains this clearly: Whatever can go wrong will go wrong.) Conversely, whatever you can do to keep the process moving and even accelerate it, the greater is the possibility that it will proceed to a successful conclusion and that you will be part of that successful conclusion.

It is important that you do not let the initiative slip from your own grasp. Remember the corollary to Murphy's Law (Holtz's Law): Disasters happen unaided; you must *make* the good things happen. You cannot depend on circumstance or chance. Hope and prayer won't do it. Only action will. Luck is a reliable factor and works for you—when you help it work for you.

## MAKING THE JOB HUNT A FULL CAMPAIGN

To use that super-résumé and the whole idea successfully, you must regard your job-finding process as something considerably more than a casual effort. For best results, it must be a full-fledged marketing campaign, with all the stops out and no punches pulled. You should plan to make at least three successive mailings to your list. Whether you use the same letter/super-résumé for each mailing or develop a new one for each mailing is less important than making the several mailings. However, it is usually more effective to make each mailing a little different from the one before it. In the case of using the methods advocated here, however, you should keep each of the letters you send out in the same philosophy as that super-résumé: short, punchy, strictly business, focused sharply. However, that is not all there is to it. Remember that one of the concepts behind this repetitive-mailing idea is to gain name recognition. Therefore, it is a definite advantage to do whatever will help accomplish that. One way to accomplish this is to have your own, distinctive letterhead for typing up your super-résumés and/or reproducing those super-résumés you may have chosen to make standard mailers, for purposes of this campaign. Here are a few ways to make that letterhead and those mailers distinctive, and yet in good taste:

1. Many large print shops who specialize in business stationery offer some quite impressive designs, some of them with gold- or silver-leaf lettering, two-color printing, and other devices which draw attention and reflect a great deal of "class" by their very appearance. You can find such vendors in the advertisements of many business magazines. You'll find such products and services offered by both printers and by large office-supply vendors. A few suggested sources will be listed in the last chapter of this book, as well.

2. You can use some of the art illustrated in Figure 11 to liven up your super-résumé and give it a distinctive touch. But it is advisable to settle on something that you will use consistently, in each and every mailing, so that it is an aid to the addressee in recognizing your super-résumé. Be careful, however, and exercise some restraint: It is easy to get carried away in this and overdo your use of graphic devices to a point of being in bad taste, an effect you do not want to achieve.

3. Design or have designed for you a distinctive *logo* for your letterhead and envelope. A logo (short for *logotype*) is a device distinctively your own—perhaps stylized initials, such as GE, IBM, and RCA use, or any other graphic representation.

4. Use paper that is itself distinctive, but be careful that it is not of a color or shade that makes it difficult to read what is typed or printed on it. Color or shade is not, however, the only way that paper can be "different" and distinctive: The paper can be different by being "deckle-edged," which refers to a ragged edge that is characteristic of certain expensive papers. It can be of special weight, since all papers are of different weights (thicknesses, that is.) It can be of different body, especially of an unusual one. For example, there is a paper that is not excessively expensive but closely resembles parchment in its texture and feel. Try to use a matching envelope, especially if you rely on the paper to be different and distinctive.

5. Draw special attention to your submittal by something special about the delivery itself, such as discreet "envelope copy." That refers to some message on the outside of the envelope itself, something you will find commonly on those fat, overstuffed envelopes that you identify as "junk mail." However, you cannot print a sales message on the outer envelope without running the dual risk of appearing to be in atrociously bad taste and possibly thus giving offense, and perhaps having your letter mistaken for junk mail and discarded promptly, perhaps without even opening it. However, you can have something printed on the envelope in bold type that says something such as PRIORITY, RUSH, POSTMASTER: PLEASE DO NOT DELAY, URGENT, or some other such words. The purpose of this is simply to foster recognition when your letter arrives for the second or third time, or perhaps even for the fourth or fifth time.

None of these things offers any *direct* help in winning the interview and the job, and don't make the mistake of relying on them for such help. But they do offer the indirect help of aiding the addressee in recognizing your super-résumé and remembering you, and that is all you should expect of these ideas—that they are mnemonic (memory-assisting).

For the very special case, such as the employer who has responded in some positive way but yet needs a bit of prodding to encourage progress toward an invitation to be interviewed, you might wish to consider some more dramatic methods, such as delivery by special messenger. Such services are available in many cities and are not excessively costly (although you wouldn't wish to spend this kind of money to deliver a large number of super-résumés). If you do this, be sure to affix some prominent label or tag to the envelope that lets the recipient know that it was delivered by special messenger. Even if this lands it in a company mailroom or on some secretary's desk, if it is addressed to an individual by name and has some prominent label or is in some prominent special outer envelope such as most express services use, it will be rushed to the desk of the addressee, in all probability. And to carry off the ploy properly, your message ought to say some thing such as: "Knowing your need for the right person is great, and your time is valuable, I have taken the liberty of rushing this to you by special messenger to help you in reaching a decision quickly. I will make myself available to you on short notice for serious discussion and swift resolution."

The story was told, in a recent seminar on proposal writing, that RCA delivered a proposal to a bank via armored car. With armed guards standing by with weapons ready, an armed messenger carried the package to the desk of a startled bank president who read the outer message advising him that the contents of the proposal were worth several million dollars and therefore the precautions in safeguarding it. The report states that RCA succeeded in winning the contract proposed by their dramatic delivery method. Of course, the method won them very special attention, and cost them only $25, the report concludes.

## LAYING IT ON THE LINE

In pursuing the job opportunity it is a mistake to be subtle or overly clever. It is a mistake to evade stating your goals directly and plainly. Do not confuse ordinary tact, diplomacy, and good taste with obfuscation—failing to make yourself clear.

You need to be clear and plain in your appeals, in your letters and super-résumés. You are in quest of a job, and are plainly offering a trade. You wish to negotiate a deal—services for money and whatever else the job will offer in compensation, and your immediate goal is to make your initial offer sufficiently attractive to provoke interest. It's not different from the grocer who carefully selects the best apples or tomatoes to put on top of the basket and even washes and polishes them carefully to make them more attractive. It's not different from the merchant who offers customers a free taste of some new delicacy, so that their interest may be aroused. Nor does the grocer make any mystery of his motives: It's quite clear that the taste is a sample intended to lure you into buying something.

Do not pretend that your second or third mailing is anything but a second or third mailing. Make it plain to your prospect that it is, in case the prospect does not realize and appreciate that fact. Use any device possible—there are several ways—but make it clear. However, also take advantage of the opportunity. Remember that every liability is an asset turned inside out: Reverse the liability, and you will have an asset. If you believe that any prospect who has not responded to your first or second appeal is a poor prospect, and that second, third, fourth, or successive mailings are a waste of time to prospects who are liabilities, consider this: The fact that you are still sending these prospects appeals is excellent evidence that you are quite serious, that you have a true interest in the organization and wish to work in its behalf, that you are determined and persistent, that you do not give up easily, that you are dependable, and so forth. Remember, it is the very fact that the employers have so far failed to respond that gives you this opportunity to build up the image after several mailings.

However, these are not necessarily automatic benefits. The prospect may or may not reason in such manner as to deduce and infer these things. In any case, it can do no harm and can only help to point these things out in some way, at least by making sure the prospect knows that this is not the first effort you have made to get attention here and discuss a trade of services for money (a job) seriously. Therefore, make sure that your successive letters carry the message.

One way is to number your letters. That, however, is pretty mechanical and even a bit subtle: The addressee may not understand what the numbers mean. A much better way is to make the matter clear in the copy itself. For example, you might open a letter along the lines of the following:

> It has been two weeks since I first responded to your recent advertisement for a full-charge bookkeeper. To refresh your memory, I offer the following:

That would be followed by either a repeat of what you said in your original super-résumé or by whatever you think might add to and strengthen what you said originally. But be as brief as you were originally and do not appear to be recriminating the employer for slowness of response to your submittal nor appear to be complaining. Try to appear to offer fresh information in a helpful vein. Here is another idea of a follow-up letter, perhaps a third mailout:

> I realize that you probably had no openings on your staff when I sent you my first and second expressions of interest in joining your company as an account executive. I am still seriously interested and eager to join your company, and contribute substantially to your success. To refresh your memory, here is a brief background summary:

There are other ways to say this, some of them even less subtle than the above, but not excessively "pushy" or offensive. For example:

> To help you keep your files up to date, here is the most recent account of the experience and abilities I wish to offer your organization as a package designer:

## HOW FREQUENTLY TO MAIL

In the case of answering printed advertisements, it is probably unrealistic to expect the advertiser to be able to sort through the responses and get back to anyone in less than two to three weeks. Therefore, it is generally of little use to follow up in less than two weeks after your initial response. In the case of "cold turkey" mailings, probably four weeks should be permitted to elapse before sending out a second mailing.

Blind advertisements pose a special problem in follow-up because they are usually addressed to a box number of the medium—the newspaper or magazine—and so are not assigned permanently to the advertiser. However, the newspaper will continue to send on the mail arriving addressed to that box number for at least four to six weeks, and experience demonstrates that many respondents answer advertising months later. Probably it would be wise to follow up an original submission to a box number about two weeks later. But responding to a blind advertisement brings up another matter.

Many people believe that it is to their advantage to answer such an advertisement only after a week or so has elapsed, on the theory that the bulk of the responses will arrive in the first few days. Therefore, their response would be buried in the pile if they responded immediately. But if they respond a week or so later, their response will be one of only a few and therefore get far more and better attention.

Alas! That is a fable like so many others. The fact is that usually the employer pays scant attention to any responses to a blind advertisement until the stream of responses has dwindled to a trickle, which may take a week or two. Meanwhile, all the résumés have been piling up, in no particular order, and will probably lie on a desk, collecting dust quietly until all or nearly all have been received. So it really makes little or no difference when you respond.

Another point: If the box number is a post-office box number, it is one the advertiser uses the year around. Therefore, you can continue to mail to that box number for as long as you wish.

## HOW TO STUDY ADVERTISING: A SPECIAL TIP

Most people seeking jobs claim that they study the help-wanted advertising to find the specific openings of interest. They study advertisements, not advertising. They, therefore, miss an important lesson to be learned: the *patterns* that emerge when you study the advertising, rather than the individual advertisements. Here is what I mean: If you study advertising carefully, you will perceive certain patterns emerging, some of which are most helpful. One of these patterns you will see is a distinct pattern of hiring by a given company, which indicates a large or long-term expansion may be underway. Therefore, it may be wise to make a special effort to pursue leads and job possibilities in general in that organization.

But sometimes a pattern of consistent hiring across an entire industry becomes apparent, and this can suggest the best job possibilities. For example, during the early years of computer development, careful study of help-wanted advertising would reveal what the industry was interested in at the time. For a period, there was a great demand for engineers with knowledge of magnetic-drum memory systems. There were periods of special interest in all kinds of specialized fields—magnetic cores, radar, stress analysis, aerodynamics, and sundry other fields. It became quite evident that one kind of specialist was in great demand, while another was in far lesser demand.

Watching major contract awards to corporations is another thing to be observant of, and these are usually reported in the business press. Again, the company with one or more new, large contracts inevitably is going to be hiring. And if they hire a great many specialists, they also must hire many support people to complement them and round out their staffs generally—a major expansion of a staff, means an expansion of the payroll, the billings, and other administrative activities, which means a need for accountants and other administrative people.

These are the kinds of input information that should guide you on where and how to mount your follow-up campaign most energetically.

# 12

# The Interview

*The moment of truth arrives for both you and the employer. This is the real selling situation, and you can be—should be—in control of it.*

## SOME FACTS ABOUT INTERVIEWS AND INTERVIEWERS

**T**HE interview is what everything has been targeted on. The interview is the first occasion in your job search which may result directly in an offer. Finally, it is the first chance you have to close, to sum up everything you have presented so far and try to consummate it all. It is, therefore, a critical event, one that requires skill on your part. But first it requires some knowledge, some awareness of reality:

Naively, most of us assume that the individual who is to conduct the interview is skilled in interviewing or is at least sure-footed and knows exactly what to do and how to do it. This is rarely the case. More often the interviewer is much less certain of what he or she is trying to accomplish than you are. In the absence of experience in interviewing and any clear set of guidelines or objectives, the typical interviewer in these situations tends to focus attention primarily on "wringing you out" on your skills relevant to the job. And perhaps even on some skills that are not relevant to the job. This is particularly true if you are in some technological field because generally the individual interviewing you is the one you are likely to be reporting to, and he or she feels most comfortable when discussing the various skills and knowledge that are necessary to do the job. In my case, most of the interviews I was subjected to were oral technical examinations (and in some cases I had to first undergo and pass actual written examinations) in electronics and its many specialties, such as test equipment, radar, digital logic, automation, and other areas, some of them rather arcane. (And some of those written examinations were general intelligence tests, such as the Otis.)

You may run into situations where you must undergo more than one interview. You may have a first interview with a personnel manager or other administrator. That is likely to be virtually an oral application, in which you are asked questions similar to those you have already answered on the company's form. And, in fact, frequently this interview consists primarily of reviewing the information you have thus supplied.

In some companies there is a behavioral psychologist who spends a day or two every week interviewing applicants for the company. The psychologist will ask questions and draw you into conversation intended to reveal whatever a psychologist believes can be revealed by conversation and answers to pointed questions. And you may have taken a test or two before that, designed to reveal aptitudes and psychological profiles.

It is also possible that you will be interviewed by a low- or mid-level manager other than the one for whom you would be working, if hired. Frequently, that manager is one who reports to the manager who will make the final decision and who has assigned the lower-level manager to the interviewing chore. Presumably, the report rendered by your interviewer will be the main determinant of whether you will be made an offer or not.

Frequently you will find your interviewer appears somewhat nervous, and perhaps quite ill at ease. Your interviewer is nervous because interviewing can be a stress situation for both parties, when neither is especially experienced in the process and both are anxious about the outcome. You are anxious because you want to earn a job offer; the interviewer is nervous because he or she tends to dread the outcome: If you are adjudged not suitable, there is the unpleasant business of turning you down, although you won't be told that bluntly, in most cases. If the decision is to make you an offer, there is the stress resulting from fear that the decision may not be a wise one— that you won't work out well on the job, and the interviewer will have to admit to having made a mistake of judgment. If the interviewer is conducting the interview for a higher-level manager, there is the stress of being judged by a superior as being wise or unwise, competent or incompetent in the inexact science of interviewing applicants for jobs.

On at least one occasion an interviewer admitted not only that he was conducting the interview for his boss, but also that he didn't know what kind of job the boss had in mind. He admitted this in a sort of lefthanded way of apologizing for the vagueness of the process and for his inability to answer the interviewee's questions about the prospective job. He simply did not know what his boss had in mind. Fortunately, this is a relatively rare situation. Here is why it is especially undesirable to be trapped into this kind of interview:

In selling, it is generally accepted as a necessity that you must "qualify" your sales prospect before investing any significant amount of time or money in making the selling effort. And qualifying a prospect means simply determining whether the prospect is able to buy what you are selling—has the money, authority, leverage, or whatever is necessary to make the purchase. If you are spending time trying to sell someone who cannot make the purchase and can't even exercise decisive influence over the sale, you are probably wasting your time and money. It is most unlikely that you will ever close the sale.

Even in those intermediate situations, where the prospect *may* be able to make the purchase—but may not be able to, also—you are risking the waste of time and money in pursuing the sales effort. You must, therefore, weigh the risk and decide whether the possibility of success is worth the risk.

This is the situation where you are interviewed by someone who is not the decision-maker, who can only recommend—you may be wasting your time. There is little or nothing you can do, however, to bypass that intermediary who has been assigned to interview you. You can only hope that either this intermediary's recommendation will be positive or that you can manage somehow to get an additional interview, higher up, with the decision-maker. There is also a special hazard here, which we'll have a look at presently.

On the other hand, you may run into an entirely different situation—one which is more the exception than the rule—in which the interviewer is confident, sure-footed, quite experienced in interviewing, and knows exactly what he or she is about and is trying to do. In many ways, that is a better situation than the other, even if it may prove to be a bit more stressful. But this is the opposite extreme of the situations first discussed, and in the average case the situation will fall between these extremes: You are likely to be interviewed by the manager who will make the hiring decision and to whom you will report, if you are hired, and that manager is likely to be someone who is not especially expert at interviewing nor especially joyful at doing it, but has some idea of what to do and how to do it.

## INTERVIEWING STYLES

There are certain distinct interviewing styles, most of them not very scientific, and perhaps not even deliberate designs, but reflections of the interviewer's own personality, uncertainty, fears, anxieties, and/or other personal characteristics. There are those, for example, who are intent on how many words a minute you can type, what you know about word processors, whether you understand Ohm's Law, how well you write proposals, and other matters, dealing entirely with the various areas of job skills. Along with this kind of question comes questions about previous employers and your duties there, in a kind of review of your résumé.

There are those who believe in what have been called *stress interviews*, in which the interviewer deliberately places you under maximum stress, testing your ability to handle frustration, pressure, and other stresses. The technique here is to challenge you in many ways, probing with apparent suspicion at all your answers, pressing hard for details, even trivial and probably long-forgotten details. I know of a case, for example, where both the President and Vice-President of a small company interviewed the applicant all afternoon, continued the interview over dinner, and then returned to the office to carry it on until late evening before letting the victim go. It was more of an inquisition than it was an interview, despite the fact that the individual was finally hired.

There are charmingly casual and disarming interviewers, jovial, smiling, informal. The interview appears to be merely a lengthy chat, and it may be. But it probably is not. You are probably in the hands of an experienced interviewer, who draws out information by a specific technique. You are probably being closely studied and carefully observed during this informal chat, when—presumably—your guard is down, and you speak frankly.

There are sometimes those interviewers who appear to identify far more with you than they do with the company. They talk familiarly about fields in which both of you specialize and about "them"—the company—what they are like, how they are to work for, what they demand, what they expect, and other conversation in a just-between-the-two-of-us frame of reference. They may be entirely sincere or they may be using some subtle means for drawing you out. The probability, however, is that they really feel more affinity and commonness of existence with you than with the company.

You may encounter an interviewer who is one of those totally organized and methodical individuals, who will have on his other desk a complete set of questions, drawn up in advance for the interview, and who will permit no deviations, but will draw you back firmly the minute you digress from the planned itinerary.

## PREPARING FOR THE INTERVIEW

Most people apparently go into an interview "cold"—without preparation. That is usually a mistake for several reasons:

You will waste valuable time asking questions to which you could have gotten the answers in advance.

You may appear more ignorant or less knowledgeable to your interviewer than you ought to be (or than he or she thinks you ought to be).

You will probably fail to take advantage of knowledge you could have gained in advance, which would have made you better able to control the interview.

The things you want to do in preparation for an interview concern learning as much as you can about the organization—what it does (services and products), where and how it operates, how large it is, how it is organized, who are the principal executives, nature of ownership (privately owned, closed corporation, public corporation, non-profit corporation, or other), and anything else you can learn about it. Perhaps you have already done much of this, as recommended earlier, using all the sources suggested. But also inquire around; among others you know who might be in a position to tell you something about the organization. You should know the name of the individual who is to interview you. Try to learn what you can about him or her through inquiry. Check with your librarian: the individual may be included in some published who's-who type of directory. (There are a large number of such directories, and you'll find many of them in most public libraries.)

Be prepared to answer questions based on your knowledge of job-related skills. Brush up especially on what the organization does. If you have been in radar design, for example, and are being interviewed by a company specializing in computer design, think out what you have learned in past employment that best relates to computers, as evidence of what you can bring to the company in technical capabilities. But also do some brushing up on computers, for it is computers they will want to talk about, not radar.

Dress conservatively. No one will ever fault you for dressing conservatively; but you may offend someone if you are too modish. No blue jeans, no matter how "in" you believe they are. Dress for the conventional, conservative, establishment's business world. If you're of the male persuasion, it's better if you don't have a beard or moustache, but if you do, be sure that both are neatly trimmed and not of some outlandish style. (Some men shave off beards and even moustaches when they are job hunting, and grow them back later.) If you're a woman, use your makeup in moderation and try to wear a reasonably conservative hair style. Cater to perceptions, even to establishment prejudices in what constitutes acceptable dress and general appearance. Those are not the areas in which to be excessively individualistic, innovative, and original.

One important area of advance preparation, the most important area, in fact, is "psyching yourself up"—developing the right mental set or philosophical attitude. This is the attitude you had or should have had when developing your super-résumé and conducting your campaign. It centers on having an adequate appreciation of your assets and capabilities, recognizing that you have something of value to trade with the employer. You must understand and accept that while the world at large regards an interview as a trial of the applicant, you must regard it differently: You must perceive the interview as two things:

1. A sales presentation, in which you trot out what you wish to sell—your personal services, for money and other compensations.
2. A negotiation, if and when the prospect appears interested enough to discuss terms for the trade.

Admittedly, the employer does not regard the situation this way. The employer prefers that conventional view in which you are on trial and he or she is judge and jury, deciding whether you are worthy and, if so, what your worthiness merits in an exchange. Were you to explain your view too bluntly, it would almost surely be interpreted as arrogance, and the interview would end abruptly. It is necessary to be reasonably tactful when selling and negotiating, of course. But it is not necessary to think of yourself as a supplicant placed on trial, and you will almost surely fare better if you have the confidence in your position that the recommended attitude ensures.

## THE RÉSUMÉ REQUEST

If you have managed, so far, to avoid giving your prospective employer a résumé, as recommended here, you have arrived at a point where the employer is going to once again ask you for a résumé. You may have, in fact, previously agreed to supply a résumé at the interview. However, it is far better if you can manage to stall further and not supply your résumé just yet.

First of all, don't bring the subject up at all, and perhaps the interviewer won't either. However, if you are asked for a résumé immediately upon entering the interviewer's office and being seated, at least try to avoid surrendering a résumé (if, indeed, you even brought one with you!). Here are a few dodges or excuses that appear to work reasonably well:

Explain that you are still working on updating your résumé, that the one you have is badly out of date and of very little help. (And for that reason you didn't bring one along.) However, you'll be happy to answer any and all questions—you'll supply a verbal résumé— and you'll send one or drop one off in a day or two. Say this disarmingly, smilingly, a bit sheepishly, and you'll probably get away with it without difficulty. (What can your interviewer do—refuse to carry on with the interview?)

Explain that you tried to write up your résumé for this interview especially, because you think the company is entitled to a résumé that relates most directly to the job opening, but you realized that you couldn't really do a decent job of it until you knew more about the company—until after you had been interviewed and had the chance to ask questions and learn the facts. And the promise to send in a résumé after the interview, of course.

Rummage around in your brief case, talking all the while, murmuring something about knowing that you have an old one here somewhere, and finally giving up the search, with an apologetic guess that you don't have one with you, after all. But anyway, it's an old, out-of-date one, and you're working on revising it. . . .

Have one prepared, if you are fearful of not being able to respond to the request otherwise, which is only partial, extremely brief, not much more informative than the super-résumé you supplied originally. Offer it apologetically, explaining that it isn't complete yet because you've been updating your résumé, but maybe it will be of some help until you can send in a completely up-to-date one in a day or two.


## TAKING CHARGE

Before the interview is more than a few minutes old, one of you, the interviewer or the interviewee, is going to be in charge of the interview. You may run into situations where you are not successful in your effort to take charge of the interview, but in probably the great majority of cases, you can take charge of the interview, if you set out to do so and go about it properly.

The first requisite for taking charge of the interview is the determination to do so, along with the conviction that you can do so. It is not something you can do fearfully or half-heartedly, but only with great confidence and a most positive approach.

The second requisite is the mental set we talked about earlier. You are not here to be put on trial and examined. You are here to complete the sales presentation you started earlier with your super-résumé, and then to negotiate, if you and the employer are both satisfied with each other. You cannot accomplish either goal if you are passive or negative. You must be positive, aggressive (tactfully aggressive, of course), with clearly perceived objectives.

The third requisite is mental dexterity. There is no preconceived plan for taking charge which is likely to work for you in every case. Usually, to take charge of an interview, you size the situation up spontaneously and devise your plan, while reacting to the conditions you encounter. Perhaps a for-instance or two will illustrate that:

One way to take charge of an interview is to steer the conversation in the direction you believe is of greatest benefit to you. If you are, for example, that radar designer interviewing for a job with a computer company, try to steer the technical conversation to whatever grounds you feel secure on. Even if you have to go back to your earlier working history to steer the conversation onto grounds where you are comfortable, do so. Surprisingly often in interviewing, you can seize and hold the initiative to such a degree that you are in control.

A second way is to ask the right questions. This has the dual effect of giving you a measure of control and of introducing some of the give-and-take atmosphere of a negotiation, which you intend this to be. It also suggests your sincere interest in the company, the interviewer, and the job.

Sometimes you can turn this to enormous advantage. There is the story of a salesman who beat at the doors of a prospect for months without getting in to see the man. Finally, one day, the salesman managed to encounter his prey for a moment in the elevator, and laid siege to him, beseeching only two minutes of time. The executive sighed and agreed, but when the salesman sat down, the executive took out his watch and laid it on the desk. "Two minutes," he said grimly.

The salesman glanced desperately around the office, spied a golf trophy. He commented on the trophy, spent the next hour listening to the executive's golf exploits, left with a large order, and was judged by the executive to be a brilliant conversationalist—as good listeners often are.

Once you can determine your interviewer's prime interests, by whatever method, it is relatively easy to steer the interview. And if you are steering it, even if the other party is doing all the talking, you are in control. Being a good listener definitely pays off, especially when you get the other party on a subject of his or her special interest.


## PROBLEMS: HANDLING THEM

One problem already mentioned is that of being interviewed by a subordinate of the individual who will make the decision. Aside from the general hazard of being at the mercy of someone who does not have direct control, there are other problems. One of them is that in such cases the interviewer may regard you as a potential threat. It is important to allay this fear and be as non-threatening as possible. Therefore, in this situation, don't "come on too strong" and assert your strengths on the job. Be low-key, unassuming, easy to work with. Don't express a cynical attitude about work and employment, on the one hand, but don't go to the opposite extreme of exhibiting a kind of career chauvinism about the company. Be careful, too, that you don't exhibit burning ambition for advancement, for this can lead the other to fear you as a possible rival in the future.

One way to play it safe in these regards is to be careful about describing past experiences with present or former employers. If you tend to portray yourself as a "hero" or "heroine" with other employers, you may very well arouse those very fears of potential rivalry for preeminence and promotion in the company.

If you are being subjected to stress interviewing, work at controlling your anger, impatience, growing frustrations, and other emotional extremes that the stress interview is presumably intended to expose. Giving way to these emotional influences is understandable enough, since we are all subject to human frailties, but it is also probably "instant death" for your chances.

Being "double teamed"—interviewed by two individuals at once—is entirely unfair, unreasonable, even unethical. Yet, it may happen to you, and you must keep your balance, and not let the tactic throw you off. Once again, this is used as a form of stress interview, and the stress-interview precautions just reviewed apply here too.

Watch out for those charmers who interview you by carrying on a low-stress, informal conversation. Listen carefully to what is said, think before responding, maintain an air of relaxed ease and self-confidence. In fact, it is wise to try to appear relaxed, at your ease, and completely self-confident in all the situations you find yourself during interviews.

If you are asked technical questions which you cannot answer, do not appear flustered or distressed at your inability to answer the question. Admit frankly that you do not know, have forgotten, would normally look that item up in a reference rather than try to remember it, or whatever appears to make good sense. No reasonable person expects you to have total recall and to be able to answer every question. In fact, some of the questions may be deliberately planted for the purpose. On one occasion an interviewer asked the applicant to "write a number in Boolean algebra." The applicant admitted that he didn't know how to do that with Boolean algebra, but offered to write Boolean equations to describe any circuits the interviewer wished to have described in that manner. The interviewer dropped the question. The significant thing here is that there is no such thing as "writing a number" in Boolean algebra, anymore than you can write a number in common, garden-variety algebra. Algebra is a method of expressing logical relationships, and Boolean algebra is used to do that in computer design. It was never clear whether the interviewer knew that and was testing the applicant, or did not himself know exactly what Boolean algebra is and is not. In any case, the applicant was wise to pretend to simple ignorance and so spare the interviewer possible embarrassment, which would certainly have been fatal for his chances of being hired.

Some of the questions you will be asked will concern your basic qualifications, such as college degrees and working experience. And if you have managed so far to avoid delivering up a detailed résumé, the interviewer is likely to ask some of these questions. Be prepared to handle any questions that you think might be deadly to your purposes. Be conscious of which are your assets and which your liabilities, and think hard about how to cope with questions that compel you to reveal or admit to whatever you think are liabilities.

## A GENERAL STRATEGY

In general terms, the tactic for coping with these problems depends on your managing to delay confronting them. Whatever you think is a liability, such as the wrong college degree for the job or the lack of a college degree, the wrong kind of working experience, the lack of enough working experience, or anything else is best overcome by first parading all your strengths and make your possible employment so attractive that your shortcomings pale and are not seriously considered. If you have made yourself so appealing a candidate for the position that the employer is fairly panting after you, he or she will no longer be greatly influenced by some factor that would otherwise have been a disastrous liability. It is, therefore, of the essence that your general strategy be always to focus on your strengths, your assets, and stall off discussing other matters as long as possible.

And even then, turn those liabilities around and make assets out of them.

One way to further this strategy is to avoid any conversational gambit or question which would inevitably lead to a question you wish to delay. If you lack a college degree or have the wrong one, don't ask your interviewer what college he or she went to or what his or her major was. That will almost surely lead to the counter-question. Even if that counter-question is not asked directly, it will produce an unspoken question—a raised eyebrow, which asks the question and all but demands an answer.

Concentrate on what you feel most comfortable with as your major strength. If it's practical experience, keep returning to your practical experience and be sure to relate all the interesting and entertaining anecdotes which illustrate and document that experience. If it's something in your military service, focus on that, and invite conversation in that area.

## HANDLING LIABILITIES

Although you delay as long as possible answering questions that compel you to admit to what are probable liabilities, there comes a time finally when you must admit that you don't have a college degree, never were actually the chief accountant, have never personally installed a microwave tower, or otherwise have some kind of presumed shortcoming in your qualifications. What then?

For one thing, never be obvious in stalling off the question. Try to delay having it asked, although you know that it will eventually be asked. But don't let your interviewer even suspect that you are reluctant to answer the question or fearful of having the matter raised at all. Once the question is asked directly, answer it directly, openly, and without hesitation. But truthfully: no evasions and no vacillation about it, at that point. And above all, no apologies.

It is important that you do not apologize nor ever in any way appear to be apologetic for not having that college degree or that specific credential, whatever it may be. Once you appear apologetic and begin to protest that you can handle the job anyhow, that you compensate by all your other good traits, you have chopped a large hole in your armor.

Trying to explain is just as bad. If you had some misfortune that prevented you from finishing college, or even going to college, so be it. If you are asked directly why, answer directly with a straightforward explanation. But not unless you are asked. If you get the direct question, "Do you have a college degree?" answer in the negative, possibly with a remark such as, "No, I didn't get the chance to go to college." Say it with a cheerful smile, and return to whatever you were discussing earlier. Don't allow an awkward silence to settle over the scene either. Just carry on.

The point is to concentrate on your strengths and ignore your weaknesses, if you have some. Sell what you have, and never mind what you don't have. You can't sell what you don't have and you can't do anything about it anyway. Don't try. Just keep flogging away at your strengths, assets, what you can offer.

Frequently in interviews, especially if you have been in your field for a time, you'll find that you and the interviewer have some acquaintances in common. Finding that out tends to create a bit of a bond, and certainly does no harm. So it is often helpful to drop as many company and project names as possible, and see if any produce a spark of recognition on the part of the interviewer. I have found often that this helps get an interview flowing along smoothly.

If you are being interviewed by a manager for whom you would be working, follow the philosophy you would in writing a résumé or selling something (for you are selling something): Inquire about your interviewer's work, duties, responsibilities, and especially problems. It is that latter area you really need and want to know about, for the best thing you can do to get this interviewer to approve heartily of your employment is to demonstrate that you can help with those problems. Unless that manager who is interviewing you is one of the rarest kind, he or she has problems, probably every day of the week. What he or she would most like in a new employee is someone who can handle some of those problems. Demonstrate—tactfully, so you don't appear to be over-ambitious and hence a threat —that you will be a big help, and you will win approval almost automatically.

Be careful in doing this. Aside from being careful that you don't appear to be so ambitious that you might be a threat to the manager interviewing you, there is the danger of appearing to be a braggart or of being somewhat arrogant. These are unpleasant traits, and even the appearance of having them is deadly. Nor must you appear to be a know-it-all, either, for that is distasteful too, and will turn most people against you. You must somehow manage to demonstrate an ability to help solve problems without appearing to brag, patronize, know it all, or otherwise reveal unacceptable traits. That means proceed with caution and manage to reflect an ability to cope with some of these problems without taking too much credit. One way to do this is to lie a little, and let others take the credit for things you may have done yourself—the reverse of the way some people do things. And don't deceive yourself about this: being too clever is a hindrance, not an aid. Far better to explain that you have *seen* this problem solved by someone in a former job, even if the truth is that you solved the problem. Take a little credit only if you can pass some of the credit to others. You'll be far better liked, and you won't appear a threat if you praise someone you used to work for and explain how much you learned from him or her.

## ASKING QUESTIONS ABOUT THE COMPANY

Some of the questions you were to ask were intended to steer the interview and control it. Some were intended to provide information to help you gauge what answers, what conversation, what remarks would help you "win" the interview. But there is another class of questions you should be asking also: You should be asking questions designed solely to help you judge whether you do, in fact, want to work for the company. Find out about fringe benefits, possibilities for future advancement, the company's own prospects for the future. If this interview is to culminate in a negotiation, as suggested, you need to know exactly what you are negotiating for. What, exactly, is the company prepared to trade for your services? Money is not the sole criterion. Look at it this way also: The company is only spending money, but you are spending your life—your years. The company can recover money, if they spend it unwisely or lose it; you cannot recover years lost, if you spend them unwisely—in effect, lose them. Getting a job does involve a real negotiation, in which you do have something to lose, if you negotiate unwisely.

## ABOUT SALARY

The question of money usually arises. You may be asked early in the interview how much you expect, require, or demand. If you answer too soon you are almost sure to make a mistake by being either too high or too low. The right tactic, if asked early in the interview about money, is to refuse to answer by delaying your answer: "I really need to know more about things, because many other factors have value. Any answer I make now about a salary requirement would be the roughest kind of guess. Can't we come back to this later?" Most interviewers will accept this rationale readily enough, and you can spend a little time fishing around, trying to decide what you can reasonably ask for.

Another way to field this, however, is to answer the question with a question, such as, "Do you have a regular scale for this job?" Or: "Do you have any specific figure in mind yourself?" But don't be pushed into a premature statement.

## AFTER THE INTERVIEW

When the interview has ended—and do not work at drawing it out; let the interviewer end it when he or she wishes to—thank your interviewer sincerely for allowing you so much time to get your questions answered and explaining your background. If you are to send in a résumé, confirm that you will do so promptly, as promised. Ask whether there is anything the interviewer would like to see in that résumé especially, something that you did not cover already. Ask whether there is anything else you can do to help the interviewer. Then try to set up the next event.

There are such sales situations as "one-call sales," situations in which you would normally be able to consummate the sale in a single call and single presentation. But there are multi-call sales, situations which can rarely be sold in a single call, and often require several calls to consummate the matter. In those situations, if you conclude a call and presentation with things left hanging—a let's-see-what-happens—what will happen is nothing, nothing at all. There will almost surely be no sale. What you must do in these situations is to always set up the next step or next event before parting company with

your prospect. And the worst possible agreement to make is to agree
to let the prospect give you a call when ready. That rarely works.
What you must do is keep the initiative; above all, do not let it pass
from your hands. And the way to do this is to set up something that
*you* will do next. But it must be something that does not permit the
prospect a merely passive role. If your next step is to send the interviewer a résumé, the interviewer need do nothing, and may very well
do nothing. If it is simply to wait until you get a call, you may have
a long wait.

In this situation, there are two things to do. The first one is to
pledge to call back. Ask the interviewer about when he or she is likely
to reach a decision, and suggest that you will call about then. Re-
gardless of what the interviewer says in responding to your question,
remark that you'll call.

After you get home, send the résumé or whatever you promised,
but also send a letter, and send that separately from anything else.
Thank the interviewer gracefully, once again, reaffirm your interest,
pledge once again to call, and then follow through: Make the promised
telephone call. And make it again, every few days, until you are
satisfied that it is of no use to continue making calls or you have been
hired. Persistence usually pays off.

Above all, don't pin your hopes on that one interview and, therefore, slow down your other efforts. Keep all your self-marketing at
full throttle until you have definitely reached agreement with someone.
Not only will this help you avoid bitter disappointments—Murphy's
Law is always at work, twenty-four hours a day, and the most attractive, virtually sure-thing offer can still fall between the cracks at
five minutes to twelve—but it will greatly strengthen your bargaining
effectiveness, since you will have the courage lent by the knowledge
that you have other strings to your bow and are not dependent on
some single hope. Never allow yourself to become dependent on a
single prospect.

# 13

## Miscellaneous Matters

*There are both philosophical and practical considerations.
Here are some of the practical, if miscellaneous, ones,
especially a means for multiplying the distribution of your
super-résumé by making up a "pocket résumé."*

### GETTING SUPER-RÉSUMÉS INTO THE RIGHT HANDS

**T**HE basic approach to job finding taken in these pages has been
to recognize the process as one of marketing yourself according
to all accepted rules and guidelines of sales and marketing. The résumé
must be constructed according to sound marketing principles, but it
must not be the instrument used for the initial approach because it
is the wrong instrument for that use. (It's much better suited to use
as the follow-up.) Instead, use for the initial approach that brief version, the "super-résumé"—"super" in the sense that it is ultracon-
densed, the résumé idea carried to something of an extreme by offering
only the most appealing element(s) of your résumé in something which
resembles a letter far more than it does a résumé. In fact, that itself
is one of its virtues: As something appearing to be a letter, it stands
a far greater chance of escaping that special purgatory reserved for
so many résumés, and is far more likely then to reach the decision-
maker directly, an eventuality much to be desired.

There is a drawback, however: You can distribute résumés freely,
carrying a supply with you at all times, but you can hardly carry
around with you a supply of brief letters to hand out everywhere. If
you are to have something to carry around with you which you can
hand out spontaneously at every opportunity to put it into the hands

of someone who may be able to help you find and win the job you want, you must either carry and distribute conventional résumés—which we have already decided is taboo (unless you disagree with me and my premise offered here)—or you must have some special version of your super-résumé which is suitable for spontaneous distribution—a pocket résumé, in fact.

## THE POCKET RÉSUMÉ

What you will do is to make up an oversize card—3 x 5 inches, minimum, although I would use one 4 x 6 inches—which bears on it your super-résumé. (See Figure 14) Because it does not resemble the conventional résumé, it is advisable here to use the word *résumé* printed prominently on the card so that there is no doubt in the reader's mind as to what it is. Of course, you can put more information in a 4 x 6 inch card than you can on a 3 x 5 inch card, and even more than in the example shown. However, it should contain essentially the same information you would put into the letter/super-résumé you mail out to specific addressees.

You can use a bit of artwork too, if you wish, although it should not be necessary, for the pocket résumé itself is such a novel way of

---

### RÉSUMÉ

Joseph T. Smith
Insurance Salesman

Happenstance Lane
Citrustown, FL 32301
(305) 555-3333

In 31 years I sold over $101 million in policies, and over the last 17 years never less than $1 million/year, but usually near my high of $6 million/year. Retired, but still in good health, bored, and wishing to sell insurance part-time. Please call or write to discuss.

---

FIGURE 14. The résumé card.

preparing a résumé that it is bound to get some special attention. At the same time, it would probably not be useful as a mailer, for it would then arrive together with the usual "junk mail" that so many of us receive every day, and might be discarded without a good enough look for the recipient to identify it for what it is.

On the other hand, if you do choose to use it as a mailer also, I would suggest the word *résumé* printed prominently on the outside of the envelope, in the hope that the word will alert the recipient, who will then not discard it. (However, it might very well get rerouted to Personnel, with the same end result.)

The primary use of this oversize card-résumé is to hand out to individuals you encounter at meetings, conventions, conferences, dinners, seminars, and other occasions. You can also use these to give friends a supply to hand out for you. But there are a few other ways to get distribution: One is to provide a supply on the literature table so often set up at meetings and other such occasions. Another is to mail them as though they were postcards, which means that they will probably get a glance at least. (That's one reason the word *résumé* must be bold enough to be recognizable at the merest glance.) And still another, if you can afford it and are willing to spend the money, is to have one reproduced in suitable publications, such as newsletters and magazines circulating to the kinds of people you want to get this information read by. And you may also be able to get such advertising free of charge by bartering your services in exchange of the advertising space. The main purpose and use of the card, however, is to carry a supply around with you in a pocket so that you have them ready to hand out anytime, anywhere.

As a variant, try using the words SUPER-RÉSUMÉ at the head of the card, which will command some attention. Or, perhaps even better, TIME-SAVER RÉSUMÉ, using some bold type in either case. This may be more attention-getting and will also serve to explain and justify the brevity and special appearance of the card. If you choose to do this, you'll see a grin steal over the faces of people you hand it to; most of them will appreciate the novelty of the idea and heading SUPER-RÉSUMÉ or TIME-SAVER RÉSUMÉ. This is illustrated in Figure 15, with different wording of the body copy and a slightly different arrangement generally. And that brings up another point: There are various things you can do with the layout and format to emphasize various points. You can experiment with the aid of a wide

---

### SUPER-RÉSUMÉ

Joseph T. Smith                                    Insurance salesman

After 31 years and over $101 million in insurance-policy sales (never less than $1 million/year but usually near my $6 million/year high in last 17 years) I retired. I'm bored, want to get back to work part-time. Call or write to discuss.

HAPPENSTANCE LANE                          CITRUSTOWN, FL 32301

(305) 555-3333

---

FIGURE 15. The super-résumé card.

variety of things you can get in any well-stocked artists' supply store. With the aid of many of these modern items you can achieve professional-looking results. Or you can seek the aid of a local commercial artist or graphic arts specialist.

## A FEW ATTENTION-GETTING ALTERNATIVES

The super-résumé card gets attention because of its inherent novelty. You can enhance that novelty by using graphic devices of various kinds, and even by paying for commercial art services to ensure a professional result. But there are also ways to accomplish this through copywriting technique. One suggestion was to use the word *résumé* in bold type, another to use the words *super-résumé* in bold type, for even greater impact. Here, however, are a few other possible headlines you might use instead that make the purpose plain enough, while adding to novelty and ability to command attention:

JOB WANTED
VALUABLE SERVICES OFFERED
OPPORTUNITY TO HIRE A HIGH PRODUCER
TOP-FLIGHT SERVICES AVAILABLE

Of course, each case offers different opportunities, and you must study your situation and especially what you can offer to identify the best possibilities for your super-résumé card. Joseph T. Smith might have designed his own super-résumé card along much different lines, taking advantage of what he had to offer, as in Figure 17.

The point is that the form has to follow the function, be dictated by the individual circumstances. This latter style (Figure 16) would probably be most effective for Joe Smith because of what Joe Smith can offer. It might not work well for someone else, who has a different kind of asset to offer.

Another point to consider is that of recognition. If you are in the computer field and seeking out connections in that field, you might get a better response by using devices that identify you immediately as someone in that field. One way to do that is through graphics (as illustrated in Figure 11). But there are other, perhaps more subtle but still effective, ways. As a computer specialist, you might want your card printed out in a style that is distinctively computer-related— by a dot-matrix computer printer, for example. Or you might design your card as a flow diagram. (See Figure 17.)

---

### TIME-SAVER RÉSUMÉ

**$6 MILLION/YEAR INSURANCE SALESMAN AVAILABLE**

| | |
|---|---|
| QUALIFICATIONS: | 31 years experience, $101 million total sales, rarely below $6 million last 17 years. |
| STATUS: | Retired, bored. |
| OFFER: | Will sell for you, part-time. |
| ACTION NEEDED: | Call or write to discuss. |
| WHERE, WHO: | Joseph T. Smith Happenstance Lane Citrustown, FL 32301 (305) 555–3333 |

---

FIGURE 16. A variant on the super-résumé card.

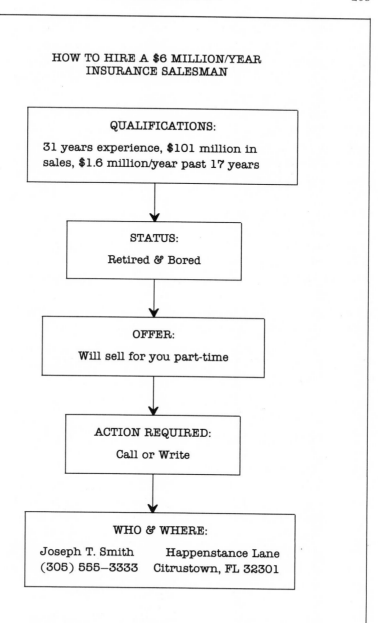

FIGURE 17. Super-résumé as a flow diagram.

But there are other fields. The accountant or bookkeeper might have a card designed in which the data appears to be on a calculator paper tape. The secretary or stenographer might use a few shorthand symbols to point to the connection. The engineer or mathematician might use some mathematical symbols.

There are also script styles which can suggest fields of specialization. There are many type styles, including scripts, old English, Germanic, Oriental, and others. All these devices and aids can help you command attention, achieve high impact, make your point, orient your reader quickly, and otherwise enhance your presentation—for even that 4 x 6 inch card is a presentation. Don't be afraid to be different. Just be sure that you are in good taste, then bore ahead at full steam.

## WHEN—FINALLY—TO SUPPLY YOUR RÉSUMÉ

The right time to supply your résumé is never. You're far better off never supplying it, if you can bring that off. It's much better to have managed to focus your entire self-marketing effort on whatever you have said in your super-résumé and in interview(s). There you have had some measure of control and been able to concentrate on your assets primarily, and minimize reference to and/or revelation of any liabilities. And the benefits of this have been both to avoid the negative effects of exposing those liabilities and the much greater impact of sharp focus on only one or two major assets, without the dilution of covering too many points.

Obviously, it is not always possible to never supply a résumé. Even in my case, I managed to get hired and be at work for several months without supplying a résumé, but the day of reckoning finally came when I was compelled to produce one. By then, of course, it could no longer hurt me in any way—and so made little difference. In fact, it was not really necessary to hold out that long, but I was testing my theories out—to see how long I could evade that supplying of a conventional résumé.

If the right time to supply a conventional résumé—what the employer will accept as a résumé—is never, there is a next-best time, which is the practical compromise you should aim at: If possible, do not produce a full résumé until you've been hired and are filling out all those forms most companies compel you to fill out when you report for work.

The point here is that once the decision has been made to extend a firm offer to you, there is no longer a valid reason to withhold your full, conventional résumé. It is at that point, in my experience, that it is the best time to surrender a detailed résumé—usually delivering it up to the personnel or administrative department when asked to fill out the company's formal application form. You may then fill in the head data—name, address, telephone number, and the personal data that would not normally appear on your résumé—and attach a copy of the résumé where the application form called for reporting previous employment in chronological order. (That practice, by the way, has proved to be acceptable to most companies.)

## COPING WITH RÉSUMÉ PROBLEMS

If you must surrender your résumé before you get a firm offer, do so, of course. But if you have problems, such as those discussed here, this is the time to address them—not after the employer has picked them up and begun to question you about them. Here are several typical problems and what do about them:

### A BAD REFERENCE

Over the course of a working career you are likely to have a bad job experience. You may get fired from a job, whether due to misconduct, malperformance, misunderstanding, inability to get along with someone, or for any other reason. (Note that this refers to being fired, not laid off.) You may have merited the firing or you may have been guiltless, but it does not matter since your record at that company will show the employer's viewpoint, not yours. And you may or may not get a reference that will harm you. (Some employers try hard not to harm a former employee, even the one who was fired.) However, you must assume that you will get a "bad" reference, and take steps.

The right steps to take are to pull the sting by admitting that you were fired from the job—simple honesty. (Remarkable how often simple honesty works better than any ploy or alibi you could think up.) This will serve to caution your new employer or prospective employer that you were perhaps not greatly admired when you left that employer. Consequently, your prospective new employer may not even bother to make inquiry there, but be content to verify your employment and satisfactory performance with other past employers. Or even if a check is made, there will be no great surprises.

The point is to be honest about it. If you have covered up the problem and a reference check uncovers a former employer's unhappiness with you or criticism of your performance there, you will be regarded with some suspicion as being less than honest and, perhaps, less than desirable. Some employers are known to disqualify one immediately for such a cover-up, no matter how minor the problem being covered up.

Of course, there is the possibility that the former employment won't be checked out at all, and admitting to a problem there may create doubts that would never have been raised otherwise. In my opinion, the risk in being totally honest is not as great as the risk of covering things up, and on balance, honesty has paid out far more often than dishonesty. It is a rare employer who will not understand such an item in your background or will hold such an incident against you, especially when you have admitted to it freely, thereby indicating that you yourself consider it minor and of little consequence.

And that brings up another relevant point: People always tend to be whatever you expect them to be and believe what you expect them to believe, if you make your expectations clear enough. In this case, you make your expectations clear by example, by showing that you've no fear of reporting the incident, and perhaps even finding it somewhat amusing or whimsical.

## LITTLE RELEVANT WORK EXPERIENCE

You may get into that familiar dilemma, the paradox of not being able to get a given job because you've no experience in the work and not being able to get the experience because you've never been able to get such a job. This may or may not be a problem, if you have managed to get a firm offer before presenting a full résumé. The reason this may not become a problem is because you have managed to convince the interviewer that you can handle the job and there is no lingering doubts or questions about it, or because in the natural course of events, the interviewing manager never bothers to read your résumé, and the personnel manager has no reason to do other than file it as an administrative routine. However, again the question of honesty arises. If you have gotten through interviews and elicited a firm offer by deceit, by manufacturing fictitious work experience, your résumé can cause withdrawal of that offer. (Such things have happened.) It is essential that you do not invent past employment, unless you want to take that risk, and risk it is.

Instead, focus your résumé—and your responses in interviews— on the most relevant items. For example, I was once interviewing a man who was applying for a job as a writer of technical training materials. The accent was more on *training* than on *technical* in this case, and my primary concern was to recruit people who were re- sourceful writers, people who knew how to research and utilize data to prepare training manuals, lesson plans, and other such end- products. This fellow—I'll call him Roy because that's pretty close to his real name—showed me a collection of yellowed newspaper pieces from a small-town newspaper in the Tennessee mountain coun- try. They were by-lined, so I knew they were his own work. I perceived that he could write well, and from our general conversation I decided that he was clever and resourceful enough to handle the work, al- though he *definitely did not have the relevant experience.* But he was honest with me about his true experience, and he was so eager to be able to spend his full time at writing and earn his living therefrom that I was persuaded to chance hiring him, despite his apparent lack of quali- fications—certainly a lack of *credentials.*

I never regretted it. Roy performed admirably. He was as clever and resourceful as I had hoped he would be, and did a fine job. Nor was his an exceptional case: More than once I hired people who did not appear to have the things we might have regarded as necessary qualifications and credentials, but who managed to persuade me that they could handle the job. Perhaps not every manager will do so, but once you manage to win an interview with the decision-making man- ager, it's up to you to *sell* yourself, and people who are able enough to become managers are bright enough to see the value of those who are really eager to succeed. (There are so many of the other kind, those who want to do enough to "get by" and no more than that.)

## REAL CLINKERS IN YOUR HISTORY

A few years ago, I received a résumé and a letter from a man who had been in prison for stealing. It was his first and only offense (at least at that time), and he admitted his guilt freely, all but begging for a chance to redeem himself at honest work. At the same time, he was qualified for a job I had open, one which would not put temptation in his way, and I invited him to come in for an interview.

I listened to his story. He made no effort to blame society at large or to whine that he hadn't had a chance. He was straightforward in asking me to give him a chance, and made it clear enough that he fully understood that he would be on trial and under close scrutiny. I concurred in that and told him without hesitation that if I hired him, he'd have to be extremely careful to be purer than Caesar's wife, for even an innocent act that appeared to be suspicious could easily be his undoing. I did hire him, finally, and he managed to perform so well and reliably that all of us soon forgot his background and observed him no more closely or critically than we did anyone else in the organization.

In his case, not only was his honesty with me the key to getting hired, but ironically enough, his problem was probably his greatest asset in getting hired. Had he not drawn my attention to his problem, I probably would not have paid any more attention to his résumé than I did to any of the others, many of which reflected qualifications equal to his.

If you are unfortunate enough to have some really serious clinker in your history, admit it, but do not make a major issue of it. Make the simple admission and go on. Handle it as a routine, as a "matter of course." As in the previous example, telegraph your own attitude and it is likely that your reader or interviewer will reflect that attitude.

## HANDLING "TRICK" OR "KEY" QUESTIONS

Some interviewers have their own pet questions, which are sometimes "trick" questions in the sense that the interviewer believes that your answer reveals a great deal about you. And it is amazing how much some of these questions can reveal about the individual being interviewed. One that is not exactly a trick question, but does produce highly revealing answers and is quite commonly used, is this: "Why do you wish to work for this company?" This is one to handle with care.

Your real reason may be that you need a job, and this appears to be as good a prospective job as any you are likely to encounter. That is, you don't *especially* wish to work for this company, but you are entirely willing to. That, however, is not the "proper" answer to give. It might impress one interviewer by its simple honesty, but it might be the wrong answer for another interviewer, who wants to hear that you wish to work for that company because it's such a great company, you've heard such great things about it, you believe that there will be opportunity, the management is modern and progressive, etc.

There is one answer that you do not wish to give—ever; it's an answer given by an applicant for a supervisory job in a computer programming firm. The applicant looked good to the interviewer, appeared to be acceptable until asked that fatal question—one to which he gave this fatal answer: He wanted this responsible supervisory job because the office was near his home.

That brought the interview to a rapid close because it convinced the interviewer that the applicant was at least naive, if not dull-witted.

## SNATCHING DEFEAT FROM THE JAWS OF VICTORY

The above is not an unusual case. Again and again salespeople are guilty of the same basic mistake of talking too much. Or too long. That is, they fail to recognize when it is time to shut up. There comes a time in every sales presentation—and no matter what your interviewer believes is transpiring, as far as you are concerned you should be making a sales presentation—when it's time to close. "Close" means bring the presentation to an end and ask for the order, in normal sales activity. If the prospect refuses to give you the order, that's a sign that it's time to resume the presentation, to clear up any question or overcome any objection that prevents the prospect from becoming your customer. Then it is time to close again. And it is not at all unusual for even the most gifted and successful of salespeople to close many times before getting the order. In fact, the most effective salespeople tend to be those who close the greatest number of times.

The problem that such salespeople overcome is that of talking too much and saying the wrong thing. It is not unusual to bring a prospect to the point of signing or giving the order, and then talking the prospect out of the order by the simple act of saying too much. Now interviewing for a job is admittedly a somewhat different proposition than selling a set of books or a vacuum cleaner. Most of the time, the prospect does not give you a decision on the spot, even if he or she has come to one during the interview. Still, it is a mistake—talking too much and saying the wrong thing, as a result—a mistake easily made during an interview for a job. What defeats some salespeople is the fear of silence. After completing a presentation, there may be dead silence. The prospect is pondering, perhaps waiting for the salesperson to say something more. Old hands at selling often comment on this situation by saying that the one who speaks first "loses." If the prospect speaks first, according to this lore, the salesperson wins the order. (Therefore, the prospect "loses" by thereby being "forced" to buy.) If the salesperson speaks first, the prospect "wins" by not buying: the salesperson has snatched defeat from the jaws of victory.

Whether this is literal truth or not, it is true in principle. A single word too much, a single word that was not necessary, a single word that was better left unsaid, can cost you the job. Here is what to do:

1. Answer all questions simply and directly, then shut up and wait for the next question.

2. Only volunteer information beyond that asked for if (a) you fear that your answer to the question would harm you if unexplained or (b) you have an opportunity to get in a really telling point in your favor. But be extremely careful—be sure that one of these is, in fact, the case.

3. Don't be afraid of "awkward" silences between questions. Your interviewer may not be sure of what to ask next, but he or she may simply be pondering your answer or waiting a moment to be sure that you have been given all the time you need to answer. Simply smile to indicate that you have completed your answer, and sit quietly. "Wait out" your interviewer if there is long silence.

Are there hazards in this? Certainly there are; nothing is completely hazard-free. But there is far greater hazard in being a blabbermouth.

There is another hazard that you should be aware of and alert for: The hazard of appearing to be one who cannot be trusted with confidential information. If an interviewer asks you for information you believe is the proprietary information of a former employer and improper for you to reveal, say so in a friendly and dignified way. Say something such as, "I'm sorry, but I don't think I'm at liberty to reveal that kind of information. I believe that it would be unethical."

The question might have been asked especially to test you, but even if it was not, this answer assures the interviewer that you can be trusted with confidential information about his or her company, should you be hired—that you are not a blabbermouth.


## REMEMBER THE THREE AREAS OF EVALUATION

Bear in mind during interviews and in all other exchanges or steps in marketing yourself those three areas of evaluation I listed for you earlier. You will always be evaluated along the three parameters, whether your employer thinks of it in these precise terms or not:

1. Job skills and/or education: How well you ought to be able to do the job, carry out its various functions.

2. What kind of co-worker you are: How you get along working with others, remembering that in most situations people work as part of teams, and your ability to work in cooperation and coordination with others bears heavily on how well you do the job, no matter how good your specific job skills are.

3. What kind of employee you are: Loyalty, honesty, dedication, dependability, and other personal characteristics that are always important to an employer. No matter how good a worker you are, you won't do if you are in constant battle with others, often fail to show up on the job, and are less than honest.


## WHAT ARE YOU ASKING AN EMPLOYER TO BUY?

The employer is aware that he or she is hiring the whole person, not just the set of job skills. Or, if you wish to put it into the reference frame you should be working from, you are marketing a whole person, not just a set of job skills. You must sell more than your specific job skills, therefore, and you must, by all means, be sure that the employer bears the fact in mind that what you are negotiating for is something more than the work that an automatic welder or any other robot could do. Perhaps an employer tends sometimes to forget that truth, just as employees do. But you must never forget it, if you are to present yourself properly.

Remember, *saying* that you are honest, loyal, dedicated, dependable, and otherwise a paragon of an employee doesn't make it so and won't convince anyone, not even a prospective employer. You need to *show* what you are, that you are all those things, by what you can report about your past accomplishments.

# 14

# Reference File

*A potpourri of remarks, ideas, cautions, names and addresses, checklists, and other useful items to refer to when the need arises.*

## SAMPLE RÉSUMÉS

**F**IGURES 18, 19, and 20 are illustrations of conventional résumés. Each includes a summary statement, an abstract of whatever the writer thought were the most important elements of the résumé. Each has the virtue of being mercifully short—one page—although in each case the résumé covers an extensive background and several jobs. Each is an attractive and businesslike layout, too, so that these are good models for conventional résumés. Note, however, that the impact of the abstracts or summaries is diluted and weakened by other features and details which demand the reader's attention.

## ARTIST'S AIDS

Manufacturers of decalcomania lettering and symbols and of various other kinds of aids that enable anyone to turn out professional-looking copy for printing include the following. If you are unable to find what you want in a local art-supplies store or don't have one within easy reach, you can try writing to one or more of these manufacturers for information:

Harvey Hostel
79991 Cherrystone Drive
Minneapolis, MN 55455

COMPUTER MAINTENANCE MGT,
MAINTENANCE TRAINING,
TRAINING MANAGEMENT

20 years military (USAF) electronics maintenance, supervision and training of up to 25 technicians maintaining
major computer systems, evaluation of training programs,
and documentation.  Honor graduate of several USAF electronic and computer schools.  Designed, planned, organized maintenance systems on unique configuration of three
computers (2nd & 3rd generation) and associated displays.

*EXPERIENCE HISTORY*
*(U.S.Air  Force from 1956 to recent retirement)*

*Aug 75 to*     *Assistant Computer Maintenance Superintendent, Tyndall  AFB*

*Sept 76*       Supervising 16 technicians, removed and reinstalled an AN/GYK
                -19,  taking over air defense of southeastern U.S.  Duties in-
                cluded responsibility for maintenance quality, spare parts supply.

*Dec 74 to*     *Electronic Computer Systems Superintendent, McClellan AFB*

*July 75*       Supervised 25 technicians, all maintenance planning and management
                for 3-computer configuration (plus displays and other peripherals).

*May 74 to*     *GP Chief, Computer Maintenance Training Section, McClellan AFB*

*Dec 74*        Planned, coordinated, supervised, and evaluated special qualifi-
                cation training for maintenance of AN/GYK-19 computer.  Personally
                provided special technical instruction.  Developed and recommended
                improvements to maintenance routines.  Supported Litton engineers
                in installation of AN/GYK-19 computer system.

*Aug 72 to*     *Electronic Computer System Supervisor (L304 BUIC), McClellan AFB*

*May 74*        Supervised preventive and corrective maintenance on computer sys-
                tems, including calibration, testing, fault-isolation, and diag-
                nostic-testing programs.

*Sept 68 to*    *Electronic Computer Technician*

*Aug 72*        Several assignments, various duty stations, maintaining computers
                and associated equipment, including training repairmen and main-
                taining training records.

*Dec 56 to*     *Radar Operator, world-wide duty stations*

*Sept 68*       Supervised up to 10 operators, monitoring, analyzing, interpreting
                radar displays, issuing radio weather advisories, and monitoring
                flights.

*SCHOOLS*

*USAF Schools on BUIC III, AN/FSQ-7, and AC&W Operator courses, representing*
*total of 69 weeks (full time) intensive electronics and maintenance training.*
*Also electronics (TV) courses DeVry Institute of Technology, Chicago.  (Gradu-*
*ated with honors from all USAF courses.)*

FIGURE 18. Résumé of retired military technical specialist.

```
Lawrence Untermeyer                              Sales
15899 Schoolhouse Lane                           Market Research
Silver Spring, MD 20907
301 555-4666


              Sales/marketing experience since 1959, including marketing
              research, supervision and training of sales personnel, purch-
SUMMARY       asing, and merchandising.  Recently completed real estate
              courses and passed Maryland Real Estate Salesman and Brokers
              Licensing examinations.

OBJECTIVE     Sales position in real estate

EXPERIENCE:

1965 - Present: College, full- and part-time, with variety of spare-time
              jobs to support college attendance--taxi driving, post office
              clerk, etc.

1961-1965:    Associate Buyer, Brown's Department Store, Washington, DC.
              Performed marketing/sales research for planning of sales, adver-
              tising, purchasing, merchandising.  Worked with Head Buyer, as
              part of team, to select and make purchasing decisions for linen,
              domestics, bedware.  Supervised, trained salespeople; prepared
              and made presentations to top management.

              Assistant Buyer.  Handled customer correspondence, inventory,
              sales coordination, marketing research, recommending sales pro-
              motions (e.g., special sales), attended trade shows.  Promoted
              to Associate Buyer.

1959-1961:    Salesman, Encore Publishers, Inc., Chicago.  National sales of
              magazines and reference books to schools, libraries, individu-
              als.  Planned, coordinated sales activities, strategies.

1958-1959:    Teaching Assistant, Morales University, N.L., Mexico.  Assigned
              to Department of English.  Tutored students in English language,
              graded examinations, translated textbooks, abstracted newspaper
              articles, magazine articles, texts.

EDUCATION:    B.A. Political Science, American University, 1970.  Real Estate
              courses Montgomery Junior College, University of Maryland.

                    REFERENCES AND DETAILS AVAILABLE ON REQUEST
```

FIGURE 19. Résumé of an individual attempting to break into new field.

```
Gregory Hawkins                              General Manager
RD 5, Box 74
Wilburtown, NC 28667
(919) 555-6565

                B.S. Economics, Plant Manager grain elevator handling
                2,000,000 bushels annually, with consistent profits
                during my entire tenure, and increasing past 2 years.
SUMMARY         Formerly VP/Manager feed, fuel, grain business, in-
                creasing sales 300%, going from $10,000 loss to
                $50,000 profit.
```

OBJECTIVE:   Management position, offering significantly greater
             rewards for accomplishment.

POSITIONS HELD:

6/70-Present:   Plant Manager, Harley Co., Wilburtown, NC, country elevator
                of 800,000-bushel capacity, with 2,000,000 bushel/year volume,
                operating under federal license.  I hold USDA Weigher's and In-
                spector's license; am responsible for producer grain marketing,
                feed and fertilizer sales.  Had additional responsibility of
                Belltown, NC elevator also during 72-73 season.  Plant profit-
                able past 5 years, and I increased profits past 2 years.  Full
                P&L responsibility.

3/69-3/70:   Registered Representative, Morgan & Smith, Member NYSE, Balti-
             more, Maryland.

11/68-3/69:  Registered Representative Trainee, Farr & Wilson.   Trained for
             examinations as registered representative.  Firm, which had
             home office in Philadelphia, decided to close Baltimore office.

3/60-10/68:  Vice President/Manager, Hawkins & Hawkins, Upper Marlboro, MD,
             feed, fuel, and grain business, which I expanded by 300%, turn-
             ing loss of $10,000 into profit of $50,000.

EDUCATION:   B.S., Economics, Wharton School, University of Pennsylvania,
             1958.

             U.S. Army, Infantry and Motor Transport Schools, Fort Benning,
             Georgia.

OTHER ACTIVITIES:  Past President, local Lions Club.

             REFERENCES AND DETAILS AVAILABLE ON REQUEST

FIGURE 20. Résumé of manager seeking executive position.

## SOURCES FOR ARTIST'S AIDS

Chartpak: One River Road, Leeds, MA 01053; Tel. 800/628–1910.

GAF Products for Design: 4601 Lydell Road, Cheverly, MD 20801; Tel. 800/638–0734.

Zipatone, Inc.: 150 Fenel Lane, Hillside, NJ 60162.

Prestype, Inc.: 194 Varernas Blvd, Carlstadt, NJ; Tel. 800/631–7790.

GAF Corporation: 189 Wells Avenue, Newton, MA; Tel. 800/225–4210.

Berol RapiDesign: Berol USA, Eagle Road, Danbury, CT 06810.

## SOURCES FOR LETTERHEADS

Among the many sources for letterheads and matching accessories (envelopes, business cards, and noteheads) are the following. In most cases, you can write or call these sources for catalogs or other literature describing their offerings.

Quill Corporation: 100 South Schelter Road, Lincolnshire, IL 60069; Tel. 1 (312) 634–4800.

Drawing Board, Inc.: 256 Regal Row, Dallas, TX 75221; Tel. 800/527–9540.

Grayarc: 882 Third Avenue, Brooklyn, NY 11232; Tel. 800/221–0618.

Lewis Business Products, Inc.: 5215 E. Simpson Ferry Rd, Mechanicsburg, PA 17055; Tel, 800/233–1190.

Mail Advertising Supply Co.: 1450 S. West Avenue, Waukesha, WI 53186; Tel. 800/558–2126.

New England Business Service, Inc.: Townsend, MA 01470; Tel. 800/225–6380.

Stationery House, Inc.: 1000 Florida Avenue, Hagerstown, MD 21740; Tel. 800/638–3033.

## WHAT YOU SHOULD KNOW ABOUT PRINTING

Until the post-World War II period, almost all printing was done by raised metal type, using a method called *letterpress*. That meant that whatever you wanted printed had to be set in metal type, using typesetting machines called by names such as *linotype* and *monotype*, which cast the letters in lead from forms. But in the case of small items, like cards, a local printer might find it more practical to set the copy by hand, using individual metal letters from a special tray called a *California case*. Most printers, even the smallest local printer, had provisions for doing this, and you had merely to bring him your copy—which could be handwritten—and a layout, explaining how you wanted it formatted.

Things have changed considerably. There is still some letterpress printing done—metal type has not disappeared completely—but by far the bulk of today's printing is done by a method called *offset*, but also referred to as *photo-offset, lithographic,* and *photo-lithographic.* It's not really necessary for you to understand all the details of the process, but this method does not use raised type, metal or otherwise, and prints from a flat surface, using a printing plate on which the image to be printed is recorded in such a way that only that image holds the ink when the ink roller is swept across the page.

The impact of this process on modern printing was revolutionary, and today it is only the larger print shops which find it necessary to have typesetting capabilities. By far, the majority of local printing shops—who usually refer to themselves today as *copy shops* and offer speedy copying and duplicating—do most of their work from "camera-ready" copy the customer brings in. Today you need prepare what you want printed in a form suitable for office-copier reproduction— a clean paste-up—and the local printer can make a plate from your copy in seconds, using a photographic method. (Hence the name *photo-litho.*) The offset printing press will print exactly what the camera sees, as the office copier does.

This makes it easy to prepare your copy. Clean typewritten copy is entirely acceptable today, since modern electric and electronic typewriters produce such clean, almost type-quality copy. But if you want the style, elegance, and greater flexibility of real type—the freedom to make some of the copy quite large and bold, for example—you still have to turn to typesetting services, although this will be a process that produces a master copy to be pasted up, rather than a form containing raised metal type.

Most printers can arrange to have your copy set in type, if they don't have their own typesetting capabilities. Or they can usually direct you to a typesetter in the area, if you prefer to deal directly with the typesetter. Or you can look in the telephone yellow-pages directory under *typesetting* and *printing* headings and find typesetters on your own. Both printers and typesetters may be able to guide you also in how to lay out your copy, if you need guidance, but it is likely that the typesetter will be more experienced in this aspect of the work. Or you may wish to turn the entire thing over to a local graphic arts shop, which you will also find listed in the telephone directory under various headings, such as *typesetting, advertising,* and *artists.*

Today's office copiers are so vastly improved over those of a few years ago that for résumés, you probably do not need to have them printed, unless you want to do them up on special paper or want large quantities printed. (Any quantity over fifty of a letter-sized sheet is usually printed more economically on an offset press than reproduced by office copier.) However, office copiers are not designed to handle card stock nor paper sizes smaller than 8-$1/_2$ x 11 inches, so for that reason alone, if for no other, it is necessary to turn to the offset press to print up your super-résumé cards (pocket résumés). However, since you should have those in quantity, you would be better off anyway using offset printing for these, even if an office copier could do them.

## WRITING HELP

There are a number of specialists in résumé writing. There are those who make a business of writing résumés for others. Of course, all claim to be the true god, the only ones who really know how to develop an effective résumé. No doubt many do a good job, as far as such a service can help. But for the most part, even a well-written and well-designed résumé is only slightly more effective than a poorly written and poorly designed résumé because résumés are so limited in what they can do for you, in most cases. It is, therefore, of doubtful value to spend a great deal of money for this kind of help.

This is not to say that it may not be useful to get some of this kind of help, to get an attractive and well-organized résumé. You do want to be able to supply an adequate résumé, when the time comes to provide one. If you think you need help in producing a résumé to meet this need, by all means turn to a résumé service for help. But do not expect what the service does will make a revolutionary difference; do not allow yourself to believe that even the résumé the service prepares for you will take the place of the sound marketing advocated in this book and, above all, do not spend large sums, such as hundreds of dollars, for the service.

To find such services, you can check the telephone directory under *writers* and *résumé service*. You will also find such services listed in help-wanted advertising, in both classified and display advertising (business/financial) sections.


## BUT IF YOU'D RATHER DO IT YOURSELF . . .

It's my opinion that you ought to write your own résumé, if for no other reason than that no one knows the subject as well as you do. The do's and don'ts of résumé writing have been covered in these pages, but to refresh your memory and to furnish you a reference source when you write your résumé, here is a summary of do's and don'ts checklist:

Do use a format along the lines of the sample résumés generally, in that your format provides generous white space, well-separated items of information, and easy-to-follow organization, so that it is conducive to swift and easy reading. Large blocks of solid text are formidable, especially when they confront a busy person who wants to speed-read your résumé and pick out salient items quickly. Don't furnish an excuse to deep-six your résumé in favor of the many others competing with it.

Do use captions and headlines, as in the samples, to help the reader identify and select specific kinds of information readily. If possible, use a different and distinctive typeface for these, but at least use all-capitals for these so that they stand out.

Use good contrast. Print in black ink only, on either white or a light pastel-colored paper. (Black and yellow are even sharper contrast than are black and white, according to tests that have been conducted.)

Keep it simple in other respects. Being arty may give you a prideful swelling, but it doesn't sell well at all. Don't try to be subtle or clever. Just communicate what you have to say as clearly as you can.

Use two pages if you must, but you are leagues ahead if you can get your story told effectively in a single page. Leave out the extraneous details and stress only the key points. But get directly to the point: no rambling introductions, no lengthy rationalizations, no excursions. Be businesslike—100 percent.

Use telegraphic style. You don't need all the parts of speech to get your message across. Skip the articles and the other unnecessary verbal baggage. But don't skip the perpendicular pronoun ("I"); that's the most important word in your résumé.

Be as specific as possible in your résumé. No opinions, positions, attitudes—just facts. Absolute minimum of adjectives and adverbs, and no comparatives or superlatives—and especially no hyperbole.

Proofread carefully. Typos and misspellings are unflattering commentaries on your work, and they will be regarded as your doing, even if you have had someone else write or type your résumé. (If you have, proofread their work before giving final approval.)

Don't include personal trivia, such as your age, maiden name, names of children, church activities, hobbies, shoe size, color preferences, and especially don't have your picture on your résumé (unless you are seeking work as a model or entertainer, in which case you would be providing 8 × 10 glossies and an entire kit). Such trivia can't help you, can hurt you, and always detracts from the important material by dilution.

Don't try to be Bob Hope. Humor is difficult, even for professionals; its usefulness in a résumé is questionable even when it is good humor, and the probabilities are that your efforts at it will come across more as banalities than as humor. Leave it alone; it's dangerous.

Be careful with graphics. They can help, used judiciously and *sparingly*—but don't get the idea that if a little graphic embellishment helps, a lot of it will help more. It works best when used with restraint and in moderation.

Don't be modest. You get no medals and no points for modesty, and your résumé is the last place in the world for modesty. Brag as much as you can, and that means as much as you can substantiate with acceptable evidence and without all those superlatives and hyperbole that appeared as a "don't" a few paragraphs ago. Stick to these simple rules, and your bragging will never appear to be in bad taste.

Be creative and imaginative, if you can. There is no law against using gimmicks, nor will gimmicks hurt you, if you follow the rules of clarity and simplicity. Take Figure 17, for example, in which a super-résumé card presents Joseph T. Smith's appeal for a job as a flowchart. Note, first of all, that the card has a headline that states the offer clearly. Note also that the card has lots of white space, is uncluttered, easy to read, organized, and even has arrows, in case there is the slightest doubt about the sequence in which to read the items. Everything possible is done to keep it simple and make it easy for the reader to follow the train of thought and get the message, loud and clear.

# Index